A WORLD OF STRUGGLE

A WORLD OF STRUGGLE

HOW POWER, LAW, AND EXPERTISE SHAPE GLOBAL POLITICAL ECONOMY

DAVID KENNEDY

PRINCETON UNIVERSITY PRESS
Princeton and Oxford

Copyright © 2016 by David Kennedy
Requests for permission to reproduce material from this work should be sent to Permissions,
Princeton University Press
In the United Kingdom: Princeton University Press,
6 Oxford Street, Woodstock, Oxfordshire OX20 1TW
press.princeton.edu
Jacket art: Padraic Manning and Kendra Lizotte, *Holding the Line*, 2012. Mixed media
on wood panels, 33" × 90"
All Rights Reserved

Library of Congress Cataloging-in-Publication Data
Kennedy, David, 1954–
A world of struggle: how power, law, and expertise shape global political economy / David
Kennedy.
       pages cm
Includes bibliographical references and index.
ISBN 978-0-691-14678-2 (hardcover : alk. paper) 1. International organization.
2. Civil society. 3. Globalization—Political aspects. I. Title.
JZ1318.K397 2016
341.2—dc23
2015012279
British Library Cataloging-in-Publication Data is available
This book has been composed in Trade Gothic LT Std and Sabon Next LT Pro.
Printed on acid-free paper. ∞
Printed in the United States of America
10 9 8 7 6 5 4 3 2 1

CONTENTS

ACKNOWLEDGMENTS

I am grateful for the remarkable community of friends and colleagues who have informed me, engaged me, supported me, critiqued me, and loved me in the years this book has been under way. My thanks first to Dan Danielsen for hundreds of breakfast and dinner conversations about every nook and cranny of my argument and more than twenty-five years of intellectual and personal partnership. Had I not met Duncan Kennedy in 1977, I would not have gotten—or kept—a job thinking about law. For almost forty years, we've pursued parallel and collaborative play in all kinds of projects: co-teaching, co-organizing, reading one another's drafts, and strategizing one another's lives. My ideas about law and everything else in this book have been generated through that collaboration. Many have been enormously generous in reading portions of the manuscript and indulging me in endless conversation about how expertise works, what law is all about, and how the world fits together: particular thanks are due to Guenther Frankenberg, Janet Halley, Sheila Jasanoff, Martti Koskenneimi, Zina Miller, and David Trubek.

I was privileged to co-teach seminars about expertise with both Sheila Jasanoff at the Harvard Kennedy School and Marjorie Garber from the Faculty of Arts and Sciences. Their very different individual and disciplinary perspectives influenced my thinking, and I am grateful for the engagement of their marvelous students and fellows. In 2009–2010, I convened the Pembroke Seminar at Brown University, a yearlong faculty/student research seminar, on the theme of expertise. My thanks to Elizabeth Weed and Suzanne Stewart-Steinberg and to the wonderful colleagues in the seminar, many of them from fine arts, media, and cultural studies.

While working on the book, I served as director of the Institute for Global Law and Policy at Harvard Law School, a global collaborative effort to stimulate innovative and heterodox thinking about global affairs. I have presented this project in various ways to IGLPers along the way, and I am grateful for the generosity of the many in our network who have taken time to share their reactions. The 2014–2015 IGLP fellows—Lina M. Céspedes-Baez, Julia Dehm, Tomaso Ferrando, and Maja Savevska—read and commented on chapter 6. My deep gratitude also to Neal O'Connor and Kristen Verdeaux for managing the institute so I could write.

I am grateful for the many helpful comments and criticisms received as I presented these arguments over the past years. My thanks to my hosts and to the participants for their generosity and engagement at the Human Rights Center at Yale Law School, February 12, 2015; the University of Cape Town law faculty, September 5–6, 2014; the Lauterpacht Center at Cambridge University Conference on Global Governance, July 4–5, 2014; the Law and Boundaries Conference at Sciences Po Law School in Paris, May 19–20, 2014; the Buffalo Law School faculty workshop, March 28, 2014; the Cornell Law School faculty workshop, March 26, 2014; the Tulane University School of Law faculty workshop February 26, 2014; the Law and Society Association plenary in Boston, June 1, 2013; the American University in Cairo Law Faculty Conference on Critical Approaches to International Law, March 10, 2013; the Rafael del Pino Foundation, Madrid, Spain, February 21, 2013; the International Graduate Legal Research Conference at King's College Faculty of Law, April 19–24, 2012; the Lauterpacht Center for International Law's Workshop on Contemporary International Law, January 18, 2012; the Welsh Center for International Affairs in Cardiff on January 16, 2012; the Gallatin Distinguished Faculty Lecture Series at the New University, New York, November 10, 2011; the Saranrom Institute for Foreign Affairs Foundation and Chulalongkorn University, August 24, 2011; the Fletcher School of Law and Diplomacy conference on April 29, 2011; the University of Colorado Law School faculty workshop, April 15, 2011; the World Economic Forum Summit on the Global Agenda, Dubai, November 29, 2010; the Global Policy Forum in Yaroslavl, Russian Federation, September 10, 2010; the University of Zaragoza, Spain, December 9, 2010; the Kormendy Lecture at Ohio Northern University, Pettit College of Law, January 25, 2008; the Temple University School of Law Workshop on Constitutionalism, December 8–9, 2007.

It would be hard to write about expertise without talking to some experts. My thanks to the mentors who have guided me through the worlds of professional practice and to the many Harvard alumni and friends who have opened their communities and put up with my questions. Glenn Ware took me into the worlds of military law, anticorruption compliance, and strategic consulting. Surakiart Sathirathai took me into the complex practice of UN diplomacy and helped me explore the work of industrial policy and development experts in his country. My good friends Helena Alviar, Alvaro Santos, Carlos Gouvea, and Arnulf Becker were beyond generous in arranging for me to meet—and helping me to understand—the development policy machinery in Colombia, Mexico, Brazil, and Chile. Many members of the IGLP's advisory councils generously responded to questions and assisted me in making contacts. Rick Samans and Michele Petrochi helped me navigate the World Economic Forum in its many forms. I have benefited from innumerable conversations with friends and former students in the human rights universe. Particular thanks to Fred Snyder for giving me my first entrée to that world. I will always be grateful that Jean Francois Verstrynge lured me to Brussels many years ago to learn about the European Union from the inside. His colleagues in the Commission, Council, and Court were generous to a fault with their time. Co-teaching with him deepened my appreciation for the practice of legal expertise in governance. I am grateful also to Cleary, Gottlieb, Steen, and Hamilton and the many partners in Brussels and Paris who let a professor look over their shoulder.

An earlier and slightly longer version of chapter 8 was published as "Lawfare and Warfare," in *Cambridge Companion to International Law*, edited by James Crawford and Martti Koskenniemi (Cambridge University Press, 2012), 158–83. The argument of chapter 1 was developed in "Law and the Political Economy of the World," 26 *Leiden Journal of International Law* 7–48 (2013). The broad themes of the book appeared in a preliminary form in "The Mystery of Global Governance," 34 *Ohio Northern University Law Review* 827–60 (2008); and "Challenging Expert Rule: The Politics of Global Governance, 27 *Sydney Journal of International Law* 5–28 (2005).

A WORLD OF STRUGGLE

INTRODUCTION
COULD THIS BE 1648?

As you drive up the mountain to Davos for the World Economic Forum, you can be forgiven for thinking this is where the world is governed: innumerable checkpoints, fancy cars, detailed instructions on what to do with your jet and where your chauffeur should park. My first time was in January 2009 as the global economy teetered. It was an extraordinary moment of uncertainty for these titans of finance, industry and government. Much seemed up for grabs and nervousness permeated the air. The Forum had just launched a Global Redesign Initiative to support what they called a "fundamental reboot" of the "global architecture" as part of their "commitment to improving the state of the world." I chaired a new Global Agenda Council on Global Institutional Governance and had been asked to consult about the global political and economic order's travails and who could do what to right its course.[1] The Forum was clear the project would not be a new Bretton Woods: no one was proposing new intergovernmental institutions. The goal was a renewed commitment to bend the tools at hand to the urgent issues of the day: rebooting the global system to strengthen "global governance."

This book is about the stories people tell themselves and one another in places like Davos and the power they exercise in doing so. Their stories are important: stories about what an economy is, what politics can accomplish, the limits and potential of law in establishing a well-ordered world. Stories make some problems visible and some actors central to their resolution. Stories are also tools of struggle, assertions about who is entitled to what, whose desires legitimate and whose do not. The technical work people undertake in the shadow of these stories arranges the world, distributing wealth, status, and opportunity.

In a world where so much is open to debate and conflict is all around us, how can it be so difficult to contest and change the things that matter? Things like the distribution of wealth and opportunity or honor and shame. Or the pattern of environmental destruction. Or the ubiquity of kleptocratic rule. The answer is not a mysterious constitutional settlement, the obscure workings of a disaggregated public hand or global value consensus. The answer lies in the strange alchemy of expertise and struggle through which our world is made and remade. The alchemy is strange because struggle and conflict have seemed inimical to expertise: matters of political difference and clashing interests that experts aim to calm, mediate, and replace by sweet reason. The world experts know is more constituted order than distributional struggle, their expertise a way of knowing what to do rather than struggling about who will win. And yet, as the world has come to be managed in the language and practice of technical expertise, expert knowledge has itself been transformed. Adopted in crude vulgate by laymen and statesmen alike, expertise has become embroiled in struggle and come unhitched from the promise of decisive clarity, the usefulness of its indeterminacy more appreciated than its analytic rigor. In our world, indeterminate language and uncertain knowledge distribute wealth and power. That is strange—and hard to render visible, let alone contest.

In studying the role of law in economic development and global order, I have been fortunate to be able to meet with all kinds of experts, listen to their stories, and observe their professional practice: international lawyers and government policy makers, factory owners, entrepreneurs and financial analysts in emerging markets, human rights activists, corporate leaders, general counsels, and risk managers from around the world.[2] I have tried to understand the world from their perspective: what are their projects, their powers, their vulnerabilities? When they tell you about their work, they place themselves on a terrain of competitive struggle and assess their powers, vulnerabilities, and strategic options. They are proud of their strategic prowess and creative in mobilizing their knowledge and institutional or social power to defeat their opponents. But if you ask them about the larger world, this terrain of struggle fades as they imagine a world that might be ordered and governed, a system that might be reformed. If you ask them what they do, they tell you about struggle. If you ask about their world, they tell you about order and system, institutional limits and appropriate procedures.

I draw on these experiences to explore the role of expertise and professional practice in the routine conflicts through which global political and economic life takes shape. I have tried to steer between bird's-eye accounts of the structure of the world system, the operations of the global economy or the constitution of the global legal order, and ground-level anthropology of people and things as they move in the world. The result is a series of midlevel observations and hypotheses for research into the role of expert conflict, knowledge and professional practice in the reproduction of an unjust world.

I use the terms "expert" and "expertise" with some hesitation because they focus attention on a class of people and a kind of knowledge rather than a characteristic role and mode of speaking, deciding and acting in struggle. As I imagine it, "expertise" is not the exclusive province of specialists or professionals, however much it may draw on ideas and reservoirs of legitimacy built up by such people. Although experts routinely imagine their work as a technical and pragmatic practice at least aspirationally removed from conflict and political contestation, the idea that "politics" is somehow different is its own kind of expert fantasy. Technical specialists shape the meaning of ideology and interest while political leaders and citizens have learned to speak the technical languages of policy. All are equally prone to irrationality, confusion, conflicting desires, and ambivalence. Criticism of the "technocratic" nature of global decision making, as I hear it, is simply a way of arguing that the wrong interests and ideologies and technical arguments have won out.[3]

Politicians, citizens and so-called experts share the experience that what they say and do expresses either their special knowledge and skill or the sum of the vectors pressing upon them rather than their discretion or decision. They are not ruling or distributing: they are advising, interpreting, informing. It is not the politician who decides, but the voice of the people, the urgency of the moment, or the interests of the nation. It is not the expert who speaks, but her expertise; it is not the layman who demands, but his rights that entitle. Expertise dictates in the name of the universal, the public good, the general will, the practical necessities of reason, or the objective truths of scientific knowledge. Sometimes it seems no one is deciding—everyone is arguing about and interpreting decisions taken elsewhere at another time by someone else. However common and appealing these ideas may be, expertise in the fields I have encountered does not operate this way. The work of legal and policy experts is all about struggle, a form of struggle in which the saying and the doing blend into one another, the knowing is partial, the universal up for debate, while the technical, the ideological and the partisan are everywhere linked together.

It is also common to overestimate the rigor of expert analytics. Ideas and analytics rarely dictate results. Experts disagree sharply with one another and are only too aware of the gaps, conflicts, and ambiguities in their analytics. Their work in law and policy is more argument and assertion than reason. Expert work is positioned and strategic, a matter of posturing as much as persuading. The voice of sweet reason is just that: a voice. A role to be occupied, a style to be deployed, a legitimacy to be claimed. As experts come to inhabit their expertise strategically, they become doubled: asserting the rigor of their analytics while embracing their indeterminacy. In this way, expert conflict and uncertainty seem to strengthen rather than weaken expert authority and significance.

I also hesitate to use the term "expert" out of respect for the enormous literature about the role of experts in governance, a literature whose concerns are largely distinct from my own. Where expertise studies have focused on what makes expert knowledge distinctive, I focus on the continuities between their modes of work and those not marked as specially qualified. Focusing on continuities also softens worry about just how to keep experts and political leaders in their respective places within a system of government. Despite the emergence of transnational technocratic rule, these concerns are also less pressing at the global level where there is no constituted political alternative and it really is expertise all the way down. I am more interested in the *how* of global expert rule: the modes of global public reasoning that arise and the significance of knowledge practices in forms of governance.[4] My objective is to bring knowledge practices and power practices into the same frame. I see expertise as the crossroads where they intersect.

I have nevertheless found the literature on expertise in anthropology, sociology, and the sociohistorical study of science instructive for understanding the knowledge practices common in global political and economic affairs.[5] The work that lies closest to my own preoccupations stresses the performative dimension of expert practice: expert work constituting the space of its own expertise. Economists, for example, do not merely study markets, they "make" them by articulating what markets are and how they function.[6] My approach has been most directly influenced by scholarship in sociology and science studies that stresses the context within which expertise arises and is practiced, from the laboratory to the boardroom, and the components of expertise that operate in those spaces, from "tacit knowledge," through shared ethics of perception, to modes of reasoning and argument.[7]

To focus on the middle space between big systems and ethnographic study, I return repeatedly to law. Law is the global knowledge practice I know best and it is certainly a visible example of the contemporary role of expertise, both as a tool in global struggle and as a promise of a reformed world. There are two further reasons to focus on law. The rise of what might be called "technocracy" or "managerialism" or "rule by experts" in global affairs has been accompanied by the legalization of ever more questions that might once have been debated and settled in other terms. The legalization of military conflict may be the most dramatic example: targets poured over by lawyers and belligerents on all sides legitimating their cause and denouncing their adversaries in legal terms. Economic policy is routinely transformed into debates about the competence or mandate of institutions with divergent ideas about what to do. A friend recently described Brazilian telecommunications privatization policy as the rapid displacement of political and technical considerations by law as ministries, foreign investors, local utilities, and citizen groups lawyered up for engagement with one another.

With the legalization of issues across the globe has come a change in law itself that may be exemplary for other globalizing modes of expertise. As legal expertise has become ubiquitous, it has become increasingly plural and fragmented. Modes of legal thought and legal reasoning have become less formal and less analytically rigorous, if also ever more complex and interdisciplinary. Legal experts have become ever less invested in the determinacy or even "legality" of their modes of analysis and advocacy. Usefulness in struggle trumps analytic rigor and formal legal status. With law's expansion has come a professional sensibility of sophistication and disenchantment. The experience of legal expertise over the past century raises the question whether this may be the destiny of global rule by expertise more generally.

By examining rule by expertise, I aim to grasp both the centrality of conflict and the importance of knowledge practices in global political and economic life. The distributive outcomes of the struggles experts undertake make expertise worth studying. The puzzle is how so much struggle fades from view as experts embody the voice of reason and outcomes are assimilated as facts rather than contestable choices. I am interested in the way experts forget their struggles and their role in distribution to celebrate their knowledge as universal, their world as ordered, their path forward aligned with progress. Modern expertise knows and it forgets—or refuses to know—its powers and its limits. When they forget—and we forget—it becomes all the more difficult to understand how this world, with all its injustice and suffering, has been made and reproduced. And more difficult to identify levers of change or experience the place we stand as a fulcrum of possibility. The result of continuous struggle is an eerie stability it is hard to imagine challenging or changing.

PART I: THE STRUGGLES OF GLOBAL POLITICAL ECONOMY

The key to expert rule is the interaction of two forces: a seething struggle for advantage undertaken everywhere at once and the operations of professional knowledge practices enlisted as tools in those struggles. People pursue projects, pushing one another around on an uneven terrain of powers and vulnerabilities, often using law to solidify their gains, expose others to risks, or exclude competitors from opportunities. As they struggle with one another, people transpose parochial objectives into ostensibly universal matters of agreement, blunting the experience of responsibility for distributional outcomes. Worlds are made and unmade, organized and disrupted—and we are governed—by the outcomes of a thousand battles waged simultaneously among firms, consumers, workers, and financiers over the distribution of gains from economic activity; among communities, families, religions, media, and political figures over the morality to be embedded in social institutions; among military planners and politicians, humanitarians, and civilians over the desirability of this war, the targeting of this village, the imprisonment of these people. Along the way, the costs and opportunities generated by climate change come to fall unevenly across the planet. The costs of economic crisis are distributed between generations, between global investors and local communities, and among workers in different sectors and different parts of the world. Risks and vulnerabilities are allocated among national economies, between families and faraway financiers.

I introduce these themes with an account of contemporary rule by expertise in global political and economic life. The territorial state and the global economy are everywhere entangled with one another. The details of that entanglement are managed, struggled over, and adjusted by experts—including politicians—working with interpretive tools that rest on a more or less conscious set of background images of their natural distinctiveness. I develop a preliminary model of expertise as a stack of ideas from general and uncontested propositions about the world to the more visible technical and ideological debates through which experts engage one another in managing the complex boundaries of political and economic life. The vocabularies of expert management translate social conflicts into expert disagreements that may be expressed in technical or more broadly ideological terms.

More familiar models of global conflict that begin with an identification of the larger scale actors—states, nations, economic classes—and structures—the state system, global capitalism—too often naturalize the actors and structures they identify when the most significant work of expertise can be the making and unmaking of actors and of the game to be played. More traditional models also encourage the notion that conflict is exceptional: normally, the world is at rest. Economics gives this impression with its "invisible hand" and "general equilibrium." So does law with its "legal process" and "constitutional settlements," or political science with "world systems" and "balance of power." In such a frame of mind, it is easy to conclude that most outcomes emerge from a "system logic" or reflect a kind of universal interest or nature. Such images align with a common tendency in expert struggle itself: to frame positions and projects as expressions of a universal rather than a particular interest. By stepping back from this kind of model, I hope to resist the temptation to treat the hegemonic outcomes of past struggle as a fixed terrain for new engagements.

The centrality of coercive struggle does not mean there are no opportunities for mutual gains, collaboration, alliance, or win-win moves. There often are: although such wins also need to be enforced and defended. Nor does it mean the pie can only be divided and never expanded through cooperation or competitive struggle. But when the pie does expand—perhaps particularly when it expands—those gains will accrue to someone. That can also be contested and will need to be defended, perhaps successfully, perhaps not. Nor does the ubiquity of struggle mean everything is always up for grabs. Most struggles have already been won and lost, their outcomes matters of accepted fact, patterns of past struggle woven into the fabric of stability. Persuasion and consensus also rest on a status of forces and are the product of coercive struggle. Struggles whose outcome can be predicted need not be undertaken to be lost or won: some struggles need only be referenced to be won decisively. It takes courage, energy, and imagination to open what has been settled for reconsideration. If we understand the ubiquity of struggle—past and present—in global political and economic life, it should be easier to summon that courage and display that energy strategically.

PART II: EXPERTISE

Expert rule mobilizes knowledge as power. The knowledge part combines commonsense assumptions about the world that may be neither conscious nor open to debate with technical and more broadly ideological material that is often disputed. But expertise is not just knowledge learned in professional study or downloaded from the culture at large. It is also a mode of work. Expert work provides the interpretive links between decisions about what to do and the context within which those decisions are made. In my simple model, experts interpret the context for decision makers and interpret the decisions taken for implementation. Controversy in this "background work" is recognized as practical reason: figuring out what to do, what is appropriate, what will work, or what is right. It takes background work to advance and justify particular positions in universal terms and to dull the experience of responsibility for those who do so. With work, it can come to seem that it really was not me: it was our policy, the will of the world, the requirements of science, the obligations of law, the requirements of sound economic management or institutional process or universal ethics and sound judgment.

The work of expertise takes place within the professional roles, entitlements, and obligations that expert communities imagine they have. With whom are they in conversation? How do they position themselves in relation to one another? These role sensibilities differ by profession. To explore these differences and suggest the range of possibilities, I contrast the position "economic development experts" imagine for themselves with that of international lawyers and human rights advocates. The development policy professional occupies a space between scientific and more popular ideas about economics, about society, history, and culture, and about law and governance. His professional posture is a kind of mediation between scientific knowledge and political practice. The lawyer's imaginary role is different, referencing the status of the material over which he presides rather than its links to scientific accuracy or political effect. Even among international lawyers, specialists in "economic law," "public international law," and "comparative law" imagine the world and their work quite differently: different histories, different projects, different worries, alliances with different neighboring disciplines.

The focus on background work underscores the co-constitutive relationship between the apparatuses of power and those of cultural narration, imagination, myth, professional argument and public reason in global political and economic life. Power is everywhere legitimated by knowledge practices that rationalize, explain, interpret and associate exercises of power, powerful people and powerful institutions with myths, ideologies, and other large ideas about values and interests. At the same time, ideals and values are rendered persuasive, enforced and trained into people through the institutional machinery of power and the mechanics of force. Foreground decision makers and background workers are engaged in a parallel and reciprocal interpretive process about what the context requires, what past decisions mean, how they ought to decide, and what should follow in consequence. Precisely because it is a two-way street—my ideas legitimate your power, your power enforces my ideas—the exercise of power, even as brute force, occurs within a discursive world of meaning. Ideas, ideologies, and myths are able to legitimate only when they are hegemonic across people with the power to halt or support that exercise of power. Understood in this way, the operations of power are expertise all around.

All expert work is contentious because it is uncertain power that needs asserting, uncertain law that requires interpretation, disputed science that requires proof or demonstration. Because their work is interpretive and communicative, experts rule by articulation. Expertise governs when their articulations are performative: when what is articulated comes to pass. To capture this process, I propose a set of tools for modeling expert articulation rooted in my experience with international lawyers, human rights advocates, and policy professionals specialized in economic development. In each of these fields, the basic unit of expert articulation is an assertion about what to do, why that seems sensible, and what will happen as a result. Experts differ with one another about each and contest the links between them. By tracing patterns that emerge, I propose hypotheses about the operations of sophisticated expertise in global management.

Background work is less a game of tight analytics than of contested vulgates. You do not have to be a specialist to play. Although often carried on by lawyers and diplomats, media pundits and politicians, it has also become something far more general, animating discussion among grassroots organizers and grandmothers, financiers and confidence men. Nor must you "believe" the language you speak. Experts routinely deploy arguments and analytics long after—perhaps particularly after—they have been disabused of their analytic rigor and persuasiveness. This is part of what makes these modes of expert practice available for global deployment, colonizing discussion among people with diverse interests, projects, and background cultural priors. With use in dispute comes the internalization of differences within the expert vocabulary and with great influence comes great plasticity and indeterminacy. A kind of agnostic flexibility has come to characterize professional fields as they become more flexible, open, and available for disputation.

I think of this kind of expert practice as at once sophisticated and jaded or disenchanted. In sophisticated and disenchanted fields, the vocabulary deployed to make, defend, and interpret decisions is composed of arguments that accommodate sharp disagreement and subtle compromise and in which people seem both to be invested and to have lost faith. There are sharp differences between alternative theories, factual diagnostics, and political commitments, and people disagree about the entailments of each theory, each political position, and each fact. As people argue, schools of thought rise and fall, mainstream and heterodox traditions clash, and subtle differences take on dramatic significance. The most accomplished experts are not surprised—or troubled—by the uncertainty of their expertise. Often they seem emboldened. People make strong arguments but seem to have lost confidence in the determinacy of their analytics. The odd thing is that it does not seem to matter. Indeed, the uncertainty and ambivalence of professional knowledge may be the subtle secret of its success. What stabilizes their argumentative practices seems to be the argumentative practice itself: a collective sensibility about what would "go too far" or fall outside the horizon of plausible expert argument. Within those boundaries, a potentially infinite terrain of dispute opens up, stabilized by commonsense wisdom about the world and the field of knowledge. This takes the discussion back to the world-making work of shared assumptions about the world to be made.

PART III: LAW

The final section of the book brings the analysis back to law, concluding with an examination of modern law in the practice of warfare as an example of sophisticated modern expertise in action. The extent to which law has become a transnational language of entitlement and disputation should not be surprising. Law of one or another kind has a privileged status in every society as a repository of that alchemy of prestige and fear we call "legitimacy." Legal ideas structure and legitimate forms of authority, and those authorities enforce and deepen law's own claim to predict and state the conditions under which coercion will back up assertions of entitlement. The same is true transnationally. The ubiquity of law as an instrument and stake in struggle owes less to lawyers than to the appetite of all kinds of people for a common—and malleable— language of engagement. Legal norms, institutions, and professional practices are the building blocks for acting and being powerful, as well as for interpreting, communicating, celebrating, and criticizing power. Legal arrangements take us inside the operations of globally distributed power as it is brought to bear in the capillaries of society.

The role of law in struggle is easy to overlook or underestimate when the focus is law's potential to tame politics into a manageable process or constitute the world as a legal order. Accounts of law's distributive role in struggle are few. In global governance discussions, law figures rather as the sinews of a constituted order, privileged tool for global problem solving, or expression of universal values. Struggle over distribution seems the opposite: a place of disorder and force, a refutation of consensus value. But the legalization of global life has succeeded: the domain outside the nation is neither an anarchic political space beyond the reach of law nor a domain of market freedom immune from regulation. The international world is the product of intense and ongoing projects of regulation and institutional management. The basic elements of global economic and political life—capital, labor, credit, money and liquidity, as well as power and right—are creatures of law. Law not only regulates these things, it creates them. They could be put together in lots of ways that would alter the distribution of power and wealth and the trajectory of the society.

People struggle over these legal arrangements because they matter. Because law consolidates winnings, translating victory into right, legal entitlements are often the stakes as well as the tools for political and economic struggle. The status of forces or balance of power between groups and social interests—debtors and creditors, importers and exporters, state traders and multinationals, local labor and global capital, military powers and their insurgent opponents—is written in law and the relative leverage of economic or political competitors is rooted in the background legal and institutional structures within which people bargain and compete. "Statehood" and "sovereignty," for example, are at once realist descriptions, a recognition of the powers that are, and an allocation of bargaining power among groups with conflicting projects: religious and secular institutions, majority and minority communities, local elites and foreign economic interests or local populations, and so on. As an instrument for asserting power over others, law is also a tool of struggle. I claim a legal privilege to put you out of business; you claim the legal authority to prevent me from combining with rivals to do so. I claim the right to overfly your territory and protect your minorities—or you may claim the right to shoot down my plane and attack my humanitarian convoy.

To highlight law's distributive significance, I place David Ricardo's ideas about the legal allocation of "rent" in conversation with his well-known analysis of the gains from trade. The allocation of gains from trade depends on legal arrangements in the sense Ricardo identified when he focused attention on the role of property law in permitting landlords to extract rent by excluding others from the gains generated on land. Legal entitlements make visible a promise of coercion to exclude others from gains they might otherwise hope to enjoy. When I place a no-trespassing sign on my blueberry patch, I express my expectation that the local police will help ensure that I enjoy the full benefit of the crop. Gains from trade likewise accrue to those with the power to exclude. Conflict over those powers also takes legal form. When the legal entitlements people assert are confirmed in practice, the powers and vulnerabilities of people in struggle are defined. As conflict continues, law consolidates gains and losses, solidifying relations between winners and losers. Over time, patterns emerge and inequalities can be reproduced or deepened. I illuminate that process borrowing Gunnar Myrdal's analytic framework for understanding dualist dynamics between centers and peripheries.

The distributive significance of law also illustrates the power of articulation. Law offers people a way to do things using words. Entitlements and powers enable when they are successfully "asserted." Law expresses power as right, and its effective assertion translates right into coercive enforcement. Law offers a language for disagreement and analysis, available for advocacy, compromise, and resolution. It provides a language of both technical distinctions and ideological assertions for debating whether this or that activity should properly be allocated to one or the other. Over time, law has become a repository for disagreements of principle, opposed ideological positions, and definitions of interest associated loosely with alternative doctrinal or institutional arrangements. Self-determination and humanitarian intervention, human rights and cultural difference, free trade and national economic development, financial austerity and growth: all these cross swords in legal terms. In specific struggles, people link these large differences to alternate interpretations of specific entitlements.

All this often comes as something of a surprise to international lawyers—or at least to the scholars who theorize their practice. It took more than a century of technical and intellectual innovation and internal struggle for international law to become a sophisticated vocabulary for contemporary global management. Practitioners and scholars were central to that development. But when they stepped back to reflect, this is not how they saw their work and their special expertise. Their work promoting the substantive expansion, fragmentation, and deformalization of international law had another purpose: to respond ever more adequately to doubts about the distinctiveness and usefulness of international law in a world of sovereign power. As theoreticians worked on that problem, technicians expanded law's scope. As they struggled with one another, they brought their differences into the materials of their shared discipline. The result is a case study in sophisticated—and disenchanted—expertise. International law today is an extremely plural and contingent field that combines a diverse technical practice with a multiplicity of orienting theories about how international law works and where it is going. What holds it all together is a kind of professional faith.

International lawyers can hardly avoid coming face-to-face with the diversity and analytic porousness of their expertise. Such an experience of legal pluralism might open the way to exploring law's role in distributive conflict and the responsibility of legal experts for the outcomes of struggle. By and large, however, this has not happened. Instead, international lawyers have transformed

pluralism into another tool for technical managers, bypassing its radical potential. The fragmentation and pluralization of the field have focused the attention of experts forward on the future world-ordering potential of law and the
prefigurative quality of its current institutional expressions without noticing
its implication in contemporary dysfunction and injustice. The attitude that
results, at once ethically confident and practically disenchanted, is inhabited
in a way reminiscent of sensibilities for accommodating both belief and doubt
within a practice of faith in Protestant religious traditions with which I am
familiar.

The lost opportunity to engage expertise as a doorway to responsible decision rather than as a substitute for ethical reflection and political choice is dramatically on display in the increasing legalization of military conflict. The last
chapter explores the practice of contemporary legal expertise among military
strategists and humanitarians in warfare as a case study of sophisticated expertise run amok. Warfare has become an expert practice illustrating the role of
assertion in struggle, the emergence of ever more sophisticated, if indeterminate, modes of expertise, and the loss of the experience of responsibility that
so often goes with their exercise. The examination of the strange dance that
arises between opponents arguing over the legality of death and destruction in
war with which I conclude this study illustrates the triumph and the tragedy
of global rule by expertise.

REMAKING AN EXPERT WORLD

In recent years, the appetite for rethinking has faded in the World Economic
Forum's discussions of global policy, risk, and governance. My Global Agenda
Council has turned to more routine questions, drafting best-practice procedures for selecting and evaluating leaders in intergovernmental organizations
and developing criteria for establishing successful multistakeholder arrangements to address global problems. What the world needs, my colleagues seem
to feel, is a mustering of the will by global elites to take on the challenge of
global management in new configurations, using new tools and attuned to
new dangers. This doesn't mean they now think the world is well ordered.
They see how uncertain and anarchic things are, how unpredictable the outcomes of their efforts, how powerless their institutions often are in the face of
global economic, political, and social change. But they have confidence in the
promise of institutional reform and in themselves as managers, technocrats,
and leaders. They shy away only from embracing their work as a positioned

exercise of power rather than management of global welfare, technocratic advice in the public interest or the articulation of universal values.

My first year at Davos, I also saw lots of demonstrators and barbed wire—one friend came back through security to the conference hall proud to have collected some rubber bullets. After returning home, I visited the Occupy Wall Street protests, participated in a teach-in at Occupy Toronto. Over the years, I've visited prisons from the West Bank to Latin America, met professionals for whom refugee protection has been a life's work, taught and interviewed human rights professionals and experts in poverty, economic development, and community empowerment. People who feel they are on the receiving end of global power are more likely to perceive a malevolent system than an open-ended terrain for enlightened leadership. Someone—probably the people at Davos—must have wanted things to turn out this way. Many people you meet at Occupy—or are likely to meet in Darfur—have wild ideas about the specific institutions or groups that are to blame. Economic instability and poverty are not problems that *escape* governance; they are the byproducts—or even the intended consequences—of current governance arrangements. Better management by today's elites would not help: they would have to be swept away.

Both Davos titans and Occupy activists have a point. The world is uncertain and open to elite management. It is also unjust, and that injustice is a byproduct of technocratic—and often enlightened and humanitarian—management. A great deal would need to change to turn all this around. In some way, insiders and outsiders are speaking the same language, inhabiting opposing roles in a common theater. From both perspectives, the ways power operates across the world remain obscure. The missing piece, I've come to believe, is the way expert ideas and professional practices of assertion and argument construct and reproduce a world of inequality and injustice. In world affairs, expertise is the coin of the realm. Whether you occupy the commanding heights or have occupied Wall Street, the work of routine reform and resistance will be carried out as a practice of expertise.

I routinely ask my students how they see their generation's project in the world. Is today like 1648 or 1919, when it seemed everything needed to be rethought? Is it like 1945 when the international order seemed to need reforming rather than remaking? Tweak the League Covenant and you have the United Nations, add lots of specialized intergovernmental institutions to coordinate and strengthen government action, replace European empire with self-determination under American hegemony and continue. Or is this like 1989, when the demand was more modest still? With communism defeated, the solutions put forward a generation before could finally be implemented. Student positions seem to reflect their background and aspirations. Those who hope to inherit the commanding heights typically split between 1945 and 1989. Those who feel their interests, politics, or national projects have been stymied by forces beyond their control opt for 1648.

I am pleased that an increasing number of young students and aspiring professionals say this is their 1648. They often have a strong, if idiosyncratic, sense that they know how the world works, who is in charge and who should be resisted. Unsurprisingly, however, many go for the middle position: reform. Add Brazil to the Security Council, sort out the democracy deficit and currency travails in Europe with another round of treaty drafting, and continue. There were reformers like this at both Occupy and Davos. The reforms they discussed were not markedly different, if expressed with a different tenor, emphasis and sense of engagement. Like many commentators, both groups tend to overestimate the potential for "global governance," the structured rationality of the global "system," and the harmony between their own perspective and world public interest.

For the reformers, the world is neither a manageable anarchy nor an unjust iron cage. On the one hand, it seems reasonable to propose reforms to global institutions like the Security Council or the World Trade Organization as if they were central to global order. On the other, it also seems obvious such institutions are not that central—things are more plural and open and confusing than that. This oscillation is repeated in countless settings. People propose institutional reforms, norms and regulations from environmental law to human rights, corporate social responsibility, or international criminal law as if a lever to move the world had been identified, while remaining intensely aware that this is more aspiration than reality. This doubled sensibility—at once earnest and jaded, committed and cynical—is also a mark of disenchanted expertise. Since the economic crisis, the European Union has attracted this kind of ambivalence. More Europe, recursively reformed Europe, seems the only way out other than seizing the gunnels and steady ahead. And yet none of the reforms seems remotely responsive to the loss of confidence and open resistance of publics across Europe.

As the plausibility of narratives about governance waxes and wanes, people on the inside and on the street enter a kind of echo chamber of reciprocal ambivalence. Experts manage in the name of analytics in which they have lost faith: protesters assemble in the name of reforms they doubt will suffice. The new language of "sustainability"—a term detached from its origins in environmental science—suggests the anxieties of the situation. An ambivalent manager class reframes their uncertainty as a matter of social-political risk management: how long can we play for time while those outside demand more before we are swamped by social unrest? Global fiscal imbalances are "unsustainable," for example, if they will lead to political rupture before they can be turned around. Global warming threatens the "sustainability" not of life on the planet, but of the economic and political arrangements people have come to think are natural.

On the outside, the forces of "social unrest" are also in the sustainability game: calculating and communicating in a parallel universe, prophesying the apocalypse in the shadow of the same ambivalences. All they need to do is hold out, hold attention, until something cracks. But no one knows what it would mean for something to crack, for an alternative to arise, for a different political economy to be constructed. There are only the usual reforms. Meanwhile, a political economy of poverty, inequality and ill health continues to be all too sustainable, reproduced through a strange collaboration between the ambivalent projects of a managerial class and everyone else. My project is not to foretell collapse, but to explain the strange resilience of arrangements so many intuit to be nearing their end.

This uncertainty and ambivalence about the world is widespread. People everywhere now understand that they are vulnerable to the decisions and actions of people far away. Their own national state is rarely able—or willing—to defend their interests or support their economic, social, and political aspirations in a globalized world. Something global must be done. There are all kinds of reforms on offer. Many seem attractive, worth mobilizing around. My students find innumerable projects to champion and worthy organizations to join. But it remains unclear, also to them, if they are remaking the world or rearranging the chairs.

The most coveted projects and proposals in my own field of international law are illustrative. It is abundantly clear that they are inadequate to the tasks they purport to address. The International Criminal Court could triple its budget and jurisdiction, the United Nations could redouble its peacekeeping efforts, the international human rights community could perfect its machinery of reporting and shaming without preventing the outbreak of genocide, the collapse or abuse of state authority. Every American and European corporation could adopt standards of corporate responsibility, every first world consumer could be on the lookout for products that are fairly traded and sustainably produced, and it would not stop the human and environmental ravages of an environmentally destructive global economic order. America could ratify the Kyoto Protocol, could agree with China and India and the Europeans on various measures left on the table at Copenhagen or Paris and it would not be enough to prevent global warming. The United Nations' Millennium Development Goals could be implemented and their post-2015 agenda realized and it would not heal the rupture between leading and lagging sectors, cultures, classes. The Security Council could be reformed to reflect the great powers of the twenty-first rather than the twentieth century, but it would be scarcely more effective as a guarantor of international peace and security. Global administrative action could be everywhere transparent and accountable without rendering it politically responsible.

Each of these efforts might be salutary. Some may be terribly important. At best, however, the implementation of these schemes would kick things down the road, manage expectations, and, by rendering the problems sustainable, reaffirm the current distribution of powers. Completing the program of international law would not renew the political economy of the world—anymore than finally "completing" the European Union would resolve the dynamics of dualism that have rocked the project from Brussels and Frankfurt on down. The project of continuing the project is part of how those dynamics are sustained. In Europe, a permanent transition toward an ever-receding goal of a "political" union sustains the technocratic separation of economic and political imperatives—and reinforces the divide between leading and lagging regions. Globally, the permanent transition toward a universal legal order of equal sovereigns sustains one after another project of hegemony. As a result, rather than a toolkit of policy solutions that might be adopted in the global public interest, it would be more accurate to see international law as a legitimating distraction from the effort to remake the politics of war or reframe economic struggle, institutionalizing an uncertain and ambivalent ideology as universal.

Over the past decades, many books and articles have been written about "global governance" to explain how the world works and how the world's institutional machinery might be strengthened.[8] Their authors tend to think like reformers, aspire to address people in places like Davos, and worry about the rising tide of social disillusion with the way the world works. They aim to explain how a disaggregated world is—and might be—governed. The phrase "global governance" signals a dream that the disorganized terrain on which people routinely struggle for advantage might one day become something more orderly, a place where problems would be solved, conflicts moderated, shared values made real. Although those who speak of global governance understand that we can't have—and wouldn't want—a global government, they share the very reasonable conviction that the global capacity to solve problems and contest outcomes ought to be improved. Somewhere and somehow, somebody could be doing for the world what governments do for the people they govern. It is this wish that has driven the substantive and geographic expansion of struggle—and rule—by expertise. And it is also this wish that sustains the viability of disenchanted rulership.

Unless today is your 1648, this does sound reasonable. When the problems people worry about cannot be addressed by local or national government, it is only natural to say that they are "global problems" demanding global solutions. When people seek global solutions, it is understandable that they would look for the kind of interest-aggregating, problem-solving competence they associate with the public hand at home. Addressing climate change, ensuring reliable and sustainable sources of energy, preventing and responding to pandemics, ensuring adequate food and clean water for an expanding population, enabling economic development, resolving cultural conflicts, addressing the threats posed by transnational terrorist networks, fighting corruption, ensuring the stability of financial system and the integrity of the Internet, protecting privacy, combating money laundering: people understand that such things cannot be solved by one city or one nation or one corporation alone. But it is also clear that they are unlikely to be resolved by the United Nations and the routines of global summitry. There is a governance gap.

In the absence of a global government, reformers have looked for functional substitutes. It is easy to think of institutions that might have something to do with ruling the world: the World Trade Organization, the European Union, the U.S. government, the major banks and global corporations, big nongovernmental foundations and advocacy groups, big governments in the developing world. Perhaps the World Economic Forum through their Global Redesign Initiative. Any or all of these might somehow participate in making and enforcing rules or resolving disputes that affect the world. As actors in all these sites reach out to engage one another, they search for a common vernacular—of common hope and personal advantage. Expertise—economic expertise, scientific expertise, legal expertise, social and political expertise, institutional and managerial expertise, expertise in the lessons of history and the universal practicalities of everyday life—fills the bill. Those who exercise the powers of expertise rarely think they are "governing the world." Their mandate and project is always far more specific, their language more universal. As a result, their powers remain obscure, the opportunity to identify and contest their rulership vanishing point rare.

To think of the "global governance" that results as the distributed action of an ersatz public hand is also an understandable dream. Lots of people have the power to change things for other people, empower them, constrain them, humiliate or honor them. Many who take my course about global law and policy are eager to find tidbits of governance in all kinds of places: in corporate social responsibility programs, civil society organizations, philanthropic initiatives—in their own summer internships. They are right to find power in all these places. But when people imagine this adding up to a system of governance, they are dreaming, reinterpreting their field of struggle as something nobler and more promising. Or they are strategizing: reframing their objectives in the language of common purpose.

To identify dispersed activities undertaken for different purposes as a functioning, if imperfect, "global governance" system is so creative an act of interpretation that one cannot help wondering about the motive for it. Calling it "governance" could be a call for accountability or responsibility. Your powers are like those of a sovereign, a sovereign for the world: wield them wisely. It could be an effort to empower: wherever two are gathered in its name, there is global governance. Go forth and govern. It could be the assignment of blame: if you are dissatisfied, knock on this door. To call something an act of "global governance" singles something out—and leaves a lot of other powers in the shadow. They are *not* governance, need not be exercised with the global public interest in mind, and ought not be contested by the dispossessed. To identify "global governance" is an effort to do something with words, to make order by assertion, as much strategy and intervention as description.

In this book, I replace the search for "governance" with an effort to map the operations of power through which our world distributes. With a better cartography of power in the world, it will be a matter for contestation and debate whether this or that actor should be honored or saddled with the label "governance." My story focuses on struggle and inequality rather than consensus and problem solving. Through the work of expertise, order and disorder—even "worldliness," if we can call it that—are distributed unevenly, even inadvertently, among nations, economic sectors or classes, issues or problems through struggles about other things. When the dust settles, some people live globally, others locally; some problems are global, others local. I have written the book with those of my students in mind who embrace the possibility that their generation could transform this world through the slow hard work of remaking the terms by which struggles are carried out, gains and losses distributed, and the status of forces consolidated as order.

The book ends by returning to the question of 1648 with which I began. Roberto Unger once described late twentieth-century expert rule as the work of "a priesthood that had lost their faith and kept their jobs." "They stood," he said, "in tedious embarrassment before cold altars."[9] This misunderstands the contemporary practices of faith among those who manage our world. Governance by expertise is rule through ruthless struggle among experts who have retained their faith and expanded their jobs. Theirs is an ecumenical, eclectic, and disenchanted faith. It is also astonishingly appealing: at once practical and promising, recognizing the world as it is with its eyes firmly planted on the world to come. Its altars are anything but cold. Its practical power and hopeful promise make every year an opportunity for modest reform and no year likely to be our 1648. It should be no surprise that those most eager to change the world would be harnessed to its reproduction. For those of my students who wish it were otherwise, this faith is the seductive obstacle. To turn back from reforms we know to be inadequate will require a refusal to take our eyes off the dynamics of struggle through which injustice is mysteriously reproduced by so many who intend just the opposite.

This, after all, is the legacy we associate with dates like 1648. That year did not transform the politics or economics of the world, although a long war in Central Europe came to an end and new commercial opportunities beckoned. Nor was it a moment of institutional reform, although the Holy Roman Empire never fully recovered. The architects of the Peace of Westphalia did not have a plan to reorganize politics for the next four centuries. If they had, it was not their plan that came to pass. Nevertheless, people remember 1648 because they associate it with the origin of the complex process of intellectual and institutional reinvention through which it came to be a matter of common sense that the politics of the world would be organized around sovereign states: a transformation that took more than three hundred years to achieve. Indeed, that was achieved only after the nature of statehood had been completely redesigned and rebuilt.

For today's generation to remake the world will be equally difficult. Uncertain expert practices and the routine aspirations for a better world that accompany them help to reproduce a world of unending struggle and unrelieved injustice. If this is your 1648, you will need to do more than nudge the managerial class to wise leadership—or protest the powers that be. To rethink and remake the world will require a thousand struggles on the plains where knowledge and power are forged and parceled out. Perhaps I will see you there.

PART I

POLITICAL ECONOMY
AND STRUGGLE

CHAPTER 1
POLITICAL ECONOMY: WORLD-MAKING STORIES

An idea about the way the world is organized can be so widely shared that it sinks into the semiconscious space of common sense. If everyone thinks the world is flat, it is unlikely someone will to try to sail around it. As ideas about the world change, different people are empowered, different projects sped forward or impeded. If it goes without saying that politics ought not to interfere in the economy, different people will be empowered to do different things than if it seems obvious the economy is always already a product of political activity. World pictures are complex and layered. When people speak about big systems like mercantilism, feudalism, imperialism, capitalism, or liberalism to characterize the global order as a whole, they have in mind lots of typical micro practices and significant players, characteristic midlevel organizational structures and political projects, as well as big ideas about what the world is like and what people in various roles should try to do. Other world pictures are less well integrated, but may also bring together small details and large stories.

The worlds imagined by different professional disciplines diverge. Do we live in a world of states—or in a global economy? Is humanity organized by culture and religion—or by levels of development? Where anthropologists see cultures, economists see national economies and global markets. International lawyers see nation-states, tempered by all their profession's efforts to transcend, organize, legalize, and govern the interactions among them. To become a professional is partly a matter of learning to see the world as others in the profession see it. One becomes how one sees and struggle over the world is also a struggle to become oneself.

The worlds people imagine and build change over time. We are losing track of boundaries that once defined a world of aristocratic families. The nineteenth-century world of hierarchically arranged races and civilizations is fading, although the early twentieth-century world of secular and religious states may be back on the rise. Imaginary worlds also have imaginary histories: the "state system" is routinely dated to the 1648 Peace of Westphalia, which is said to have turned a world of religions into a world of sovereigns. In fact, it took another three hundred years to build a world whose politics were organized along state lines. During that time sovereignty and statehood meant many different things. Nevertheless, origin myths are as important for world building as they are for religions, families, or cultures.

Different worlds have different senses of time, of things that are recent and distant, urgent and inconsequential. For some the future stretches out majestically, for others we are living in end times. International lawyers and policy professionals who work to build the machinery for global governance often imagine a kind of middle distance in which their partial efforts will add up to a more perfect global public capacity. People have different ideas about what drives the present—a clash of civilizations? The rise of Asia? And different ideas about what we can expect and what would count as progress.

Many contemporary books about the world begin by nodding to the powerful economic, social, and technological forces of "globalization." The world is interconnected, local problems have become global, global problems have become ever more threatening and intractable. This kind of world cries out for governance, counsels cosmopolitanism, and places parochial concerns in a past we can no longer afford. History challenges an ill-equipped governance system and managerial class: will we rise to respond? There is a lot of truth in such stories, although one also encounters stories that stress the rise of fragmentation and sectarianism in today's world. As I was finishing this chapter, the *Boston Globe* ran a prominent feature headlined "The Great Deglobalizing: Our Interconnected World Is Shrinking Back toward Its National Borders—And That's a Problem."[1] Author Joshua Kurlantzick of the Council on Foreign Relations urged his readers to worry that our world was plunging into protection and isolation, citing falling cross-border capital flows, trade volume declines, rising hostility to immigration, and an upsurge in populist nationalism. Stories of both kinds are told for a purpose: to embolden those seeking local self-determination or, in Kurlantzick's case, to redouble the countervailing efforts of cosmopolitans. The goal is not only to "get it right" on global trends, but also to encourage action and support one or another broad orientation among the policy class.

As a result, ideas about the world are often hotly contested. Decades of argument about whether the world is warming, how fast and why reflect the intuition that getting people to think it is warming will make it easier to mobilize resources to do something about it. Or, to take an example from economics, if for a generation everyone thinks an economy is a national input/output system to be managed, and then suddenly they all become convinced that an economy is a global market for the allocation of resources to their most productive use through the efficiency of exchange in the shadow of a price system, lots has changed. That is also governance, the exercise of power, the reorganization of possibilities for people in political and economic struggle. We can expect that people would periodically try to bring these large images into conscious dispute as they struggled for advantage, developing the rhetorical tools to promote one grand idea against the other.

It is a staple practice of the policy intelligentsia to argue for an adjustment in background ideas about how the world works to make some kinds of policies more likely, others less defensible. Thomas Friedman's bestseller *The World Is Flat: A Brief History of the Twenty-First Century*, for example, was a prominent earlier intervention in these background images.[2] He urged leaders and the informed public to update their conception of the world: nations matter less, economic ties matter more, distance matters less, communication technologies matter more, political divisions matter less, knowledge matters more, the poor have more opportunities to compete, bulky consolidated political and economic actors are less likely to succeed. Friedman sprinkled the book with suggestions about how appreciation for these facts should change priorities for business and government.

Each image that conjures a world also suggests a project, a practice. Someone must see it, say it, divine its meaning, communicate what is to be done and mobilize others to do it. A "balance of power" story casts the "balancing power" in a heroic role, stabilizing the global order, rather than as an unreliable ally struggling for advantage. To imagine a world and read its implications for human organization is work: creative and imaginative work, interpretive and diagnostic work, programmatic and practical work. And work in a setting where others are seeing different omens, auguring different meanings, proposing different projects. This is not only interpretive work. It is also necessary to build the scaffolding, the institutions, the media enterprises, the academic institutions, the professional guilds from which the world can appear this way and from which such projects can be undertaken. To build such structures is also to empower people—create people—who see things from this perspective. The existence of the United Nations with a tall building in New York and thousands of employees reproduces the world seen by its creators among those who work in its shadow. The UN secretary-general brings the authority of his office to bear on the world through the structures of diplomatic life. But the world imagined by his office and reinforced by the community of diplomats is also brought to bear on him, on his goals, projects, and capabilities. It is hard to function at the United Nations without seeing a world of "member states" and global problems and trying to invent technical programs for their resolution.

WORLD-MAKING STORIES: BACKGROUND IMAGES AND REFORM TRAJECTORIES

Stories make the world not through direct implementation by devoted acolytes but through a complex interaction with technical knowledge and professional practice. To explore how that might happen, let me begin with a dystopic and common interpretation of what have become the well-known challenges posed by economic globalization. Imagine the following story, which I have cobbled together from a variety of recent left liberal and progressive opinion pieces and news articles. It combines a range of "observations" and focuses on the problematic separation of economic life from political control.

What is going on in the world today? A rapid process of factor price equalization and technological assimilation has allowed people everywhere to aspire to a refrigerator and an air conditioner, along with the public and private institutions necessary to realize those ambitions. On the one hand, globalization has opened the world to miraculous economic possibilities and focused national politicians on providing the essential conditions for economic stability: fiscal responsibility, a strong and reliable private legal order, and security. But change on this scale is profoundly destructive and relative income equalization is an extremely uneven business. A global economy is not a uniform economy. Things turn at different speeds. Millions of people are lifted up. But people are also left out. People are dragged down. When people turn to their sovereigns for help, the results are terribly uneven. Some are too big to fail—others too small to count. Workers, consumers, businesses large and small turn to the nation state for support against the competitive pressures and uncertainties of global markets. Some are given golden wings and strong armor. Many find there is little their sovereign will do.

Unfortunately, neither the creative destruction of global economic flows nor the instability and vulnerability to shocks are amenable to management on the scale of our political life. Governments everywhere are weak, buffeted by economic forces, captured by economic interests, and engaged their own economic pursuits. Global economic actors are increasingly asked to take on public responsibilities beyond their mandate with no incentive to assess the choices they face from the perspective of political constituencies or world welfare. As the weakness of governments has become visible, politicians have learned to operate in the shadow of disenfranchised and disillusioned publics who have lost faith in the public hand. Political life has drifted into neighborhood and transnational networks, been diffused into the capillaries of professional management and condensed in the laser beam of media fashion, transformed into a unifying spectacle. The inability of politics to offer public interest solutions to policy challenges has encouraged political cultures ever less interested in doing so. Politics has come to be about other things: symbolic and allegorical displays, on the one hand, and the feathering of nests on the other.

Meanwhile, unmoored from stable political management, the global economy has become volatile and destructive, veering from boom to bust set free from the stabilizing hand of sound regulatory management. The relative mobility of economics and territorial rigidity of politics have rendered each unstable as political and economic leadership have drifted apart and political leadership has everywhere become peripheral to economic management. In short, the disconnection of economic and political life threatens the sustainability of contemporary political and economic structures.

That all sounds pretty bad. If we accept this interpretation of globalization and want to do something to change it, the story suggests we focus on institutional design. The recurring theme is actors operating in structures unsuited to their tasks: the scope of political power and the range of economic activity are mismatched. An obvious path for reform would be to build global "governance" capabilities, render corporate actors responsible to social concerns, empower new nongovernmental actors to regulate and monitor transboundary activities, and so forth.

Such a story lets many people off the hook. Indeed, its usefulness as apology should make us skeptical. It reinforces a tacit division of labor between economic and political institutions, neither of which appears responsible for the outcomes. No wonder the most powerful governments fail to meet the demands of their constituents: their failures are the product of forces beyond their control. Nor are the institutions of global economic life responsible. From financiers, entrepreneurs, and corporations to black-market traders in drugs, arms, and remittances, economic actors are only doing what makes sense, given their interests and mandate. They can undertake social tasks as a philanthropic exercise in "social responsibility" but have no political responsibilities in this domain. The "global economy" is also a place of necessity: a natural force of "creative destruction" responsible for demolishing industries, impoverishing workers, and disempowering governments. No actual person did anything.

The reforms suggested by such an interpretation are also not very promising. If we want change, we would either have to alter the system structuring relations between economic and political actors or somehow encourage "enlightened" leaders to rise above the constraints and incentives of their position to do something unnatural to their role. Each is very difficult to imagine. Wise leaders rising above their mandate across the world? A structural change in the "state system"? At Davos, even in crisis they shied away from a "new Bretton Woods." The transformation of global corporations and banks into politically responsible substitutes for government? The emergence of citizen alliances powerful enough to constrain both governments and private economic actors? All very unlikely.

At the same time, each of these things could be *attempted*. You can establish an NGO to monitor global value chains. You can urge governments to cooperate where interests are shared: combatting terrorism, improving airline safety, collecting taxes. You can convince corporate leaders attentive to reputational risk to prioritize social responsibility. There is work to do that can be understood as a "first step" toward remaking the global system of political and economic actors. You can get a job—or at least a summer internship—doing these things. And what alternatives are there, given this story? How else could the challenges of globalization be addressed other than by this kind of reform: awakening private actors to public responsibilities and strengthening public actors able to operate above and beyond the existing constraints of national government? Although many people who write stories like this urge structural reforms in the strongest terms, the result is a kind of tyranny of no alternatives other than reforms you probably intuit are unlikely to do the trick.

Part of what makes this story seem compelling, if disheartening, is its reliance on differences and distinctions that seem natural and fact-like. Globalization is problematic because it heightens the difference between "economic" and "political" structures and actors. In legal terms, the first are "private" and the second "public." The story stresses the urgent need to link them more effectively: to find public actors able to regulate outside borders, to find private actors willing to act in the public interest. The commonsense notion that public and private actors or political and economic structures are distinct and different runs deep. It is shared by people with very different, even opposing, interpretations and reform proposals. People who love globalization and people who want an even sharper separation of economic life from political oversight share the commonsense idea that these domains are different.

But the differences between politics and economics or public and private are ideas. Each is more "ideal type" than sociological truth. Such abstract differences cannot help but exaggerate the homogeneity of both global economic and political life. In fact, all governments do economic things and all corporations do political things. All public authorities exercise power tacitly and explicitly outside their "jurisdiction." A low-wage export strategy works only if it penetrates foreign markets where wages are higher: if the wage rate bargained in the shadow of local rules "applies" in otherwise high-wage foreign markets through the movement of goods. All corporations "regulate" the activities of their employees, customers, and business partners. Or, to be more precise, all so-called governments do things we could easily interpret as "economic" and vice versa. These designations are the product of contested interpretation.[3]

FOREGROUNDING THE TECHNICAL WORK OF EXPERTS

Getting beyond the tyranny of hapless reform requires bringing the routine interpretive work through which these designations are made and contested to the surface. It is this technical work that *already* makes and unmakes the boundaries of political and economic life. The more we understand what experts and professionals do when they argue and contend with one another about just where the boundaries should be, the clearer it becomes that global dysfunction arises not from the nature or structure of "politics" and "economics" or from the abstract historical force of globalization, but from expertise: from the global knowledge practices for their differentiation, interaction, and management. The interplay of politics and economics is easily forgotten because the technical work of linking them is understood by those who do it to be knitting domains together or balancing forces that are otherwise distinct and opposed.

The creation of a market is not an exercise of unrestrained factor mobility. Factor mobility is a relative thing: which factors can move under which conditions is determined by legal, social, and cultural mores and institutions. Global economic life is a patchwork of sectors and regions, some of which are tightly integrated, others invisible and impenetrable to one another. The boundaries are everywhere disputed as people struggle for market access and market protection. The active work of national institutions in maintaining global economic life could also be undertaken in various ways. National governments provide the currencies, manage the central banks, regulate the banking, insurance, and transport sectors, construct and empower economic actors, enforce the contracts and property rights and arbitration awards, provide security, and define the lines among white, gray, and black markets.

Just how and where and for the benefit of whom these arrangements should be settled are matters of conflict that are typically resolved as matters of more or less. *How* independent a central bank? How effective a tax? How tolerated the black market or the demand for corrupt payments? These adjustments are not made by architects of the global system. Resolutions emerge from struggles among people in particular institutional settings trying to gain or hang on to an advantage. In those struggles, technical and professional modes of reasoning, debating, and deciding are used both to make and to unmake the boundary between "politics" and "economics" or to settle it in different places. These struggles are undertaken in specialized languages—often of law or economics—which are only loosely tethered to the more familiar terms of broad debates about the desirability of linking or delinking economic activity from political contest, although the way people interpret the trend ("globalization" or "deglobalization") can affect who wins in such struggles, who is able to imagine moving a boundary this way or that, and which arguments have wind in their sails. The lines that are drawn and the balances that are struck are tentative. Whether they harden into necessity or get remade tomorrow will be determined by appetite and the power of those who stand to benefit and lose.

To establish a corporation capable of global economic activity, for example, is not simply a matter of shielding investors from liability and excusing the corporation from political responsibility so it might cleave only to the pecuniary interests of shareholders. It is a complex matter of degree: how should the obligations of shareholders and managers be balanced, what role for workers, what form of ownership, how much liability for which kinds of damage, what duties of care are owed to consumers and populations where corporations are active? An abstract commitment to "disembedding the economy" cannot determine how to settle these questions of degree, although people who favor increasing shareholder control may extol globalization and economic disembedding while those who would increase corporate responsibility to other interests may also denounce globalization and advocate greater local political control.

There are technical arguments here: about what is "efficient," about what a corporation "is," about how rules about these matters will interoperate with other parts of the institutional or rule system. Sometimes one or another solution may seem technically obvious, the expression of universal reason. Everyone may understand the requirements of "efficiency" or the best way to avoid "agency costs" similarly, or these may be matters of dispute. This is the space for benchmarks, best practices, indicators and rankings: "objective" measures of what needs to be done. When they are disputed, technical choices may also be framed to reflect large debates in the larger public arena: should we embrace globalization or not? Sometimes people argue about questions of corporate structure, for example, as if the nation's place in the global economy is at stake: workers on the corporate board will erode foreign investment and ensure that we cannot compete, closing off the opportunities opened up by globalization. Whether these midlevel arrangements are debated and settled in technical terms or through broader debates, the discussions take place in the more or less conscious shadow of commonsense ideas about how economies and polities ought to be arranged. These may be invoked and contested directly, but more often they lie dormant in accepted wisdom. The relationships among commonsense, broadly debated choices about the world and the nation's place in it, and the technical in the professional work of establishing, differentiating, and linking economic and political arrangements are the puzzle to be understood.

The professionals who struggle over these matters do not see themselves as architects of global order. Few are motivated primarily to implement large abstract ideas—"disembed the economy" or "reverse globalization." They are usually pursuing advantages of one or another sort for their ministry, their client, their political party, their profession, their faction or school of thought. They may simply be seeking validation as the experts who knew how get to it right. When they reflect on their work in general terms, their self-conception is often quite benign: doing their best to manage the problems before them. The hypothesis I explore in this book is that their work is nevertheless world making. If the natural separation of the global economy and national politics is common sense among experts debating how and when to link them, their technical work may keep the separation going no matter how committed everyone is to ensuring their productive association. The result would be a strange double practice that somehow unravels in the routine work of day the enlightened objectives experts have seen themselves pursuing the night before.

The global political and economic arrangements that result are surprisingly sturdy for all the talk of crisis and worry over sustainability. Terribly unjust, subject to crisis, environmentally unwise, everywhere politically and economically captured by the few, and yet somehow impossible for anyone to alter or escape. My hypothesis is that this stability arises from the relative invisibility and imperviousness of the world of technical management to contestation. The large stories people advocate to explain what is happening and urge people to action—globalization/deglobalization—float free of the numerous small-scale calculations made in their shadow, all of which are contested matters of more or less rather than hearty endorsements of one or the other. People may struggle over these issues as if they stood at the Rubicon, but they do not, and in some part of their professional sensibility they also know that.

SHIFTING THE STORY, CHANGING THE TECHNICAL TERRAIN

A sudden shift in the story can reshuffle the available technical choices. In crisis, elites sometimes double down on arrangements they favored beforehand and sometimes are emboldened to move the pendulum the other way. For people in an expert community, the sum of the vectors can feel like momentum and the balance of power in many small struggles may shift. When planes hit the twin towers in New York on 9/11, lots of struggles were already under way between projects advanced in the name of "security" and those advanced for other reasons. Suddenly, a thousand tug-of-war standoffs lurched toward security. The terrain had shifted. But do we live in a new age of "security states"? If you Google "globalization" or "governmentality" and "security state" you will find many authors who think we do. Although their interpretations may become hegemonic—like "globalization"—for the moment, this remains a battle cry useful for raising alarm about surveillance and a growing military-industrial complex.

The 2009 global economic crisis had a similar effect. Suddenly each country, each city, each firm seemed to need a global political economic *strategy* after all. Politicians scrambled to figure out how to strengthen the competitive hand of their cities, regions, nations, and favorite economic sectors. The hegemony, if it had been that, of neoliberal orthodoxy applauding a global market liberated from local political distortion and national politics disciplined by the needs of that market was on the wane. Strategic engagement with the global economy was not a new idea, of course. The technical knowledge was available to give shape to argument about how to have a strategy. Paul Krugman had published *Strategic Trade Policy and the New International Economics* in 1986.[4] In development economics, theories of "dynamic comparative advantage" were already being taught as "modern growth theory."[5] These theories had been digested into programs of action. Aspiring policy makers learned that countries should seek to climb a natural "ladder of comparative advantage" from resource-intensive activities, through unskilled labor-intensive and skilled labor-intensive, toward capital-intensive, and finally R&D- or knowledge-intensive industries.

> In the higher rungs of the ladder, the exports are of . . . goods in which comparative advantage is not simply natural or historical but has been acquired. Michael E. Porter and Krugman stress the creation of comparative advantage in new products through proprietary knowledge, innovations, investment in human capital and physical capital, and the realization of economies of scale in production. Such sources of comparative advantage are dynamic, involving a process of economic transformation and the creation of comparative advantage in differentiated goods through technical capability and learning by doing.[6]

After 2009, these ideas entered the programs of political parties with new vigor. Policy makers everywhere tried to create, protect, and promote local winners—if only rarely effectively—sometimes with a vague promise of transfer payments to compensate local losers. To strategize one's insertion into the global economy required promoting local winners and stimulating "a process of economic transformation" through which new winners would be created to move "up" the ladder. It is easy to imagine all kinds of interests presenting themselves as the key to climbing that ladder and many disputes arising about the allocation of resources among possible winners undertaken in the language of strategic trade and dynamic comparative advantage. The new language of strategy—with its own set of technical considerations—was available for appropriation in struggle.

In one country, one city, one region after another, one now hears the same refrain: we will invest in new technologies, new industries, new educational programs and new infrastructure to become winners in the high-tech global knowledge economy of the future. Even a country like Qatar, with the world's highest per capita GDP and an unparalleled opportunity to develop on the back of resource-intensive industry, has come to pursue a national development plan oriented to becoming a "knowledge-based economy." Regardless of the rents available in oil or the cost of human capital development, the direction for enlightened government seemed clear: to reduce reliance on oil and gas and to stimulate the emergence of new industries and communities based on knowledge and innovation. This is what it means for a large-scale story to have momentum. Exactly how to do this was open to technical assertion, argument, and struggle. Which knowledge industries? Supported in what way? Success measured by what criteria? The larger meaning of the turn to strategy also remains open to interpretation. The rise of national strategizing could, of course, be interpreted as "deglobalizing." But it could also be argued that the strategic turn *increased* the ruthlessness of global economic—and political—competition. After all, if the public hand is everywhere to be a force multiplier for leading sectors, nations, regions, the turn to strategy would also heighten imbalance and inequality in the global economy, harnessing everyone more tightly to its competitive edge.

INHABITING A SOPHISTICATED TECHNICAL STORY

I had dinner a couple of years ago with a leading European politician—a Social Democrat—after hearing his impassioned speech promoting a high-tech green industry strategy for left parties worldwide. I asked whether he really thought it was possible for every nation to be a highest tech, greenest, innovation-driven knowledge economy, any more than everyone could be the lowest wage manufacturer. No, of course not, he admitted. Then why didn't he say that? Why had he encouraged the opposite? Because the point was to inflate a balloon that would change the balance of political legitimacy in the internecine battles that are the routine work of government. He would go back to the office and face one after another debate with opponents, bureaucrats, and specialists from his ministries or from Brussels and Frankfurt about all kinds of things and he wanted to strengthen the arguments he would deploy in those discussions by heightening their presence in the public realm.

Why, I asked, would *those* people believe such a strategy plausible? They probably would not, he imagined—they were as sophisticated as he. But they might think that was how politically motivated publics would see it. And they might not worry about its overall plausibility—they would be debating much more marginal adjustments, after all. But why, I wondered, would the balloon rise among the public? How could so unlikely a promise seem like a plausible political program for so many? Don't laypeople also see, or at least suspect, that speeches like his are justifications for mobilizing resources behind the successful, deferring rather than underwriting the promise to compensate? Perhaps they do. But maybe they also sense that nothing so dramatic will happen anyway. And perhaps people think that is how politicians and bureaucrats would frame choices that mattered to them in other ways or for other reasons. The sophisticated idea at work here is a strange mirror among a public, a political class, and a technocracy all speaking a language they find less than compelling because they imagine it convinces or motivates other people while also understanding that the choices being discussed do not require the story to be more than vaguely plausible and loosely relevant to what they hope to do.

Two things missing from both the visible public debate and the bureaucratic struggles that invoke it would be an examination of the arrangements though which some economic activities become marked as "high-value" objects worthy of public strategy or private investment and the semiconscious assumptions about political and economic life shared by everyone involved. Let us imagine the kinds of debates my politician might face when he engages the technocrats in government. The occasion will be something specific. Is public investment needed, or ought it to be avoided to ensure a robust airline or high-tech industry in our country? Should we guarantee these loans or consider the strategic impact of this public procurement? These issues will have technical dimensions and will be framed by whatever debates are moving the political class at the time. Perhaps whether the nation should resist globalization with strategy or embrace it. Or, if my friend's trial balloon flew, whether the nation should invest in high-tech green industries as a path to prosperity.

Other things that might have been debated will have settled into common sense. Perhaps no one is debating whether the world is globalizing or deglobalizing or everyone is taking "austerity" and "structural reform" as desirable. At the technical level, it could also be that no one is contesting whether airlines and high tech are, in fact, high-value industries. This may be seen as a question of fact: on the ladder of comparative advantage, strategy can get you to "high-value" industries, but you cannot rearrange the ladder so that different industries are "high value." You should just ask an economist which they are.

The arrangements that make some activities high value and others low value are institutional and often legal. Economic activities are called "high value" because people who do them, under current arrangements, can exclude others and capture a higher share of the global gains from undertaking them. Those who are excluded, bypassed, or outcompeted will capture less. In "low-value" activities, those who do them have little or no authority to exclude others and must compete ruthlessly on price. This also depends on legal and institutional arrangements. For example, the international enforcement of intellectual property law, however imperfect, makes technological innovation a high-value activity when compared with low-skill labor, but only as long as low-skill laborers are put in global competition with one another by legal institutions regulating corporate employment practices, migration law, unionization, and more. The meaning and global impact of intellectual property law, like the regulation of corporate labor practices, is the frozen settlement of earlier debates that may have been, at the time, similar to those we now imagine about guaranteeing loans to aircraft manufacturers or investing in infrastructure to create "hubs" for high-tech start-ups or scholarships for people who will become entrepreneurs rather than engineers or farmers. It is just that these earlier debates have faded into matters of fact.

EXPERTISE: A FIRST PICTURE

This suggests a crude preliminary model for the work of knowledge in the making of policy as a loose stack of debates. At the top—or maybe buried most deeply in common sense—are settled understandings about the world: globalization. Then come open questions about what to do: Is national political strategy wise or unwise? Should politics embrace or try to harness globalization? Although these debates are often readily associated with political or ideological terms (right/left; free-market liberalism/social democracy), they are heavily influenced by the loose expertise of public intellectuals and academics that have been taken up by the political class: austerity or countercyclical investment? This is as true of military as of economic policy: sanctions or surgical strikes? Deter or defeat the enemy? Hearts and minds or overwhelming force?

These broad debates, in turn, are loosely tethered to open technical questions about how the boundary between public and private action ought to be settled in particular cases. Should the treasury guarantee the loans? Should the government push back against Brussels austerity? New debates of this sort arise repeatedly: over the wisdom or necessity of "internal devaluation" and "structural reform" as a strategy for growth. Or over more specific details: on what schedule will public investment in this industry generate growth sufficient to increase tax revenues to repay the loans? All kinds of decisions can be debated as part of the "knowledge economy" strategy. Should the Boston public transport system remain open all night? Only on weekends? Not at all? In 2015, the debate was conducted not only as a question of "what kind of city we want to become," but also in terms of what was needed for a robust knowledge-based high-tech economy. Young innovators would settle in other

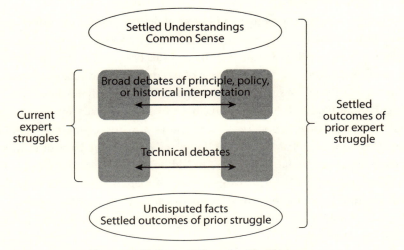

Figure 1.1 Professional Expertise: The Elements

cities, it was alleged, if the subway was not available to whisk them to late-night socializing.

Beneath all these debates lie a set of taken-for-granted facts that are the naturalized outcomes of earlier debates. Is intellectual property protected forcefully? Are worker wages and terms of employment open to collective negotiation? The geography of a city often appears natural: industries here, residences there, bus lines and transport hubs in these locations, good and bad schools allocated in this way. Each of these, along with the allocation of powers to alter or preserve them, is the outcome of an earlier set of contested choices that have now faded.

The processes by which some large conceptions and the outcomes of some prior struggles are naturalized as part of the factual donnée is difficult to uncover. I think of it as a process of hegemonic consolidation, and I review some standard critical tools for reversing this kind of naturalization in the coming chapters. To ask how hegemony arises is to participate in its erosion. Simply to name the idea as a "common assumption" or matter of background common sense suggests that it might not be. The relationship between the middle tiers of debate is easier to study: how large opposing conceptions of economic and political life are transformed into or become associated with technical questions of more or less. This is where technical arguments about efficiency or innovation or competitiveness touch larger ideological discussions about local strategy in a global economy and opposing considerations of interest.

The bridge between conceptual and technical debates is the transformation of principled alternatives into points on a line and vice versa.

Strangely, it seems impossible not to cross this bridge. It is hard to resolve a clash of swords between "a market free of interference" and "a government attuned to market failures and strategic opportunities" cleanly because these are Potemkin abstractions. In the world, they are always already mixed together and what seems like boundary work is always a matter of more or less. On the other hand, it is hard to do the boundary work on the basis of technical knowledge alone. If one could, there would be no boundary work to do: the outcome would have been clear to everyone. If there is work to be done, it is difficult for experts not to arrange themselves around the choices presented on the basis of their loose affiliation with large commitments or interpretations of the world situation.

Perhaps as a result, debates at all these levels blend together. So long as large debates and technical questions are disputed and have not yet fallen into common sense or been naturalized as fact, people at all levels combine professional analytics and institutional tools with invocations of broad interpretations of context, interest, or ideological commitment in their debates about who should do what. The terms of intellectual property protection can be contested by reference to large-scale debates about globalization. The global structure of political and economic life can be transposed into the key of technical necessity: what innovation or efficiency requires or what property is.

The dispersion of struggle has increased the significance of professional and quasi-professional modes of engagement that communicate transnationally, retain sufficient status to be effective, and are themselves uncertain and fragmented enough to sustain multiple insistent projects simultaneously. On the one hand, choices that may seem ideological or political (liberate the economy/strengthen the state) come to be discussed in more technical terms. The European Union offers the most obvious example. Debates between nations (Finland vs. Greece, Germany vs. Spain) or between center/right economic liberals and center/left social democrats are transformed into debates about the requirements of austerity, the demands of a single currency, entitlements of various stakeholders, or the free-rider problems that may follow rewarding rather than punishing the profligate. At the same time, these large debates can be dissolved into matters of more or less in specific circumstances. Exactly how should the Greek bailout be adjusted? Who should take how much of a haircut? And, of course, these can be reframed as direct political confrontations: Greek national dignity demands this and no less!

This is as true at the local as at the national level. The long bankruptcy proceeding in my hometown of Detroit was a constant oscillation between absolute claims and technical details. On the one hand, absolute entitlements (the "rights" of investors, residents, pensioners), political priorities (residents or faraway banks, hard work rewarded or canny investments, current residents or retirees elsewhere), and large debates about "what kind of a city are we?" On the other, all the detailed ways in which claims could be measured and adjusted, losses shared, compromises reached. All those involved came to speak the language of "fairness and justice" alongside the technical jargon of Chapter 9. In one sense, the European politician at my dinner table was right: inflating a balloon in public debate may cascade down through thousands of smaller struggles just as technical wisdom can colonize the public debate. Meanwhile, all those involved will find it difficult to contest the big ideas and prior battles that lie off-limits in common sense or expert knowledge.

This is contemporary rule by expertise. When people think about the significance of technical reason in contemporary economic and political life, their reaction is often to demand its displacement by democracy: to replace technical management by political control. But politics has become part of a technical world, an expert performance in its own right shielding the worlds of institutional management from contestation. For the critical animus to become active, it needs to be translated into the available vocabularies of struggle. It must learn to become expertise in a world where experts differ sharply and yet somehow together seem to sustain arrangements of astonishing inequality and injustice that no one claims to have intended. Unfortunately, the effort to "replace technocracy with democracy" has a lot in common with the effort to "link economy with politics." It leaves unexplored the assumption that they are essentially different while shielding from controversy the process by which earlier struggles had settled this as technical and this as political.

BIG IDEAS AND SMALL CHOICES: THE EXPERT VOCABULARY

However much ruling experts may doubt the possibility of disentangling economics from politics or try to set the balance between them correctly, something in the way they set the frame may nevertheless set national politics and global economics off on divergent paths. Deeper commonsense images of what an "economy" and "polity" are queer the pitch, overwhelming the more congenial sense that it all comes down to a sensible balance among institutional arrangements that are inevitably entangled with one another.

MAKING AN ECONOMY GLOBAL

How do elites imagine an "economy"? Although it is common to think of an economy as something nations have—the German economy, the Japanese economy—when people think of an economy as a "market," it is difficult not to think of it as something that can be scaled up or down. And to think that scaling up is generally good. Ever more people, products, resources, and ideas ought to be able to find their markets in the shadow of a common price system across ever greater distances. As a result, when putting an economy together, it is a good idea to try to link as many things together as efficiently as possible at the national, regional and global levels. People I have encountered in the global managerial class blend these ideas: although national economies do wise need management, it would be better if they could be knit together into some kind of common market.

It was not *always* common sense. A mercantilist sense for the global economy as a space to be secured by political control was quite different. In the first half of the twentieth century, elites imagined "the economy" far more exclusively in national and colonial terms. Nor is a sense for the virtue of a geographically expansive economy unshakable. For many years, a foreigner listening to German elites discussing economic policy would have heard a great deal about the European and global economies. A few years after the economic crisis, a retired German ambassador invited me to his home in Berlin for dinner with an array of political luminaries. As the discussion went on—I the only foreigner—I was struck that everyone who mentioned "the economy" quite clearly meant "the German economy." When I pointed this out, my host admonished the table— our foreign guest asks a serious question about Germany's relation to Europe. The conversation turned on a dime as the guests competed to demonstrate their European and global bona fides. Nevertheless, something had shifted in the taken for granted.

To the extent a geographically expanding economy is common sense, it is the result, at least in part, of ideological struggle. Since the Second World War, many among the policy elite, aghast at the consequences of the Great Depression, have remembered the world of nineteenth-century liberalism in this way and have sought to build their way back to it institutionally.[7] Innumerable projects have been launched and defended as contributions to realizing this vision, from the European Union or the General Agreement on Tariffs and Trade to a library of bilateral and multilateral trade and investment treaties, although each in its technical details reflects a distillation of various ideological influences. However diverse the genealogy of these institutional arrangements, some version of this vision has fallen into common sense, even for those whose conscious ideological and political commitments run the other way. Economies *are* markets and markets are more effective mechanisms for the efficient allocation of resources the larger they are.

At the same time, elites also realize that even this very general and limited vision has always been more idea than reality and has always been contested. Indeed, as it has fallen into common sense, it has also fallen into ideological disrepute. All but the true believers realize the nineteenth century was not like this and that the world's economic life remains fragmented along lots of lines, for good and ill. Local and sectoral specificities, informal networks, oligopolies, barter, intraenterprise trade, market failures, bottlenecks and other anomalies remain ubiquitous today. Not everyone plays by the rules. Markets can be ruthless and the weak must be protected. Markets can fail and their failures must be compensated by policy. Efficiency is no guarantor of growth, which must be midwifed by strategy. As a result, it is *part* of the background consciousness of ruling classes that the virtuous destiny of economic life is an ever more undifferentiated global market in which goods and services follow prices to more productive uses. But it is *also* part of their background consciousness that this idea is partial, has limits, and ought to be tempered or opposed outright. An idea—but a qualified idea. Common sense, but available for disputation in particular situations.

The (qualified) idea of a global market has been understood to bring with it dozens of practical corollaries. Economic activity can happen on a global scale only if the institutional arrangements are in place to support it, just as political activity can be concentrated territorially only if the institutions responsible for political life have distinct jurisdictions. A national politics requires a "state." A global economy requires a range of different institutions that may be constructed in different ways. A system of "world prices" seems to require that exchange rates be either stable or extremely fluid and accompanied by legal arrangements to manage exchange risk. Private actors—investors, employees, managers, corporations—need to be capacitated to operate globally. Local arrangements that could make employers feel they should hire from among a particular union or corporations feel beholden to specific locations or constituencies should be relaxed. Economic entities themselves should be able to be reconstituted and unbundled, able to be reorganized, parceled out for sale and redeployment. Supply chains, information channels, labor markets, investment patterns ought all to be rendered global through institutional and legal integration. The legal arrangements necessary to keep all this going should be protected from interference by local political and judicial authorities.

These institutional arrangements are not absolute requirements. They may be put together in a variety of ways that allocate power, status, and wealth in various ways. As a result, the details of their construction are matters of controversy, at least until one or another pattern becomes best practice or common sense. Experts come to these practical details with the idea and its qualifications and criticisms in mind. As people argue about the details, people who oppose the neoliberal disembedding of economy cross swords with those who favor the insulation of markets from political meddling. Even where there is sharp disagreement, however, the disembedders would not abolish the state, nor would their opponents favor the national regulation of everything. Both must decide which and when in the shadow of a general sense that an economy wants to expand and all politics is local.

In drawing the lines to put these subordinate institutional arrangements together, experts move back and forth from ideological to professional argument, drawing on technical distinctions of various kinds. They may aim, for example, to treat national regulations that compensate for "market failures" differently from those that do not although the analytic for deciding which are which is uncertain in the extreme. People who want stronger national regulation see lots of market failures; those who favor a global economy unleashed see few. As vulgates for engagement, technical distinctions are often effective even where the technical analytics and empirical basis for deciding how to proceed are not particularly robust. If they were robust, people would not have needed to debate the matter.

A common technical frame for setting the boundary for political interference in economic matters is to assess whether a particular territorially enforced policy *distorts* rather than *supports* market prices. If so, it ought to be eliminated or harmonized to establish a stable background for global market transactions. This frame is not alone. There are well-known exceptions and trumps. Even if it does distort, a regulation may be warranted for reasons of public health, safety, or public policy. Each of these brings along another set of technical arguments and analogies. Market failure analytics is also situated in a broader set of argumentative frames: strategic growth arguments, for example, may be raised to regulate even in the absence of market failures—or may themselves be defined by the existence of an otherwise uncompensated market failure.

Nevertheless, from the European Union to the General Agreement on Tariffs and Trade and the World Trade Organization, experts approach national regulatory and administrative measures in this very general spirit: public action—or private monopoly—that distorts the market is presumptively improper. This background idea frames debate about specific institutional or regulatory outcomes. Convincing your government to oppose foreign regulations that hamper your business strategy means making the case that these regulations are "distortive," while a regulatory terrain that would permit you to garner a larger portion of the gains from economic activity represents a "level playing field." For whatever reason, this seems to work better than saying "I could capture more of the gains from trade if they abolished that regulation." Although assertions of direct commercial interest are certainly made when American industry speaks privately with the US trade representative, everyone seems to understand that the national and international legal and diplomatic framework for making claims rewards arguments couched in technical terms of market "distortion." Within this frame, other arguments are harder to make. For example, that your growth strategy requires delinking from global markets, discrimination against foreign economic interests and local protectionism. But there is also no need to make such arguments if the "market-supporting/-distorting" vocabulary is malleable enough to find market failures in need of compensatory policy around every corner.

As the market-supporting/-distorting distinction is interpreted and implemented across dozens of institutional settings, a professional sensibility or common sense emerges about the substantive and territorial limits of public power and about the scale and naturalness of economic flows. Exercises of public authority that support the market travel more easily than those that regulate or otherwise distort the market. Private rights, understood to lie outside or before politics, travel very easily—if you own something here, you own it when you get off the plane somewhere else. Public policies, the stuff of politics, do not travel, except as necessary to support the broader market. Political institutions have the legal authority to enforce private agreements and private rights established elsewhere, although they cannot regulate beyond their borders. In this spirit, regulatory regimes understood to support the market—criminal law, financial regulation, antitrust law—are routinely enforced extraterritorially, while those understood to distort market prices—labor law, environmental law, or antidiscrimination law—are not. These distinctions and institutional arrangements also sink into common sense.

In particular cases, the distorting/supporting analytic is rarely decisive. It must be argued. People *argue* that enforcing their contractual entitlements will support market exchange even as it impedes other potential transactions and opportunities. Other experts may argue the other way: to enforce these contracts would hinder competition and distort the market. Establishing the privilege to discriminate or union bust on foreign job sites requires an *argument* that labor or antidiscrimination laws are public regulations that do not travel rather than implied terms of contract law that should. People supporting or seeking to limit the independence of transnational financial activity argue about the "private" nature of finance and the relative importance of public respect for private contract. Just as there is no robust analytic to decide what is market-supporting and -distorting, there is no clear analytic to differentiate public power from private right. Even when you do not see the state "acting," it may have set the terms for private action. Ultimately private rights are simply promises that the state will intervene to enforce a duty on another actor. Public power and private power arise and act together.

Arguments about things like this nevertheless establish a kind of bandwidth within which people debate what governments and private actors are and do. As these arguments are resolved this way or that, global economic life comes to be consolidated around what come to seem the natural limits of territorial government and public law regulation. For this to happen, there does not need to be an analytic for distinguishing market-supporting from market-distorting. This apparently technical distinction can rest happily on unexamined cultural and political mores. Nor does there need to be an ideological conviction to liberate markets from political oversight. It is enough that differences of opinion can be transposed into a technical vernacular of argument and professional management and become the stuff of regulatory strategy and struggle. As a political ruler operating in the shadow of the rough consensus that emerges from these struggles, you find your interests and authority defined and managed by the expert votaries of various institutional sites who interpret your mandate by resolving arguments made in these terms.

LINKING POLITICS TO POLITIES

Is there a political corollary? For all the differences among national institutional arrangements, the global managerial class has a common set of intuitions about politics and the structures it requires. A basic starting point is the association of politics with a "polity": a community of people associated with a geographically defined territory. This general image hosts a variety of different sentiments. It seems natural that citizens should prioritize affiliations with others inside their polity and identify their political aspirations with the competences of government. One should expect to care less about things going on in other polities and to have less ability and less entitlement to affect them. At "home," politics is primarily the work of a specialized class of people— including "politicians"—who have or aspire to have government power in states: hence the equation of politics with the work of government. Institutionally, governments are organized as vertical channels of authority and accountability between citizens and rulers. Political authority is a matter of mandated competences and geographically specific jurisdiction or power. People exercise authority as a specialized competence delegated to specific institutions: legislatures, judiciaries, cities, transport ministries, lobbyists, county sheriffs, and dog catchers. No one exercises political power except as a role occupant and the horizon of political possibility is defined by the technical tools and jurisdictional limits through which roles are defined.

Like images of economic life, these are part ideological commitment and part common sense, although the naturalness of national politics is more settled as fact than the desirability of an ever more geographically expansive market. Still, the national political form is understood to be partial and contestable. Experts know well that politics is not the monopoly of states and that state boundaries are not the horizon of ethical fellow-feeling. As a practical matter, other affiliations and intermediate groups trump the relationship between individual citizens and states. The centrality of the national state in political life has been and continues to be disputed, perhaps particularly among those who participate most directly in the management of global political and economic life. International lawyers, for example, furiously denounce "sovereignty," even as it remains the cornerstone of their edifice.

Nor has the nation-state always been the obvious frame for "politics." The state as polity is a work of imagination and an institutional achievement. International law remembers the origin as the promise of the 1648 Peace of Westphalia. In diplomatic and political history it is more usual to point to the rise of European nationalism in the second half of the nineteenth century, setting in motion a process of global political reorganization that reached the majority of the world's peoples only in the second half of the twentieth century. Political elites in every country have their own story about the cultural and institutional origins of their nation as polity.

For most of the world's citizens, a national government of delegated powers and specialized competence linked to a territorial polity remains more idea than practical reality. Political struggle in every country is far more confused. Alternative affinities define politics for lots of people who disagree intensely about the wisdom of yielding to "national" authority. Informal loyalties, tribal and ethnic affiliations, economic alliances, and transnational solidarities matter everywhere. Private and economic actors not mentioned in constitutions have enormous political authority. Like the interconnected efficiency of global markets, the state's monopoly on political life has been resisted and remains imperfect. The even rows of flags in front of the United Nations cover a multitude of different national political arrangements, even if every one of them has an anthem, an Olympic team, and national flower.

The idea of a national polity is made real through innumerable practical institutional details to deepen the links along a vertical axis between rulers and their constituents and to define the boundaries of territorial and institutional competence. In the process, both rulers and ruled are transformed: both must respect the national legal and cultural constitutional settlement. The governed should understand themselves as citizen constituents of rulers, expressing their political wishes through the responsive channels made available by their polity, responsive to their nation's demands and proud of its virtues. Rulers should perfect their expertise and respect their mandate. This may mean respect for a scheme of divided and specialized competences or the intensification of representational links to local constituencies through mechanisms of accountability and transparency. Or it may mean rising to the challenge of service as a charismatic strongman. In one contemporary formulation common among global elites, "good governance" means respect by those in power for the specificity of mandates based on specialized knowledge, the separation of governance functions and established hierarchies of responsibility for a given territory, as well as ruler responsiveness to local constituencies, encouraged by citizen empowerment, transparency and other machinery of accountability. One could imagine counternarratives linking good governance to just substantive outcomes, rapid economic growth, or successful military vindication for historical slights to national honor.

These objectives may be achieved by institutional arrangements that empower and disempower in various ways. Like the construction of a global economy, the institutional consolidation of politics in governments is the product of ongoing technical work and argument. Reconstituting people as individual citizens of specific states requires a range of technical innovations from passports to voting privileges. From the eighteenth century, the vernacular of rights—civil rights, human rights—redefined justice as an appropriate relationship between an individual and a state. Political significance was slowly leeched from intermediate social groupings as newly specialized political parties were formed to link individual citizenship to the political organs of the state. Civic institutions that might once have played a political role—professional guilds, unions, tribes, religious sects—were either assimilated to national political parties or transformed into cultural and economic rather than political institutions, their members unleashed to engage with the national political world as individuals. Linguistic, religious, and other minorities were accommodated either by recognizing their demands for political autonomy through secession or, more commonly, assimilating them into a national polity as citizens with enforceable individual and minority rights. Governments were assembled in capital cities, capable of sending and hosting diplomatic representatives.

Just as markets need not—indeed cannot—be fully integrated horizontally or disembedded from political authority, government need not—indeed cannot—fully consolidate its authority vertically. Although each state did come to have a flag, a national museum and a "traditional" costume, these covered a wide variety of different local arrangements. Nor are these arrangements exclusively territorial. Boundaries are everywhere officially and unofficially porous, jurisdiction a fragmented arrangement of powers more local and more expansive than territory, local conditions affected by powers elsewhere. National authority over citizens must be squared with sovereign authority over territory whenever people travel or their activities have effects elsewhere. The power of adjacent polities and the complexity of social life on the ground make state power everywhere a matter of more or less. In specific situations, people argue over what is appropriately within the jurisdiction and mandate of which authority. These power struggles about what a public agent should and should not do are routinely undertaken in a technical vernacular of accountability, jurisdiction, and mandated competence. The details are different in each country. They may be a matter of intense local veneration or popular indifference. Disagreement about who is part of the polity turn into debates about federalism, subsidiarity, separation of powers, states' rights, home rule—or succession. Over time, a kind of common sense emerges about what it is reasonable or wise for government to do and the appropriate horizon of responsibility for leaders alongside a more or less settled sense for the distribution of powers and mobilities implied by the "territorial" nature of political authority.

The fantasy arrangement of the political world into "states" also shapes what people understand as *world politics*. At the global level, politics is not a vertical relationship between a sovereign and a polity. No such thing seems possible, and it makes no sense to speak of a global ruling class aggregating interests and responsible to a global polity. International politics means the diplomatic and military conversations carried on by word and deed among official people linked to governments and anybody else seeking to influence their behavior. All the other activity that occurs around the world is something else—commercial activity or cultural activity perhaps, but not "politics." This idea carries a bias: international politics is imagined as a predominantly horizontal engagement among putatively similar polities. There are power struggles, of course, with winners and losers. But the basic structure is not one of vertical authority. In this sense, international politics is like a global economy: a terrain for interaction rather than a relationship of domination.

In that international conversation, the representatives of national polities deal with their counterparts as best they can. As people argue with one another about who can do what, they search for common vocabularies to appeal to one another. The search for a common terrain of argument has encouraged a drift from overt expressions of interest and threats of violence toward more technical modes of expression. The authority of "science" may be useful to settle political controversies just as economics may lend the terms used to build a global economy a patina of objective analytic rigor. The attraction of quasi-technical and grandiloquent ethical vocabularies is obvious: they can be asserted as matters of universal accord. That "shocks the conscience of mankind" and contravenes "general principles of law recognized by civilized nations"! The development of a common playbook of arguments encourages the fantasy that disparate polities are part of a common "international community" of shared values and common sense. This is itself an appealing idea of great strategic use. Diplomatic specialists are quick to assert that their interests and actions express the universal interest, as US President Barack Obama did confronting Syria: "I didn't set a red line. The world set a red line." But there is no "world" to draw lines: only arguments by people positioned in separate polities that their line is universal.

Lawyers and other specialists have developed a variety of technical vocabularies for debating the limits of a territorial "sovereignty" when one bumps up against another. People argue about who is in charge by asking where something happened, whose territory was affected, or who has violated whose sovereignty. The answers are rarely decisive. Where something "happened" and whose "sovereignty" was implicated are often matters of perspective. When citizens travel abroad, it is analytically impossible to deduce from the nature of state power whether and when the link between a sovereign and his subjects should or should not take precedence over the link between another sovereign and his territory. Sovereignty is about both territory and citizenship in different measures. But the vocabulary need not be decisive to operate. By meditating on the abstract nature of sovereignty—how imaginary absolute powers relate to one another—people have generated all kinds of seemingly principled limitations and authorizations. Perhaps one sovereign "impliedly consented" to the other's action, or one sovereign "abused" his rights at the expense of another or failed to engage in "good faith." Perhaps the reciprocal nature of intersovereign discussion suggests limits to the kinds of claims one sovereign must be expected to entertain: they must be important, grave, the nationality of those involved linked in a genuine way to the legitimate interests of the sovereign demanding a response.

Public officials at all levels also make diverse claims to exercise juridical, administrative, and legislative jurisdiction in every state. The delimitation of jurisdiction is anything but a straightforward deduction from the nature of statehood or sovereignty or the nature of territory.[8] In the absence of global rules determining who has jurisdiction over what, political and legal professionals have devised a variety of technical ways to talk about opposed jurisdictional assertions. Public international law proposes that each authority weigh and balance a series of factors to ensure their exercise of jurisdiction is "reasonable," factors as wide-ranging as how important the case or value or interest is to each state, whether the exercise of jurisdictional exercise might lead to discord or conflict among sovereigns, and more. To give a sense for the breadth of considerations that might be marshaled to justify setting the boundary between assertions of jurisdiction, consider the Restatement (Third) of the Foreign Relations Law of the United States (1987), which articulates the law on "jurisdiction to prescribe" as an interaction between a series of approved "bases" for asserting jurisdiction (territory, nationality, effects in the territory, and "conduct outside the territory by persons not its nationals that is directed against the security of the state or against a limited class of other state interests") and the requirement that no assertion be "unreasonable." The reasonableness of jurisdictional assertions should be assessed in this way:

> Section 403.2 Whether exercise of jurisdiction over a person or activity is unreasonable is determined by evaluating all relevant factors, including, where appropriate:
>
> (a) The link of the activity to the territory of the regulating state, i.e., the extent to which the activity takes place within the territory, or has substantial, direct, and foreseeable effect upon or in the territory;

(b) The connections, such as nationality, residence, or economic activity, between the regulating state and the person principally responsible for the activity to be regulated, or between that state and those whom the regulation is designed to protect;

(c) The character of the activity to be regulated, the importance of the regulation to the regulating state, the extent to which other states regulate such activities, and the degree to which the desirability of such regulation is generally accepted;

(d) The existence of justified expectations that might be protected or hurt by the regulation;

(e) The importance of the regulation to the international political, legal, or economic system;

(f) The extent to which the regulation is consistent with the traditions of the international system;

(g) The extent to which another state may have an interest in regulating the activity; and

(h) The likelihood of conflict with regulation of another state.

Section 403.3 When it would not be unreasonable for each of two states to exercise jurisdiction over a person or activity, but the prescriptions by the two states are in conflict, each state has an obligation to evaluate its own as well as the other state's interest in exercising jurisdiction, in light of all the relevant factors. . . . A state should defer to the other state if that state's interest is clearly greater.[9]

Argument about such matters opens a broad terrain for professional struggle over the meaning of sovereignty, the bases and reasonable limits of jurisdictional authority. Shared ideas about what is "reasonable" matter a great deal in such discussions. A question that remains off the table: whether the exercise of public power would or would not be in the global public interest. This is simply not anyone's remit to ask. Political affiliations and concerns that are more difficult to articulate in vertical language of sovereigns and territories are harder to remember, inhabit, or defend.

THE OUTCOME: A WORLD POLITICAL ECONOMY OF EXPERT MANAGEMENT AND STRUGGLE

The relationship between politics and economics is a matter of interpretation and perspective. The smallest market transaction—a T-shirt sells in Ghana—can be interpreted to illuminate the politics or the economics of the planet.

Alternative disciplines or professions become associated with divergent interpretations of the same transaction. Economists and politicians understand the scale and "logic" of a T-shirt sale in Ghana differently and embed it in a different social, institutional, and intellectual context. The practical differences between economic and political institutions emerge as a byproduct of the routine professional making—and unmaking—of an infinite series of small-scale technical distinctions experienced as matters for subtle balancing rather than sharp line drawing: between public and private, national and international, family and market, between regulations that support the market and those that distort market prices, or between acts of the state that enforce private rights and those that burden them with regulation, alongside a parsing of considerations affecting the reasonableness of linking the sale to various interest and territories.

It is important to understand that this legal practice has been a joint product of economic and political ideas and expert work. An infinitely scalable economics of efficient markets and a politics of ever deeper links between local rulers and local citizens have been fiercely promoted, criticized, and transformed into intermediate institutions and doctrinal schemes for their technical accommodation. The analytics that have developed to manage these relationships are shaky. Both market efficiency and good governance rest on shared background ideas about the "normal" polity and the "normal" market. The practice of reasoning in these terms may not, in the end, be logically or philosophically satisfying. The results may also fail to persuade. As a practical matter, however, the practice is sufficiently plausible that experts find it possible to argue effectively with one another about whether something goes "too far" in one direction or the other. As those people draw lines in specific situations, professional specialties emerge devoted to each domain that default to drawing the line in one way rather than another. International private law experts think differently than those focused on transnational regulation. The professions responsible for the management of public and of private law, or of market making and market regulating, have grown apart and now themselves occupy different institutional sites. Divergent styles of technical interpretation harden the differences between domains that no one thinks distinct.

If we return for a moment to my left/liberal dystopic worry about a global economy slipping the leash of local politics, the reform proposals it suggested might be considered in a new light. That story channeled reform energy in two quixotic directions: hope for leaders who might step outside the boundaries of existing actor mandates and institutional structures, or change the responsibilities of both political and economic institutions to reverse their functions.

Neither seemed likely, but each seemed possible to attempt. Bringing the expert work that lies behind the construction of these actors and structures into view opens an alternative. Perhaps the commonsense ideas and best-practice technical findings that frame both broad public and narrowly technical debates could themselves be contested and altered.

Doing so would require a thousand technical shifts in each institutional form from more to less and less to more. It might also require that positions that now lie out of bounds be brought within the range of plausible expert argument. It is possible to imagine the governance professions undertaking their routine work against a different set of background ideas about both economics and politics. Imagine politics delinked from polity, spreading horizontally to diverse sites of potential contestation. Imagine an economics whose destiny was local, linked to the well-being of communities. Against this background, the routine boundary work of the governance professions might be quite different: aiming to reconnect the political and the economic while fragmenting the space of economic activity and multiplying the modes through which politics is undertaken. As ideals, these images of political and economic life need not be any more plausible or analytically satisfying than an economics delinked from political life to reverse the direction of technical work.

To reorient the work of governance professionals so radically seems utopian: reversing their apparent commitment to a global economy and a national politics. Yet the broad critiques of each are familiar and arise routinely in argument about how far to go in particular situations. Such a program would already be familiar to the world's leading risk managers who have seen the dangers of overintegration in economic life. Financial risk management today often requires the reintroduction of stopgaps and go-slow provisions against the damage of contagion and the volatility of speculative flows. Supply chain risk management now requires the reintroduction of inventories to guard against the disruptions of a tsunami here or a nuclear accident there. It is easy to imagine continuing on this path: reintroducing institutional forms of economic life linked to territory and to the constituencies whose economic and political possibilities rise and fall with their location: public unions, publically owned enterprises, corporate forms responsive to public policy as well as shareholder profit, banking and credit reoriented to local economic development. Large-scale regional institutions—central banks, development banks—might be reorganized to be more responsive to diverse local economic and political imperatives, their investments delinked from world market benchmarks. We can imagine reorienting professional work along these lines because it has been done before. Intermediary organizations that now seem like pure economic irrationality and inefficiency only a generation ago were spaces of political engagement: professional monopolies, corporations linked to local stakeholders, unions forcing negotiations over the forms and costs of public goods.

This is a thought experiment—a story to focus attention on the significance of expert work and the background ideas experts carry in their heads for the structure of world political economic life. It took a long time to organize the world in nation-states and then to build a global economy. They were not built to implement an idea. They may have been managed into their current form by professionals and experts, but they also emerged from struggle. Building a national public politics across the planet had a strong emancipatory dimension: slaves, women, workers, peasants, and colonial dominions obtained citizenship in relationship to the new institutional machinery of a national politics. For all the vulnerability, instability, and inequality wrought by the effort, the global economy has also lifted hundreds of millions from poverty while enriching tens of thousands, some beyond imagining. People have struggled to bring it about and are invested in its stability. These things will not be unbuilt easily—or reversed by new professional ideas. Changing them will require struggle. And yet, where to begin? The opportunities for meaningful struggle are hard to identify because the quotidian management of a vertical politics and a horizontal economics so often absorbs the energy of contestation in routine boundary work. The next chapter explores the relationship between the chaotic struggles that animate global political economic life and the work of the professions. Thereafter, I examine the nature of expertise in more detail before turning to law's role in distribution of gains and the dynamic reproduction of inequality as a case study of the relationship between the knowledge work of the technical professions and the struggles of global political and economic life.

CHAPTER 2
STRUGGLE: TOWARD A CARTOGRAPHY OF ENGAGEMENT

Global political economy rests on expert knowledge practices. But it is not all ideas, dialog and persuasion. The knowledge practices of experts are undertaken through conflict and struggle that are ruthless, unceasing and often violent. Knowledge work encourages, defends and legitimates harm: diseases untreated, businesses bankrupted, families destroyed, cultures unraveled. When international law—or any other expertise—"legitimates" warfare conducted according to its precepts, killing, burning and maiming people become easier to undertake. The means of expert struggle are every bit as ruthless. Although knowledge work often begins with words, experts assert, persuade, and implement their knowledge by coercion, not only when they send missiles as messages, but whenever they mobilize political or economic power behind their arguments and claims. In expert work, the saying, the insisting and the enforcing blend together. In this chapter, I describe an approach to placing the modes and strategies of expert struggle at the center of our picture of how the world works.

A more conventional way to locate the work of expertise in global conflict and competition would be to look for experts "inside" a larger system of actors engaging one another competitively or coercively. After training in political science, for example, we might begin with a large picture of the international system. Depending on the strand of political science one preferred, it might be a "balance of power" system among states with analogous "national interests" or a multilevel game in which more types of actors compete and cooperate, their orientation to the system a function of diverse cultural preferences and institutional arrangements. Or it might be something more communicative and constructivist in which the actors and the system reinforce and regenerate one another. Political actors would struggle and clash—or work out a more or less stable modus vivendi. After training in economics, by contrast, we might begin with a picture of the world economy in which welfare maximizers interact in the shadow of a price system or of a trade and finance system through which national economies jostle for advantage. Economic actors would compete for market share or work out profitable modes of collaboration. The competition among them would generate the creative destruction of capitalism. The pattern that emerged might be a relatively stable equilibrium or stand on a knife edge. However we imagined the system, conflict and cooperation would take place among the rival political or economic actors who were understood to inhabit it.

In such a picture, the work of experts would indeed be the work of ideas and words: analyzing, explaining, informing, advising. We would look for them *within* the system: counseling actors, interpreting their powers and the limitations of the structure, resolving disputes, offering their knowledge on questions actors thought relevant. Legal professionals would do these things with legal expertise: explaining the rules, the limits, the powers and perquisites of actors in the system. The big story would be about the global economy or political system, the major actors the nations or national economies or preference maximizers. As they struggled for advantage, experts would stand behind them, whispering, interpreting, taking care of the details. Were experts to become central to the story there might even be a problem: in politics, a technocracy problem; in economics, an agency problem or the loss of "consumer sovereignty."

In the contemporary world, expertise and the practices of experts have merged with the calculations of economic and political actors. To understand that reality, I develop an approach to conflict in global affairs from the inside out, foregrounding the knowledge practices of experts in the making and remaking of actors and structures through struggle. I propose a cartographic model of expert struggle from the perspective of those who engage in it. The central axis is coercive struggle over the allocation of value. People pursue conflicting projects by mobilizing their respective powers to coerce adversaries into foregoing gains.

I focus on law and legal expertise to illustrate possible roles for expert knowledge in this kind of struggle. Legal rules, legal arguments, and professional practices offer a route to understanding the formal and informal arrangements that affect the allocation of gains in global economic, political, or cultural life from the perspective of people making and enforcing assertions of entitlement or authority against one another. As they go along, they generate identities for themselves and allocate powers and resources in ways that might be interpreted, with the benefit of distance or hindsight, as constituting a system. Seen this way, activity that might otherwise seem a technical practice *within* a system can be understood as generative of the "actors" and "structures" that populate the systems imagined by more conventional modes of analysis.

STRUGGLE: DISTRIBUTION THROUGH COERCION

I begin with a vague image of people pursuing projects on an abstract terrain. I look out the window and imagine a beehive of continuous struggle among people. I focus on "people" rather than more familiar abstract and institutional actors like "states" or "corporations," "capital" or "labor." These are all abstract things, labels attached to people for a purpose. And I start with a very simple image of a "terrain" on which projects could be pursued, rather than the elaborate structures of a "state system" or "global capitalism." Whether the actors are "states" or "corporations," nations with interests or consumers with preferences may be part of what is at stake in the struggle. Convincing people that they are operating within a "global market" or a "multipolar world system" may be something people would want to do to strengthen their hand or weaken their opponent.

On the terrain where people engage, struggle is an iterative affair best understood dynamically. There is a preexisting status of forces, on the basis of which people come into struggle with different powers and vulnerabilities. They fight to capture gains and exclude their adversaries from things they value. They also fight for an improved starting position in the next round, struggling over the ability to lock in gains and defend their dominance. As a result, no struggle takes place among equals on a level playing field for long. The fault lines between winners and losers mark the outcomes of past struggle and affect the alliances, affinities, oppositions, and trajectories for the next round.

Struggle is most usefully imagined as binary: us and them. This is a familiar starting point: at their root, political, economic, social, or psychological interests are antagonistic. This was Hobbes's state of nature: a war of all against all.

Hereby it is manifest that, during the time men live without a common power to keep them all in awe, they are in that condition which is called war, and such a war as is of every man against every man. For war consists not in battle only, or the act of fighting, but in the tract of time wherein the will to contend by battle is sufficiently known; and therefore the notion of time is to be considered in the nature of war as it is in the nature of weather.[1]

Locating the root of economic activity in self-interested competition is familiar. Here is Adam Smith:

> It is not from the benevolence of the butcher, the brewer, or the baker that we expect our dinner, but from their regard to their own self-interest. We address them ourselves not to their humanity but to their self-love, and never talk to them of our necessities, but of their advantages.[2]

For Clausewitz, the absolute nature of war was the theoretical jumping off point. However much the fog of war may moderate or obscure the antagonism, in his view, strategic thinking begins with the recognition that if the enemy has an interest, your interests are opposed, across the board. If the enemy is well informed and seeks a pause, it must be to your advantage to advance.

> I will not begin by expounding a pedantic, literary definition of war, but go straight to the heart of the matter, to the duel. War is nothing but a duel on a larger scale. Countless duels go to make up war, but a picture of it as a whole can be formed by imagining a pair of wrestlers. Each tries through physical force to compel the other to do his will. . . . War is thus an act of force to compel our enemy to do our will.[3]

War, as Clausewitz imagined it, is not unlike other domains of political and economic life:

> We therefore conclude that war does not belong in the realm of the arts and sciences; rather it is part of man's social existence. War is a clash between major interests, which is resolved by bloodshed—that is the only way in which it differs from other conflicts. Rather than comparing it to art we could more accurately compare it to commerce, which is also a conflict of human interests and activities; and it is *still* closer to politics, which in turn may be considered as a kind of commerce on a larger scale. Politics, moreover, is the womb in which war develops—where its outlines already exist in their hidden rudimentary form, like the characteristics of living creatures in their embryos.[4]

Clausewitz is hardly alone in placing opposition and conflict at the heart of political and economic life. Carl Schmitt famously identified the true nature of politics as the encounters of friend and enemy.

> The specific political distinction to which political actions and motives can be reduced is that between friend and enemy. . . . The distinction of friend and enemy denotes the utmost degree of intensity of a union or separation,

of an association or dissociation. It can exist theoretically and practically, without having simultaneously to draw upon all those moral, aesthetic, economic, or other distinctions. The political enemy need not be morally evil or aesthetically ugly; he need not appear as an economic competitor, or it may even be advantageous to engage with him in business transactions. But he is, nevertheless, the other, the stranger; and it is sufficient for his nature that he is, in a specially intense way, existentially something different and alien, so that in the extreme case conflicts with him are possible. These can neither be decided by a previously determined general norm nor by the judgment of a disinterested and therefore neutral third party.[5]

In one after another field, however, what begins as foundational opposition is muted as actors are constructed and take their places in larger systems. Conflict and struggle become exceptional, order across a constituted system the norm. With the Leviathan or the social contract comes political order. An invisible hand transforms self-interested struggle into a productive market. The idea that system supplants struggle makes it tempting to attribute the results to a master system logic, historical necessity, or human nature rather than to a process by which wins and losses are routinized and reproduced.

Clausewitz suggests an alternative. For him, it is only the primacy of the *political* objective on all sides—the interests of those in struggle to yield or continue—that tempers the absolute opposition of militaries. This is how it looks to people pursuing projects. One foregoes gain either as strategy or in defeat. From a system perspective, the outcome may be growth or environmental catastrophe, but for people with projects, there will be winners and losers. To speak about the system and its logic can only be a strategy: to orient or justify oneself or talk one's opponent into a corner of necessity.

And people do habitually obscure the distributional significance of what they seek by emphasizing the benefits that will accrue to all mankind: we intervene here in the name of the international community, to defend universal values and humanitarian imperatives. People take territory in the name of historic or religious entitlement and invade as problem solvers. A counterclaim in the name of sovereignty will also be pitched in universal terms: if you can intervene here, anyone could intervene anywhere. Expert vocabularies that have "gone global" seem to share an ability to frame particular demands in universal ethical, scientific, or legal terms. You must do this because this is how things are. The fact that asserting a legal entitlement is always to frame one's interest in common agreement and benefit contributes to law's global usefulness.

Although there may be changes in the status quo that would unequivocally make everyone better off and no one worse off, these remain rare in practice. When claims are framed this way, it is easy to overlook those who do, in fact, pay a price. When human rights campaigners oppose the death penalty, for example, it is easy to lose track of the fact that success will bring costs: for sovereigns unable to choose the punishments they prefer, for victims unable to achieve the retribution they may seek, for other prisoners should life without parole become more common. Placing struggle rather than system at the center of the story encourages opposing interests to be identified and the costs and benefits of alternative projects to be assessed.

Struggle distributes when resources, powers, statuses, or virtues are allocated among people, all of whom seek them. It takes coercion to make distribution stick: to prevent those who wanted what they did not get from taking it anyway. Adversaries must be coerced to surrender or forego gains they would otherwise have garnered. In economic terms, to exclude them from your market, to put them out of business, force them into bankruptcy—or simply compel them to pay you a bit more than your costs of production. In political terms, to bend them to your interests, force their submission to your truth, compel their acknowledgment of your authority.

If you can do that by talking to them, excellent. Warfare is but one instance, one tactic, one tendentious label applied to particular struggles and adversaries. Even war is not only or even mainly a matter of bombs, bullets, or boots on the ground. Sometimes threats can work. Sometimes the Security Council—or the global financial system—can do the work for you. Enemies can be coerced by economic rearrangements, physical changes in the landscape, shifts in the arrangement of allies and enemies, changes in community sentiment or in the economies of honor and shame, legitimacy and illegitimacy, or the application of effective administration. As the neologism "lawfare" suggests, war can also be waged by law: law as a weapon, a strategic asset, a force multiplier. As a result, global struggle is a matter of persuasive arguments, strong armies and big bank accounts at the same time. It is at once a material struggle waged with words and a struggle over values and ideas waged by force. Bargaining power is as much a matter of knowledge as leverage is a matter of persuasive authority.

When distribution is accomplished without the use of force, the coercion may not be obvious on the surface. But it is there. When people agree or go along, the discourses that persuade them may reflect a hegemony forged in an earlier distributional settlement. Or, under the terms of earlier settlements, those who need to agree may not be those who pay the price. A great deal of global

struggle is undertaken with words whose effects reflect the sedimented authority of prior wins. Gains are won or lost by classification in shared vocabularies:
this is a private dispute, whereas that is a public matter; this is political, that is
economic; this is national, that is international. Or by the framing of a dispute:
this crisis is a horizontal political struggle between regional alliances, whereas
that one is about enforcing the will of the whole world against an outlier.

Such claims are often made in legal language because law is a site where
words can be made real as coercion. The assertion of a legal entitlement or a
claim to legal authority relies—tacitly or officially—on an enforcement power.
Force is somewhere in the mix, often in the implicit background thinking
where people take formal and informal, direct and indirect pressures into account. They might be thinking about the coercive power of the state, of their
families, economic partners, communities, traditions, or religions. Formal and
informal legal norms attest to the coercive authority of those who stand behind them. The law we can see forms a Bayeux Tapestry of past conflict and a
prediction of coercive pressures that might be brought to bear in the future.

THE PERSPECTIVE OF PEOPLE IN STRUGGLE

When people think strategically about their own projects, they grasp the dynamics of global struggle without exaggerating or naturalizing the "system"
within which it occurs. They do so by focusing closer in, on opportunities
for gain, vulnerabilities to their competitors, levers by which they can render
the terrain more hospitable to their objectives. This requires attention to the
available political or economic vernaculars and institutional arrangements for
identifying and securing gains. How are resources, authority, and status distributed, when and how do those distributions become more or less stable, and
how do those inequalities affect what happens next? What levers are available
to ensure—and increase—my share?

If you work for a large oil company, you may wish to increase your firm's
share in the gains from the exploitation of oil reserves in the developing world.
The number of levers that affect the price of oil and allocation of gains from its
extraction is practically infinite. If we were to start with a "system," it would be
very unclear which system to pick: the geopolitical system, the world financial
system, the transport system, the international tax system, the legal system, the
land tenure system, the "oil system"? People constituted as actors in all these
systems may have the power to help or hinder your effort to increase your
share of the gains from oil exploitation.

A savvy person would begin with a 360-degree audit of the terrain, identifying the widest range of people in various systems who might be enlisted as an ally or should be feared as an adversary. You might start with a rudimentary sense for the people and entities that might be relevant: other oil companies, one or another government, a local community, some politicians, some shareholders, a rebel group, various people inside and outside the nation. This is a tentative list. There would be lots more—banks, governments, political parties. To sort them out, you would need to understand their projects—are they adverse or complementary—and their powers and vulnerabilities. Then you would need to inventory the coercive tools available to you to press for advantage on this terrain. If there are gains to be had, how can they be locked in? Are there opportunities to play for advantage in the next round by consolidating your powers? For strategic actors of all kinds, the greatest challenge is often knowledge: gaining an overview of risks and opportunities and turning that knowledge into strategy. Who are the competitors, where are the markets, where and how can gain be extracted and retained? What are the risks? A cartography of risk is often the work of "due diligence" required before engagement. Who are the regulatory players? Who are your business partners? But this is just one piece of the puzzle. Frontline players must not only do the diligence to ensure compliance with various legal regimes. They must also remain alert for strategic opportunities and be trained in the arts of political, economic, and legal combat. A better word might be "strategic awareness." The goal is internal and contextual awareness in diverse and distributed business environments where supply chains are lengthy and business partners many and diverse. Law provides a kind of guidebook to the global terrain of struggle. Economic actors push their competitors from the market and harness the public hand for advantage by asserting and enforcing entitlements. Politicians mobilize and promote private or parochial interests as the public interest with the institutional machinery of regulation and administration. Public and private actors engage the legal terrain strategically, seeking to make their standards the global standards and to defeat arrangements that would impede their political or business strategies. Over time, victories and defeats on the terrain of law add up, reproducing patterns of empowerment and disempowerment.

Corporate risk managers and business strategists understand that transnational commerce takes place across a terrain of multiple and shifting rules, standards, and principles of behavior that present opportunities and pose risks. The rate of return in a given market, with a given business partner, or in a given sector rests on a legal foundation. When that foundation shifts, calculations must also shift: think of new export or financial controls in an important market. Where law poses risks, compliance—or moving elsewhere—can help to avoid liability, the reputational damage of becoming entangled in prosecution or suit and the costs associated with defense.

For thoughtful businessmen, the regulatory terrain is also more than a risk to be mitigated. The global legal environment is also a variable to be managed and an asset to be harnessed. You can seek to replace unfavorable regulations or substitute for them by developing your own internal or sector-specific private standards. You can harness the regulatory terrain as a competitive asset. This is the lawfare part of the story: regulation as a barrier to your competitor's market entry. What business would not like to see its standard imposed as the industry standard, the national standard, the global standard? Regulation can be an offensive weapon—slowing competitors' speed to market, entangling competitors in compliance or litigation. Or a market asset, as where compliance functions as brand enhancement. There is something Clausewitzian about this—where regulation is an asset for you, it is a liability for your competitor, and vice versa. The person responsible for thinking about regulation across the business environment is often called the "compliance officer." That person may be—often is—a legal professional, perhaps the general counsel, perhaps not. A better title might be "regulatory strategist," charged with aligning regulatory and business strategy in the global governance struggle. Legal experts play a parallel role in military circles and are forward-deployed ever more routinely. With lawfare comes the engagement of legal professionals in military strategy. With struggle over gains from economic activity comes the engagement of regulatory professionals in business strategy.

The role of law as a strategic tool for capturing gains is easy to see in the distribution of economic gains across global value chains: firms struggle with one another to increase their bargaining power by seeking to insulate what they contribute from competitive pressures while ensuring that those with whom they bargain confront robust competition. Your firm may have intellectual property in the product of the value chain and your suppliers may compete with one another in an environment where all firms have the privilege of access to low-wage labor and workers have no rights to bargain collectively, either within firms or across the industry. The arrangement of public and private law in a world of legally independent sovereigns allows you to secure the advantages of weak foreign labor law while defending your intellectual property abroad. You may also have exclusive access to a link in the distribution system, strong brand recognition among consumers, exclusive arrangements with retailers, or all of the above. To the extent local and international antitrust policies permit this level of exclusivity, you may cut your suppliers off from negotiation with others along the chain: they must make a deal with you.

Your suppliers may try to gain an advantage vis-à-vis each other by being faster or more reliable, having knowledge of your needs, or securing privileged access to financing, transport, labor, or raw materials. These "competitive advantages" will also be reflected in and dependent on legal and institutional arrangements. Some may be protected by administrative license or may be embedded in more or less exclusive contracts with development banks, local investors, or local governments. The relative productivity of their labor force may reflect a variety of networked relationships, access to housing, educational and health services, local family structures, tolerance for labor unrest, relations with local safety and other inspectors. Their know-how may be reflected in employment contracts or secured simply by defense against trespass within their property. They may have developed relationships with local regulators that speed their time to market or smooth their compliance with other local regulations. They may have obtained—through purchase, license, or custom— entitlement to land for their factory that secures access to transport or labor.

As your suppliers strengthen their hand relative to their competitors, their advantages may come to be embedded in long-term contracts with you that give them further room to maneuver against their competitors. The result is an allocation of the overall gains from production among your firm, your financiers, your shareholders, your consumers, your workers, your suppliers, and all those who are unsuccessful at entering this value chain at some point. That allocation will not be equal, nor will it be an objective reflection of everyone's "productivity," unless we are careful to note the extent to which productivity is itself a function of entitlements, bargaining power, and strategy.

We might imagine the terrain across which one might assess the powers and vulnerabilities of people in a global value chain by arranging the various actors on a field constituted by legal and other arrangements for capturing and allocating gains. We may come to the picture with a strong sense for who the actors "in" the chain are as well as a variety of suspicions about their relative powers. In "the value chain" for textiles, for example, we might find assembly workers in textile companies, a series of transport and other middlemen, global retailers, and the various institutions of finance, insurance, and advertising they rely on to move product to consumers. There is no obvious reason to put these actors "in" the chain and others outside it. Governments, media, labor unions, trade negotiators, and hundreds of other actors affect the relative prices of goods and services passing up and down the chain. A judge in some far-off country may suddenly make an antitrust ruling that shifts the balance of power between global retailers and other distribution systems sharply.

A cartography of power, opportunity and risk for people in this business would need to take these other actors and strategic moves into account. If we look through the constituted actors and soften the boundary of the value chain, many others will come into view. The point of focusing on "value chains" rather than corporate forms was precisely to understand more clearly how power is exercised and value distributed across a production process by softening the boundaries of the corporation to include all those with whom it has direct or indirect, formal or informal, contractual relations. There is no reason to stop here if we are looking for the levers that affect the distribution of value. Stopping here would place the world of media pressures and reputation as well as the entire regulatory terrain out of focus. The most savvy players are always on the lookout for moves, risks, and opportunities outside the frame.

International high politics might also be interpreted as a set of struggles and bargains whose outcome depends on formal and informal norms, expectations, and institutional arrangements. Take the controversy sparked in 2013 by Edward Snowden's disclosure of US government electronic intelligence-gathering practices. Prior to the disclosure, we could assess the status of forces. Public sovereigns had—or thought they had—various authorities to eavesdrop under international and national law, reinforced by local and global social expectations. Numerous companies and government agencies participated in the provision of global Internet and telecommunications services by license, contract, the exercise of legal privilege or simple convention. Public and private entities in many countries had access and sought access to electronic data both publically and secretly. Public, private, and government knowledge about these efforts was distributed in diverse ways. While some had become matters of public and political controversy—alleged Chinese corporate and military espionage aimed at US companies, for example—most had not.

Snowden's disclosures shifted the terrain. His global political power to do so resulted from his legally privileged access as a private contractor with Booz Allen holding a US security clearance, a power that could be exercised only against the background of the firm's disciplinary process (he was immediately fired) and the US government's legislative, prosecutorial, and enforcement jurisdiction over him, discounted by his ability to use the global airline and communication system to flee the jurisdiction, engage the interest of other governments whose interests diverged from the United States, and stimulate public reactions by supporters and opponents worldwide who had a variety of instruments at their disposal to register their interest in what happened to him, what happened to the United States, the future of electronic surveillance, and the innumerable other issues raised by various actors in the aftermath of his disclosure.

An enormous variety of existing legal and institutional arrangements influenced the distribution of power among these actors in the days and months that followed: rules about travel and extradition and asylum, rules and informal expectations governing the media in different countries, the corporate structure and regulatory environment for telecommunications, the Internet, and social media platforms. The many actors jostling for position after Snowden's disclosures were already in conversation and struggle about innumerable other issues. The distributions of authority on the contemporaneous agendas for discussion among China, the United States, Ecuador, Russia, the European Union, the telecommunications industry, the US Congress, and so on also affected the bargaining power and position of these actors. In short, Snowden's exercise of power took place in a complex terrain allocating political authority, economic possibility, prestige, and legitimacy among innumerable actors. As the incident played out, people—including Snowden—struggled over the distribution of political gains from what had happened. They did so with very different powers at their disposal, and the outcome shifted the distribution of those powers.

Economic and political struggles over distribution are conducted not only through the peaceful assertion of entitlement or persuasive bargaining. Whether explicit or implicit, threats of violence and coercion are also in play. My exercise of legal rights and privileges can put you out of business, destroy the value of your investment, increase the chance of your death by accident or disease, ruin your marriage. Public actors enforce entitlements coercively and exercise their power through calibrated applications of force. Whether in families, communities, or international political, cultural, or economic networks, the threat and use of coercion and violence not sanctioned by the state is a routine part of local and transnational bargaining.

The "high politics" struggles over the future of the Ukraine—or Syria—have involved the repeated threat and use of force by various local and international players. As in the Snowden case, we might begin by identifying actors with interests in the shape of Ukraine's future or in the relative stability or instability of political and economic conditions that could be affected by developments in the Ukraine. It would be a long list with wildly diverse capabilities to affect one another. As a global struggle over Ukraine's future began to unfold, major geopolitical actors ("Putin," "Europe," "NATO," "America") had levers to pull: military threats and deployments, both overt and covert, economic threats to withhold access to financial services or energy resources, media arguments about history and the reasonableness of their behavior. Each of these threats rested on the legal entitlements and institutional capabilities through which they could be made real and on the cultural persuasiveness of arguments for their appropriateness. Each of these actors was constrained, pressured, and persuaded by a range of commercial and social actors, from media commentators to energy conglomerates, with their own levers to pull. All were vulnerable to a shifting situation within Ukraine itself, in which an unstable array of forces struggled for momentum. Everyone tried to deploy powers and precedents won in earlier conflicts and to reframe the situation in ways favorable to their interests. As in many global conflicts, the use of force—whether by major armies and local extremists—was everywhere in play as a threat, a promise, and an event.

A CARTOGRAPHY OF PEOPLE AND THEIR POWERS

How might this approach, familiar to people engaged in struggle, be more systematically pursued in academic inquiry? The first step in a cartography of struggle is to identify people whose interests or projects might be adverse or complementary to one's own. Beginning with people rather than the many entities into which they might be organized—nations, corporations, governments, religions—foregrounds the plasticity of these institutional forms. Although most global political and economic struggles involve institutions and collectivities, when we say that corporations and nations and religions do things, we mean that people are speaking, exercising authority, making claims, cooperating or fighting with one another in their name. How people speak and act in the name of abstract collectivities is affected by institutional arrangements and by the ideas people have about what is to be expected in these roles. These arrangements are often contested by legal or other expert arguments about what "sovereignty" or "limited liability company" means, or what governments and corporations can do. Legal instruments may also be deployed to transform a public institution into a private enterprise—and back again.

Starting with people bypasses the temptation to develop a "theory of the state" or a "theory of the corporation," any more than a theory of the "international system" or the "global economy." All of these imaginary places are terrains within which people struggle with one another over their respective roles, capabilities, and entitlements. Over time, consistencies and routines develop, but the most strategically aware approach these with caution: perhaps there is a way to do something different this time, to make the corporation into something different, to have the people running the state take it in a new direction.

In whatever institutional form they confront one another, people struggle with very different powers and vulnerabilities. These differences can be washed out when the focus is on the institutional actors rather than the people who act in their name, particularly if we imagine entities with parallel legal forms—"corporations" or "nation-states"—as equivalents. Much will depend on the powers and vulnerabilities of particular individuals or their position on other social groups and institutional structures rather than the abstraction in whose name they act. Power in struggle is also an imaginary thing, often claimed by and attributed to people in accordance with the perceived importance of the "system" within which they seem to operate. If you come at the "financial system" from the "human rights system" or the "social welfare system," you may have less luck than were you to come from the "security system" or the "corporate system." The relative ability of the "international political system" and the "global economy" to empower actors in a struggle with one another is one way to picture what "global political economy" is all about.

It is helpful to think of people coming to struggle with little backpacks of legal and other entitlements, powers, and vulnerabilities. This is equally true of people who occupy roles in "public" and "private" institutions. Like people in corporations, the employees, agents, and leaders of the state have legal backpacks. In this respect, "capital" and "finance" are no different from "labor." Capital may come with entitlements marked "property" and labor may have entitlements marked "contract," but each is a set of legal relationships that could, at least in principle, be put together in a variety of ways. One backpack may be enormous, the other meager, but neither is natural or foundational. Starting here avoids the temptation to assume the priority of one or another type of actor: the state or the property owner or the worker, for example. Everyone is just a person with a backpack.

A CARTOGRAPHY OF VALUE, GAIN, AND COERCIVE DISTRIBUTION

People with backpacks pursue "projects." A project is something a person wants to achieve or obtain. Projects determine what people will count as a gain or loss. Although it is routine in economic analysis to focus on money and in political analysis on power, people pursue all kinds of things in arrangements that might be characterized as economic or political or both. They seek affiliation and opportunities to differentiate themselves from one another; affirmation of their identities, in their own eyes or reflected back from others; dignity and honor; status of one or another sort; and so on. People in the oil world might pursue national prestige, market dominance, or technical prowess as well as profit. In global political and economic life, people may want love or room to maneuver. They may want to victimize or be victims, to dominate or control. Theirs may be a project to kill or a project to heal; to break down or build up.

Struggle is not all about pleasure and power. It is always surprising to discover that some people—even entire professions—seek marginality, even misery. People sometimes seek to remain weak, just as they sometimes seek humiliation or submission. Many, for example, would rather denounce power than exercise it, even if the denunciation is not likely to change things. Nor are projects all about winning and dominating. Some want to cast away wealth, to relinquish power, or to be constrained. Not everyone seeks to be an industry leader or dominant player: some are more comfortable as franchisers. Not every employee seeks the highest wage or most prestigious and responsible position. Nor does every firm seek to increase its market share or every nation its relative power. What people seek—along with who they think they are, their role, mandate, or identity—is routinely reimagined in light of the powers and vulnerabilities they have in their backpacks and is shaped by the institutions and social groups within which they find themselves and on behalf of which they undertake projects. Sometimes, of course, the relevant "value" to be distributed as gain will be money or power. In analyzing the oil-extraction industry or mapping distribution across a global supply chain, for example, it may be sensible to follow the money, although savvy actors will always have their eyes open for other potential gains and losses.

The next step is to identify sites where value becomes available for distribution as gain: where money or power or anything else one seeks can be captured. At what points—geographical points, institutional points, temporal points in the production process—are people able to transform oil into money? The crucial point is that value—what people seek—becomes gain when people are successful in obtaining and defending it: when it has been distributed. Approaching things this way avoids the need for a theory about the origin of "value" in economic or political life. Political power does not emanate down from a sovereign or up from individual right. Neither property nor labor is the ultimate source of economic value. People in the institutions of "capital" and "labor" approach one another at a site where they think gain might be won with backpacks of powers and liabilities. The outcome of their engagement will be a distribution of gain. A "theory of value" is a story people tell to naturalize their interests: to place *their* potential gains outside struggle. I focus rather on people with backpacks: what they seek is value, what they obtain is gain. At each point of potential distribution, projects become relational: other people will need to be enlisted, defeated, persuaded, or sidelined for one person to capture the value as gain.

In distributional struggle, other people are either helping or getting in the way. It may be hard to tell who is doing what, of course. Military professionals can be found arguing for restraint and humanitarians for more vigorous applications of force for lots of reasons relating to the specific conflict and their broader objectives. But whether you are a humanitarian or a military professional, whether you argue for more or less robust use of force, the strategic question is whether your position, if adopted, will strengthen or weaken your team or theirs. Of course, people can be wrong about the consequences of their strategy. Military professionals (or humanitarians) arguing for more or less vigorous applications of force may end up weakening their position vis-à-vis their opponent. Argument about whether and when that happened is all part of how people on all sides of a conflict struggle over the levels of force to permit or encourage.

People struggle by drawing on their backpack of powers and the available modes of engagement. Seeking market share, historical vindication, profit, or political power, they argue, posture and denounce, exercise whatever authorities and privileges they can muster or threaten. And sometimes they turn to violence. It may also be possible to struggle over the distribution of authority to obtain and retain gains or to change the terrain so one's own projects are easier or less necessary to pursue. Wherever value becomes gain, there will be coercion, whether formal or informal, overt or tacit. Someone had to yield. The coercive force need not be violence—it could be an institution, a fence, or a hegemonic mode of persuasion. Some coercive instruments will be clear—claims of sovereignty or ownership, terms of investment, tax systems—and others may be both difficult to assess and open to change: media pressure, threats to withdraw from the terrain or to withhold capital or labor. Both the "value" to be captured and the "coercion" necessary to exclude might be spiritual or material, individual or social, formally recognized or informally enjoyed.

A very rudimentary snapshot of the "oil system" in operation might identify people, their varying opportunities to assert control over the generation of value from oil extraction, production, and use, and their characteristic modes of engagement. Perhaps people grant and receive rights to explore for oil, assemble financing and technology for its extraction, transport, refinement, and sale. An initial entitlement to transform oil into cash may then give rise to numerous sales, payments, and transfers. At each point, we can track the distribution of gain. A local community with the political or physical power to disrupt production or tarnish the image of larger players may extract a new school, road, or housing. Investors will receive returns on capital lent, governments will share in revenues from taxation, licensing arrangements, payments for the provision of public services. Inventors will share revenue from technology deployed.

People with projects look for the points of value creation and opportunities to harness coercion to capture what they value as gain. The search for coercive distribution will often lead to the legal system: legal entitlements and permissions that depend on the powers and forbearances of the state or other authorities. People buy things with enforceable contracts, put their neighbors out of business without sanction through the exercise of legal privilege, mobilize their friends to capture the mayoralty, and prosecute their enemies through the institutions of the political process. Legal entitlements will authorize actors to deploy the coercive machinery of the state to enforce their share in the value generated by the exploitation of the oil. When investors threaten to withhold capital from future projects if they are not paid, their threat rests on a legal privilege to do so. The tacit threat of boycott by the investor class rests on a similar privilege as well as all kinds of shared ideas about how "investors" behave and what they demand, need, and think. Informal and black market pressures are also at work. In a world of reputational risks, media pressure can be more effective than law. If Bloomberg says investors may flee, investors may flee.

An imaginative person might see opportunities to reframe the situation by reconfiguring actors—even reconfiguring himself—to identify new opportunities for value creation from which others might be excluded. Entrepreneurship and diplomatic ingenuity are all about looking for opportunities to enter the value chain or apply leverage others have not seen. The clearest example is tax planning, which often involves rearranging the legal forms through which value is generated and captured to reduce the amount claimed by a public authority.

Much will depend on the conditions of uncertainty and plasticity in the situation. How open to manipulation and reconfiguration are the forms of value, the tools of coercion, the identities and powers of the actors, or the institutional arrangements within which they interact? How much work is required to make that potential visible or effective? The answers will often lie in the tools of engagement rather than in the nature of actors and institutions. How effective are things like bargaining, paying people off, contracting, threatening violence, going to war, arguing, protesting, denouncing, exercising rights, demanding bribes, or threatening to exit at changing the situation in one's favor? What can be done with legal reinvention or military action? Can property be turned into contract? Enemies into allies? Can contractual entitlements be sold as property? Can the terrain of engagement be expanded or force concentrated at a single point? How easily can corporations be rearranged and restructured? Can humanitarian action be a force multiplier? Under conditions of uncertainty, assertions about all these things might be unsettled by argument or transformed with leverage.

A viewpoint from which identities and institutional structures, forms of value and modes of coercion are all central and malleable is familiar from legal practice. Each of these points has a legal foundation that may be rearranged. Actors can be reconfigured and new actors brought on stage. Regulatory change can shift the status of forces, just as the terrain may be shifted by technology or new modes of organization and production. Value can be reimagined, one form transformed into another. It is not only money that is fungible: so often are things like status, legitimacy, shame, and authority. Coercive levers will vary in their availability, their certainty, their legitimacy, their effectiveness. People will have powers they do not use or realize they have, and will seek to use powers they turn out not to have. Of course, not everything can be shuffled around—and not by everyone. The capacity to maneuver is itself a value to be distributed. People are playing a game on at least two boards: pursuing their project and struggling over the ability to remake the terrain upon which their project is pursued.

STRUGGLE WITH WORDS AND THE POWER OF IDEAS

Professional vocabularies often provide the arguments and images for interpreting and contesting who and where one is, who can do what, who has what authority over whom, who can call upon the cavalry to what end. A vernacular for making claims may be fine grain—an interpretation in conditions of uncertainty of the specific powers, privileges, and other entitlements of people in particular circumstances. Law is often about this. But a vernacular—including the legal vernacular—may also comprise large background ideas: about what an economy is, what a nation is, what war is, what politics is about, and what power is legitimate.

When the Obama administration announced a campaign against the Islamic State of Iraq and the Levant (ISIL) in 2014, they were careful with labels. Was it a "war"? How could it be described to affirm the president's warlike level of personal and political commitment to the endeavor while reassuring the American people that he would not commit "ground troops" to "another war" in the Middle East? The commitments of allies, the engagement of the American Congress, the media's benchmarks for evaluation, the significance of the United Nations, the enemy's appreciation of the level of threat: all these were affected by the choice of vocabulary. And that choice shifted from week to week as partisans on all sides adjusted their strategies.

The ideas that are deployed in struggle may be shared narrowly within a profession or more broadly in culture. They might be abstract principles and magic formulas: general propositions asserted to defend more specific policies and choices through lengthy, but weak, deductive chains. Or distinctions presented as natural that turn out to be matters of judgment or political choice. They might be favorite policies and policy projects, promoted with or without evidence or clear analytic connection to expected benefit. Or widely shared attitudes, analytic moves, favorite arguments that seem decisive or need no refutation, but which could be contested.

Because the ideational frame for engagement can be a force multiplier, these background ideas are worth contesting. In war, it is clear that if your objective and means are thought illegitimate by those with the power to get in your way, you will have a harder time of it. Unsurprisingly, people on all sides go to great lengths to frame their violence in the available vernaculars of legitimacy: as legal, as sacred, as defensive, as the enforcement of global values or the reaction to legitimate grievance. This is equally powerful in economic life. I lobbied you and contributed to your campaign, but I did not bribe you. I sold my expertise and capitalized on my relationships, but I am no influence peddler. Although I put you out of business, I did so using only my legal rights and privileges. Setting up shop next door, I mobilized my relationships and entitlements, using my larger market presence to demand lower prices from suppliers and advertise to your customers, my relations with bankers to borrow when you could not. I outcompeted you—but I did not ask my uncle to pay you a visit with a lead pipe.

The ideas undergirding a mode of engagement are most visible when they are contested, usually by people motivated to identify and refute ideas supporting claims made by their opponents. But a great deal of background "knowledge" about how the world is will be common sense for all parties, at least until someone contests it. The boundary between the free speech of campaign finance and the corruption of bribery lies somewhere in between. People intuit the loose analogy and slippery slope between them, but stand to one side or the other, marking the difference in careful compliance with technical rules.

In national political life, the arguments that define ideological alternatives often become routinized to the point that contest rarely disrupts the institutional balance. At the global level, there is often less common ground, particularly in asymmetric conversations. The vernaculars of contestation may be fewer and more specialized, but the perspectives brought to the table are more diverse. This puts enormous pressure on the expert vocabularies that have globalized: they must be coherent enough to be recognizable across great differences and plastic enough to be inhabited by diverse interests and actors. Many public modes of discussion common at the national level have a hard time in global debate. Struggles that might easily take shape as a contest between "government" and "business" at the national level, for example, translate poorly to the global arena. For one thing, there is no global government. Diverse forces claim to act in the name of global governance, but these might as easily be corporate as public entities. There is a global economy, but all the economic actors are also local to particular countries, sectors, cities. Governments struggle with one another and are often internally divided and fractious. All are available for instrumentalization by economic players—some, of course, more directly and completely than others. Public forces are as prone to shield private action as to regulate it. Business interests also differ and harness political and economic tools in their struggle with one another. All economic actors rely on legal entitlements protected by states—from property rights to administrative licenses and regulatory guidelines. And many perform so-called public functions—not just avoiding or influencing regulation, but making and enforcing it. Business is as likely to seek regulatory protection as to condemn the protection of its adversaries. And public/private partnerships are everywhere.

Rather than business and government or private and public, the broad thematic of global struggle often resolves into a confrontation between interpretive frameworks rooted in local and global control. In a world of vertical politics and horizontal economics, this could be a clash between economics and politics: is this properly a subject for local political control or for global economic management? One of the reasons global governance seems technocratic is the association of the technical with all that is not political and that is therefore proper to horizontal management. The local/global discussion may also take the form of a debate between two frameworks for understanding a situation: as a horizontal clash of opposing particulars or as a vertical opposition between universal norms and particular interests. We saw this vividly in the international crisis sparked by rebellion in Syria. Some framed the issue as one of global norms disregarded, others as a geostrategic clash of religious sects and regional and global powers. Trade wars are similarly framed both as universal norms demanding local compliance and as competitive struggles between opposing economic interests and nations. In this sense, the struggles that animate global political economy are routinely conducted as struggles about the proper boundaries of global political consensus or economic management on the one hand and local political prerogative and economic gain on the other.

Law often provides the site and language for undertaking these by now stereotypical debates. International law is routinely explained as the law "governing relations among states." It is also, and more importantly, the vernacular used to distinguish the local and global by marking the line between the political and the technical or economic, or the line between universal/local and local/local conflicts. Although these lines may be quite clear, people are always pushing and prodding at them. Does genetically modified food present an issue of local political choice or is it a matter of global technical resolution? This question will come up in all kinds of settings: local courts, international institutions, diplomatic discussions, media commentary. Is military engagement here or there the expression of the intervenor's national interest or the enforcement arm of global normative commitments? Although the answers may differ, in many settings they will be clear. But there will also be elements of uncertainty, settings in which—and audiences for which—there will be room for argument. A strategically able struggler will focus on the sites where either clarity or uncertainty makes it possible to garner and enforce gains.

If we put this picture together, we could say that global struggle is an interaction of people with projects, engaging one another on a terrain so as to generate, garner and preserve gains others are forced to forego. The available modes of engagement will be variously plastic to their efforts. However intuitive this may seem to people who are engaged in global struggle—and to their lawyers—it is less common in social scientific work. But it need not be. The most effective people engaged in global struggle think this way routinely. They identify points of opportunity and vulnerability and focus on the available moves. Multinationals know they may need to change the rules of the game—or change their own structure—to make a profit. So do terrorists and operational commanders in the military. Theirs is less a world of actors and structures than a terrain of moves, points of pressure, and vulnerability. This is also how things look to professionals specialized in the modes of engagement themselves—people like lawyers and military strategists. They look at situations for opportunities to make and hold gains using the tools of their expertise. If a client needs to be reconfigured, they may recommend doing so. If there are wins to be had by changing the game, they are also often masters of the rules.

CARTOGRAPHY AS AN ANTIDOTE TO THE LIMITS OF SYSTEM ANALYTICS

The more conventional approach to modeling global political or economic activity aims to understand patterns of regularity in the behavior of actors in structures to generate rules of thumb for the dynamics of various types of system: national or international markets, diplomatic balance of power systems. The results can be enormously helpful. The tools of neoclassical and institutional economics, international relations theory, systems theory, public choice and game theory, or strategic studies are crucial for understanding the dynamics of global political economy.

By focusing first on the powers, vulnerabilities, and strategies of people with projects in struggle with one another, however, I aim to compensate for some classic limitations of the actor/structure/system framework. The most crucial for my purposes are the tendency to reify the actors and structures one sees, a bias toward order, and the potential to overlook the knowledge work of experts with the result that their shared logic is treated as the logic of the system itself.

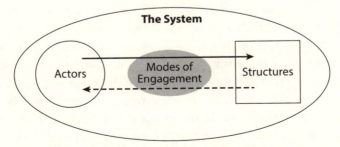

Figure 2.1 A Classic Model: Expertise Fades from View

REIFY THE ACTORS AND STRUCTURES

It is easy to overestimate the importance and stability—even the existence—of the actors foregrounded by the structure one identifies as well as the structures those actors see around them. One can even naturalize and overestimate the significance of human actors. Nature, pathogens, and weather—like institutional arrangements—fall into the background as elements of context or structure.[6] The actors you see affect the conflicts you notice and the modes of engagement you treat as paradigmatic. That nations are understood to be the primary actors in the international system is the outcome of knowledge work framing global affairs as an "international system" in which "nations" interact. People who understand their role to be representing a "nation-state" have expectations about the moves they can make and what others might do that reflect what they have learned about how the international system works.

British international relations scholar Hedley Bull described his now classic book about order in world politics as "an inquiry into the nature of order in world politics, and in particular into the society of sovereign states, through which such order as exists in world politics is now maintained."[7] The interaction between a conception of the actors and of the system within which they operate is visible in his opening definition of the "order" he intends to analyze:

> By international order I mean a pattern of activity that sustains the elementary or primary goals of the society of states, or international society. Before spelling out in more detail what is involved in the concept of international order I shall first set the stage by indicating what I mean by states, by a system of states, and by a society of states, or international society.[8]

When actors are defined by their role position in a system, it is difficult to see "behind" them to bring their "subjective" desires and preferences into the analysis. Things like "national interest" or "consumer preference" can be read in the behavior of actors but the process by which actors are constituted as desiring subjects remains frustratingly off-screen. Although the tendency of economic modeling to exogenize the origins of demand in the black box of consumer preference has been criticized by institutionalist economists at least since Thorstein Veblen, it has so far been a losing battle. John Kenneth Galbraith, for example, proposed to recognize the extent to which demand may be a function of production rather than its mysterious source. "As a society becomes increasingly affluent, wants are increasingly created by the process by which they are satisfied. . . . Wants thus come to depend on output."[9] Although intuitively obvious, this kind of observation is difficult to reconcile with a system model that requires much to be exogenized for the system's regularities to be successfully modeled and analyzed. Institutionalism can go only so far. This makes it difficult to speak about the agency of ideas, from professional common sense to broad ideological commitment, in shaping what people do as they struggle with one another. It is all too common to picture the impact of ideas as a straightforward capture: the actor becomes the agent of the idea, belief, or ideology. The role of ideas is rarely this straightforward however: people are ambivalent, often assuming something at one level of consciousness that they work assiduously to overcome at another. Their identity as an actor is often itself at stake as their ideas contend with one another or are contested and validated by others.

Focusing on macro-level systems, one can miss the moments when people contest the rules of the game and remake the actors in play. As a result, the midlevel processes by which individual actions aggregate into systemic patterns remain obscure. They can be modeled, but their mechanisms remain sociologically indistinct. This is most clearly evident in writing about global political economy that merges public choice or game theory models of political processes like voting with equilibrium theories of economic behavior to generate models of global trade and production.[10] Equilibrium theories, whether in game theory, mathematics, or economics, model the dynamic through which the moves or choices of individual actors in a system compound toward an equilibrium of one or another sort. As these models have become more complex, they have struggled to take various anomalies, disruptions, and path dependencies into account. Their limitations as sociology, however, remain those that characterized Leon Walras's process of *tâtonnement* or "groping" through which he imagined a simultaneous or successive process of adjustment among individual economic agents leading toward an equilibrium matching supply to demand.[11] As he formulated the outcomes of iterative trials in 1892,

> We shall always be nearer the equilibrium at the second trial than at the first. We enter here on the theory of trial and error, such as I have developed in my work, and by virtue of which we arrive at the equilibrium of a market by raising the price of commodities, the demand for which is greater than the supply, and by lowering the price of those, the supply of which is greater than the demand.[12]

Like other images of dynamic movement toward equilibrium, *tâtonnement* could be modeled mathematically but offered only the metaphor of iterative "groping" as sociological description.[13]

One result of inattention to the lived mechanisms by which actual people struggle with one another can be an underestimation of the available strategic opportunities and the importance of the modes of disagreement and struggle people discover as they engage. Diplomats may think they represent "nations" in an "international balance of power system," but that does not mean they do—or that it is the only possible terrain on which they might engage one another. These might be the least imaginative diplomats: innovators might see other possible systems and other roles for themselves. Actors may be raised up, constituted, transformed, or eliminated in the course of coercive struggle over the distribution of value. Their identity as agents may be part of the value, the stakes in struggle, just as it may be a coercive force. The same is true of "structures" within which "agents" operate. They may also be constituted and transformed, and may be the precondition, the stakes, or the outcome of struggle among actors. Focusing on the mode of engagement provides the opportunity to understand the processes by which actors and structures emerge as outcomes of struggle.

TENDENCY TO OVERESTIMATE ORDER

The bias toward order is puzzling given that economic life and political life are both thought to have their origin in conflict: in the nasty and brutish world before Leviathan, in the inexorable clash of clan and class, or in the scarcity that sets economic actors in competition with one another. One of the great puzzles of modern social thought is the alchemy by which an insistence on the inexorable centrality of conflict evaporates as people offer accounts of economic patterns of regularity and political systems characterized by order and constitutionalism. Political scientists and economists have developed a range of stories about how conflict conduces to order, its rules of operation, its relative stability and potential for disruption. Diplomatic and military historians explain how great and not so great powers can be expected to behave in a "balance of power" or "hegemonic" or "balance of terror" system much as economic models explain the regularities—even equilibrium—of a global economy. Hedley Bull's international relations classic said it clearly in the title—*The Anarchical Society: A Study of Order in World Politics*—an anarchical society generates order.[14] Only in disruptive crisis, war, or revolutionary overthrow does conflict predominate. In my picture, global economic and political life throws off stability as victory and defeat. It takes work to interpret the outcomes as constituted order or functioning system rather than a conflict flash frozen in institutions.

If you begin by identifying a set of actors and then imagine the structures within which they engage, it is not surprising that conflict would come to seem exceptional. Actors and structures at rest seem stable, coherent, or settled. Engagement—and conflict—arises when someone does something and surely only some of the things people rouse themselves to do will be conflictual. And only some of those conflicts will be disruptive of the "system" represented by the actors at rest. Much that people do will reinforce the system or simply take place "within" it. Actors and structures are constituted through engagement. But conflict is always already there, frozen perhaps, but there.[15] Their positions at rest are the outcome of those prior struggles.

If you are looking for patterns of order, it is also easy to overestimate the significance of agreement, collaboration, consensus, or persuasion. Actors regularly do cooperate, agree with one another, affiliate, transact, discuss, and persuade one another. But their collaboration, like conflict, takes place on a terrain of distributed power and legitimacy. Agreement, like argument, is undertaken in a vocabulary whose effectiveness arises from its relative hegemony. Every collaboration rests on a status of forces and every persuasive argument rests on a canon of the plausible and the persuasive. Even where there is cooperation and consent, moreover, people get hurt. Often other people, people who have been the intended or accidental casualties of someone else's collaborative strategy.

In both conflict and cooperation, people engage one another strategically, vaguely or vividly aware of a background of alternatives, implied threats and available options. Hedley Bull's picture of international relations as an ordered society is often juxtaposed with the more hardheaded "realism" of those less sanguine about the prospects for cooperation. Hans Morgenthau is a classic counterpoint. His *Politics among Nations: The Struggle for Power and Peace* places political power and political conflict front and center:

> International politics, like all politics, is a struggle for power. Whatever the ultimate aims of international politics, power is always the immediate aim. Statesmen and people may ultimately seek freedom, security, prosperity, or power itself. They may define their goals in terms of a religious, philosophic, economic or social ideal. . . . But whenever they strive to realize their goal by means of international politics, they do so by striving for power.[16]

Among participants in global politics, Morgenthau then argues, patterns can be identified. The most important, both historically and theoretically, is the "balance of power."

The aspiration for power on the part of several nations, each trying either to maintain or overthrow the status quo, leads of necessity to a configuration that is called the balance of power and to policies that aim at preserving it. We say "of necessity" advisedly. . . . It will be shown in the following pages that the international balance of power is only a particular manifestation of a general social principle to which all societies composed of a number of autonomous units owe the autonomy of their component parts: that the balance of power and policies aiming at its preservation are not only inevitable but are an essential stabilizing factor in a society of sovereign nations; and that the instability of the international balance of power is due not to the faultiness of the principle but to the particular conditions under which the principle must operate in a society of sovereign nations.[17]

Morgenthau places the "balance of power" alongside other theories of "social equilibrium." Each "signifies stability within a system composed of a number of autonomous forces."[18]

Two assumptions are at the foundation of all such equilibriums: first, that the elements to be balanced are necessary for society or are entitled to exist and, second, that without a state of equilibrium among them one element will gain ascendancy over the others, encroach upon their interests and rights, and may ultimately destroy them.[19]

Although Morgenthau was doubtless using the words "entitled" and "interests and rights" in a quite general way, we can see where law fits in the story: it is part of the assumed background on top of which actors and society engage one another. Placing law in the foreground forces attention to the process of struggle through which precisely *these* "elements" became entitled to exist with *this* set of "interests and rights." Had these struggles had other outcomes, there might be a different system or "society." As long as these struggles continue, there would be no reason to suppose movement toward an equilibrium—or there might be multiple possible equilibria.

The broad bias against direct engagement with distributive conflict encourages a variety of fantasies about the benevolence of political and economic struggle. It is obvious that economic competition can be destructive—people can be put out of business, their families ruined, their self-esteem crushed, the efforts of a lifetime defeated. It is comforting to imagine that economic growth or the gains from trade will benefit everyone and to search for the institutional conditions that maximize those gains, however they may be distributed. People call it "creative destruction," hope the resources released will be redeployed more productively and the lives destroyed somehow compensated through the reallocations of the political process. Their distribution is, in any event, a question for politics or a reflection of social values rather than something of direct concern to economics.

On the political side, it is easy to overestimate the opportunities for "win-win" solutions to address "global problems" and strengthen the "international community" as a whole without regard to how the costs of these gains will fall. It is easy to speak about the pursuit of human rights as if their enforcement would raise everyone to a cosmopolitan order of equal dignity rather than requiring some to forego privileges that others might be rendered "equal." Even people nostalgic for "class analysis" remember its association with "solidarity" more readily than its association with "conflict." As people engaged in economic competition and political maneuver know all too well, however, the world rarely distributes gains so evenly or lifts all boats.

Working in these academic traditions, it is easy to lose sight of the midlevel arrangements through which political or economic gains (and losses) are distributed and focus instead on the benevolent fantasy of an invisible hand or a disaggregated but functional and promising as-if global sovereign hovering above routine political or economic conflict. It is understandable that people would come to global affairs with an image of struggle taking place beneath the watchful gaze of a sovereign public hand. This takes some of the sting out of struggle: a benevolent father is standing by. Within a polity, it does seem possible to imagine political struggle as a way to "aggregate interests," deliberate about what constitutes "the public interest," channel and limit the harms that can result from private conflict and economic competition. It seems plausible to imagine the brutality and dynamic instability of economic competition softened by the regulatory hand of governance, attuned to the general welfare. Although sovereignty, like patriarchy, rarely lives up to this fantasy, the thought is nevertheless reassuring: perhaps you can arrange your constitution to empower a public-spirited ruler and minimize the potential for capture by faction or despot. On the global stage, however, this reassuring thought is harder to sustain. There simply is no global public hand or deliberative demos standing by to articulate universal values, attend to global welfare, or solve problems in the public interest. Nor is there a constituted order through which struggle over economic opportunities and political powers occurs and the potential for capture might be minimized. The idea of a global order immanent in the chaotic political and economic life of the world is open-ended enough to support many interpretations and claims about the locus of disaggregated global sovereignty. One result is a powerful temptation to nominate oneself as an agent of world order, global welfare, and a universal ethics. European legal scholars, for example, are far more likely to insist the global legal order has a discernable "constitution" than are their American colleagues. It is not hard to see that it could strengthen their hand as professionals, and the hand of their middle-power nations, were their claims to be borne out. The opportunity to govern—to make your sense of the good the public good, your allocation of opportunity decisive—is up for grabs. All purportedly global norms and institutions are made by winners, demand allies, and create losers.

THE TENDENCY TO OVERLOOK THE KNOWLEDGE WORK OF EXPERTISE

A significant drawback of the actor/structure/system framework in social scientific work is the tendency to treat expertise as a marginal part of the story, relevant only when expert ideas capture the will of system actors or the technocratic process torques the system's routine operations. Even complexly constructivist system analytics is prone to this tendency. We might acknowledge that characteristic state system actors and modes of engagement do not precede the establishment of a state system, nor can their form be derived from the "nature" of such a system. The words "state system," we might acknowledge, are simply an interpretation of what happens as these elements are produced and reproduced in a particular way. We might agree that people acting in the system reproduce this interpretation and the systematicity of their world. People in a system think they are in a system and therefore are in a system. Unfortunately, this is the kind of insight that is easily said and then forgotten. It is interesting only if people could think and then be the system in different ways, and if we could understand how that might occur. Focusing on expertise is helpful precisely because experts within a system do imagine the system differently and might remake it differently. In part, this is because they are not just system actors: they inhabit parallel professional and personal worlds that may see the system differently and struggle to make it different.

One of the most useful ideas in the contemporary literature about global affairs is the notion that global political, economic, and social life can be interpreted as occurring in a plurality of "regimes"[20] in which patterns of behavior appear to follow different imperatives, reflect different limits, and constitute different identities. Rather than an "economic market" and an "international political system," one might imagine, for example, a global "sports system" or "health system" or "trade system" each combining elements of national and international economic and political activity in different ways. This has several advantages. Conflict is easier to picture, particularly when struggles occur along lines of differentiation among regimes: people who imagine themselves within the global health system will approach the availability of generic drugs differently than people in the trade system or intellectual property system and conflict about what to do will also pit these regimes against one another. Moreover, the idea of plural regimes draws attention to the divergent values, objectives, and worldviews of people inhabiting different institutional cultures within and across large-scale world systems. The institutional and rhetorical practices of the European Union, for example, have influenced elites across Europe: speaking a common language of "comitology" and "subsidiarity," framing their proposals as steps toward the shared objective of a "common market," they can seem like strangers in their national political and cultural contexts. The world system, one might say, is one of regime conflict, its constitution the norms and institutional arrangements structuring that conflict. In a world of plural regimes, people acting in more than one regime may themselves have diverse identities, interests, or modes of engagement. As a result, one might expect a world system fragmented into functional regimes to be less of an iron cage and more the constructed product of communities of people through strategic engagement with one another.

Despite these advantages, regime thinking is nevertheless prone to overestimate the structuring power of regime logics rather than to see regimes as ongoing social products of human minds interacting and people struggling.[21] The logic of a regime is no more a fact to be discovered by analysis than the structure of a world system. These are labels one might apply to a way of acting or advocating for a purpose: to stigmatize it as a mechanical false necessity, to praise it as reason itself, to differentiate it from other ways of proceeding. The reality of imaginary regime/systems like the "market" or "balance of power" or "the European Union" or the "world of sports" arises from the shared perceptions and practices of people who reinforce that framing for their interactions. The "trade system" is a shared interpretation of particular institutional players and typical maneuvers as "trade policy" or a "trade war": how to interact, with whom to ally, whom to oppose, what to value, and how to achieve it. Conflict "among regimes" raises competing claims for the hegemony of the shared ideas associated with one or the other group of experts.[22] Rather than "regime conflict," it might be better to say that the regime-ness of a regime may be among the things at stake in struggles among people.

The key point is not simply the socially constructed nature of systems and regimes. They are socially constructed by a particular kind of activity: the work of expertise. This knowledge work may be subject to independent scrutiny and may be deployed along different trajectories with different potential system results. The systematicity of the system is not only a byproduct of expert work. It is also a strategy whose form will vary with the projects for which it is deployed. One way to think of this would be to say that regimes and systems are internally diverse and populated by people from adjacent or even adversarial regimes pursuing their own projects in their own ways. The regime—its agenda and logic and boundaries—will itself will be plastic to the peregrinations of those within it. When statesmen engage one another as representatives of "states" in the "international system," their mode of engagement might blend the language and practice of diplomacy, law, and war. Each of these is a distinct profession with its own body of knowledge, set of practical skills, history of the possible and the unachievable, and set of institutional alignments tethered to other actors and other imaginary systems beyond statecraft. How these will intersect with the projects of statecraft is hard to predict.

Attention to law helps make this visible. States and nations are legal institutions put together differently at different times and places. "War" and "peace" are legal statuses that may be more or less distinct and may relate to one another in a variety of ways. "Sovereignty" or "statehood" may be thought to precede and authorize their legal form, to be dependent upon its authorization or simply to be the sum of legal entitlements. "Public" powers may be the exclusive prerogative of sovereigns or may be parceled out among various personal, corporate, and other authorities. Borders may be firm or porous, national polities more or less exclusive. Minorities may be accommodated in a variety of ways, within states, as separate states or regions of disputed status. All these choices advantage some and disadvantage others: unsurprisingly, they have become matters of struggle. As a result, the struggles of international political life are about the frame of the system as much as they occur within it. Attending to legal variations and points of choice helps to endogenize struggle about the actors and structures that together constitute the state system. Legal arrangements, like other expert work, provide the missing link between actors acting and the structures of systems emerging. The plasticity of law highlights the possibility to contest these framework ideas in the institutional arrangements that make them seem natural or immutable.

There is a parallel story on the economic side. When economists place "competition among wealth maximizers under conditions of scarcity" at the center of economic "markets," they are imagining actors in a system without acknowledging the process by which those actors are constituted, placed in relationships with one another, and offered various powers and vulnerabilities for use in their competition with one another. The constituent elements beneath this economic imaginary—property, contract, corporations, credit, money, labor, public regulation—are legal institutions that could be arranged in a variety of ways. Which people are capacitated for commercial engagements, how they may pursue their preferences in competition, what institutional forms are available under what regulatory constraints: all need to be determined. Is slavery permitted? Is bankruptcy debtor or creditor friendly? Is a global value chain one corporation or many? How are responsibility and authority distributed along the chain? How easily can private actors generate liquidity? May women or children work? May workers bargain collectively? Must property be used to be retained? Must contracts be fair to be enforced? Arranging economic institutions differently will benefit and disadvantage different people and may generate equally efficient (or inefficient) outcomes with very different growth trajectories or levels of inequality.

As a result, struggle in economic life is more than competition among economic actors. It is also the process through which competing actors come to be constituted and empowered relative to one another. The idea that law arises "inside" and "after" the emergence of a political or economic order whose roots lie in struggle and scarcity gets in the way—and contributes to a false sense for the inevitability and naturalness of economic outcomes, "flows," and "forces."

The boundary work that goes on between regimes is no different in kind from the struggles that occur "within" a system about what it is and might become. A focus on the interstate system and the global economy can naturalize the difference between "economics" and "politics" in ways that erase the knowledge work that occurs as people contest the boundary. Lots of human activity might be framed as "political," reflecting choices about the public interest or generating winners and losers among people, social groups, and ideological commitments. Similarly, in some sense everything is "about scarcity" and might be recast in economic terms. The vocabulary for distinguishing political and economic activities is extremely plastic and the arrangements that consolidate the boundary are open to strategic engagement. Law provides a robust vocabulary for both making and contesting the designation of an actor or activity as political or economic, public or private, collective or individual, local or global.

Calling what someone does "political" or "economic" is an argument, a move in a struggle, a strategy. Espionage, for example, might seem like a strategy of national economic competitiveness and development for China while seeming to the United States like a political intrusion of public power, monies, or military or espionage powers into economic trade. Interpreting activities as economic or political can alter who is enabled to do what to whom and get away with it. The boundary work performed by law may provide a model for investigating the work of other knowledge professionals who mediate between actors and structures.

In this chapter, I have proposed to focus on expert struggle—a blend of knowledge work and coercion—to illuminate global affairs while avoiding some characteristic pitfalls of efforts to observe or theorize political or economic "systems": overestimating the stability and singularity of the actors and structures made visible by a particular system picture, allowing a bias toward order and coherence to mask the ongoing impact of prior and current struggle, and mistaking the shared ideas of people for a logic of the system. Focusing on the ubiquity of struggle is half the story. The other half is to understand the way expert knowledge operates to constitute actors and shape structures while serving as a tool for people pursuing projects to capture and allocate gains. The next chapters develop a framework for investigating the shared knowledge practices of experts who inhabit the institutions of global political and economic life.

PART II

EXPERTISE

CHAPTER 3
WORLD-MAKING IDEAS: IMAGINING A WORLD TO GOVERN AND TO RESIST

It is easy to see that professionals bring knowledge they have learned to bear on problems people present for solution: doctors, priests, lawyers, financial advisors, and life coaches all approach a family in crisis with different tools, frames of reference and experience. The same thing happens at the global level: economists, lawyers, scientists, religious leaders, politicians, businesspeople, and bankers come to global problems with diverse values, experiences and knowledge about how things work and what to do. But the image of experts bringing prefabricated knowledge to bear on world problems captures only a part of the role expertise plays in world making. The knowing, the doing, and the world making are more entangled than that. Background ideas about the world—often experienced as "facts" rather than "ideas"—shape the world before people set to work on the problems they see with the knowledge they have.

World-making ideas cannot be downloaded wholesale from the cloud. They arise through interaction and struggle. In one sense this is quite obvious. People bring to one struggle attitudes, values, and professional habits that have been effective and persuasive before. Today's tools reflect yesterday's victories. John Dewey described "logic" in a similar way.

> Now I define logical theory as an account of the procedures followed in reaching decisions . . . in those cases in which subsequent experience shows that they were the best which could have been used under the conditions. . . . It follows that logic is ultimately an empirical and concrete discipline. Men first employ certain ways of investigating, and of collecting, recording and using date in reaching conclusions, in making decisions; they draw inferences and make their checks and tests in various ways. . . . But it is gradually learned that some methods which are used work better than others.[1]

Dewey uses the words "best" and "work better" in the context of problem solving or reaching a conclusion. In the context of struggle, what "works" is what persuades or successfully coerces an adversary to yield or relinquish gains. Pictures of the world that are effective in this sense arise not only from past battles that may be studied, but through ongoing struggles where opposing world pictures frame alternate paths forward. In this sense, the world-making power of expertise is relational: world pictures that comprehend and shape the world and its problems are calibrated to the position people in struggle wish to occupy. To see the world this way is to see me in this place, you over there, and the path ahead down that road. As struggle proceeds, these become the available worlds, debate between them a terrain for engagement.

In the next two chapters, I explore the specialized knowledge, professional work and argumentative practices of professions involved in world making and management. In this chapter, I offer an interpretation of commonsense ideas about the world, its problems and the potential for governance that recur among professionals I have encountered—lawyers, economists, businesspeople, scholars and policy makers—who worry about and wish for better collective management of global problems. To illuminate the way world pictures arise in relation to one another, setting the stage for debates about how to proceed, I develop an ideal-typical contrast between the background ideas and professional postures of people who imagine themselves as "insiders" and "outsiders" to global rulership.

Ideas that become common sense are rarely formulated directly. Spelling them out requires a kind of imaginative and empathetic reconstruction. Listening to people arguing or watching them engage the world, one must step back to ask what they could be thinking or assuming about the world. What must they be taking for granted to be engaged in this conversation? Nor is background consciousness a set of propositions in the form "the world is flat and we shouldn't try to sail around it." It is more a pastiche of themes and orienting frames that bring some things to light, place others in shadow, and suggest a way forward. The elements are hard to separate: ideas about the world, the global problems that call for solutions, the nature of governance and leadership at the global level, and ideas about their own role.

Generating a common vision of a world to be governed is both a communicative and performative work of the imagination and a technical institutional project. Seeing a world, people build institutions that seem suited to it, design tools to act within it, empower leaders to address the problems they think it has. In doing so, they bring that world into being and make it visible. With those tools, from that institution, this world can be seen. This double-edged activity is a kind of reasoning, a way at once of comprehending and shaping the world. Technocrats, citizens, journalists, soldiers, bureaucrats, statesmen, poets, and priests all participate, scripting roles for themselves in its future. In world making, everyone is also tempted to fashion a stage on which they would be players, and to do the work on the self that is necessary to become players on the stage they see before them.

Forty years ago it was common to say that the most meaningful product of the space race was a distant photo of planet earth. Environmentalists, world federalists, pacifists, and cosmopolitan humanists of all kinds latched onto the image as evidence of a deep truth: ours is one world, we are one humanity, planet earth is our only home. This idea was not yet hegemonic among the world's political, commercial, and cultural elites: the photo pushed things along. Without a space program, perhaps without a Cold War, without *Life* magazine, we might not have had those photos at that moment in that way, and the idea may have arisen differently, at a different moment, or have seemed less suggestive or compelling. To be effective, the image had to be singled out, given meaning, and then settle into common sense. Resting there, it could be called upon as grounds for doing one thing rather than another. The photo's currency arose from its allegorical power to make visible what some had argued and others resisted. As the idea of worldliness it expressed sank into the consciousness of elites, its power faded into cliché. Of course this is one world . . . and so we must act.

Against the background of common sense, there remains plenty of room for disagreement about just *how* to act: in the next chapters, I explore the development of alternatives and modes of argument within a common framework of expertise. In debates about what to do, people mobilize—and sometimes contest—background images of the world that have settled into common sense. Even where people differ only marginally about how to proceed, they often accuse those with whom they disagree of ignoring what should be obvious. Seeking a slightly higher carbon price than you, it is tempting to claim that your preference ignores the threat of global warming all together.

The consolidation of one picture rather than another distributes authority, access, and legitimacy. As a result, the image that emerges from such debates reflects a status of forces. The idea—associated with 1648—that relations among states are secular represents a historic defeat for all those who yearn for a more religious world. Likewise the idea that all one can hope for on the global stage is "interfaith dialog" and reciprocal respect. When the space photo made "one world" a cliché, people pursuing more parochial projects were disadvantaged relative to cosmopolitans and environmentalists whose projects could be hooked to the coattails of the one world idea. Some came to share the new elite consciousness and continued their struggle by developing positions within it. For many, this did not seem possible. Rather than simply people with a different view about what to do, they now stood "outside" a world picture shared among the elite. They would need to come to terms with a world whose common sense they did not share. As people do this, they often develop a counterpoint set of propositions about the world, its problems, and the changes necessary for things to get better. This opens the way for argument between those who feel they are on the "inside" and those who experience themselves to be outside, beneath or peripheral to the world as it is now ordered.

A classic, if also tragic, historical example of the distributive impact of one-world ideas from my own field of international law is visible in the influential teachings of Francisco Vitoria, a Spanish theologian and jurist of the early sixteenth century. His writings were the space photo of his day, urging a conception of global humanity that included the newly discovered peoples of the new world. They were also human, he reasoned, cultivating land and organizing themselves in political communities, and were bound alongside Europeans by universal natural law. They had obligations as well as rights, including the duties of welcome and hospitality for friendly commerce and obligations to hear the gospel. Where they violated these obligations or heard the gospel clearly but failed to convert, the Spanish were empowered, as arms of the universal law, to discipline and conquer them by force.[2] Facing this kind of universal world, indigenous peoples needed a strategy, as they have throughout the ensuring centuries. Their strategies have varied—war and rebellion, assimilation, working to reform and adapt universal doctrines to their own ends. Their various strategies were also projects of communal identity, placing them within, without, or alongside global order and its common sense about the world as it is.[3]

The world-making activities of global elites are shrouded by self-evidence: their commonsense world is the world. As they work alongside the World Economic Forum in its commitment to "improve the state of the world," today's insiders take as given a world with common problems demanding that they rise to the challenge of global management. They focus on who might do what. People they can identify—whom they may even know—can pull these levers and act in the general interest, if only they have the right information, the requisite political will, the appropriate ethical orientation, or simply the right "incentives" and the necessary institutional structures. Those who can see themselves ruling can focus on the machinery of rulership, the institutional practices and doctrines of judgment and action. Their world can safely be assumed—until it may suddenly not be. Better global governance is necessary to manage problems before they present a challenge to the sustainability of the system itself.

On the receiving end, political, economic, or military coercion does not feel like technical management. Nor does technical management always seem like a public good. If you stand outside the project or promise of global governance, your interests adverse to its success, you will see a different world. Problems are not global or general, action in the public interest not what can be expected of enlightened elites. There are winners and losers: powers to the former, problems to the latter. The insider picture of a new world to be wrought by technical management and managerial self-improvement will seem like apology for the status quo and legitimation for their position in it. "Improving the state of the world" may seem like empire in the making. From the outside, even the problem of "sustainability" looks quite different. Poverty, environmental damage, inequality, and so forth are, from this perspective, all too sustainable. The problem is the system's capacity to reproduce exclusion, immiseration, or resource depletion.

I have imagined insiders and outsiders as ideal-typical positions or postures toward the world-making projects of an age. The world pictures of insiders are rarely fully settled into common sense: they still need the space photo as the Spanish needed Vitoria. Nor are outsiders unable to assimilate or argue forcefully in the insider language of problem solving. The opposition nevertheless marks the boundaries and provides the terms within which debate and conflict over more specific world-making projects occurs as experts arrange and rearrange images drawn from this stock. Each picture of the world comes with an allegorical vocabulary for identifying global problems and an orientation to solutions. In struggle, these can be attached to particular projects in all kinds of ways as people debate who should do what.

THE WILL TO WORLDLINESS: IMAGING AND RESISTING A WORLD TO BE GOVERNED

There are certainly points of overlap. People for whom global governance is an aspiration or present danger are among the most likely to see the world as a whole. Many—perhaps most—people look out the window and see only their neighborhood, their profession, their industry, their family. The animus to see "the world" may lie in an ethical or social experience of cosmopolitan humanism—all men are brothers—or social exclusion—the world is against us. The roots may also lie in fear. On the one side, urgent problems amenable only to global solutions demand that we see the world whole. On the other, our local difficulties have roots in a malevolent global order that must be resisted wholesale.

The one world of universal humanism imagines the world's people united in consensus, shared values, one civilization: the opponent is the outsider. Rule making, naming and shaming, or invading represent and enforce humanist civilization against stray states or dictators who "shock the conscience of mankind" or violate "fundamental norms." This is the vocabulary of humanitarian assistance and the international human rights movement, of the "responsibility to protect" and the international battle against terrorists, pirates, and traffickers. When insiders say that the "international community" is taking action, they are not thinking of the strange echo chamber of diplomats, journalists, and civil society advocates that keeps that phrase aloft, nor of the leading powers who act under that umbrella. They are expressing their vision: a world made whole through consensus taking institutional form to "protect civilians," denounce outsiders, or mount sanctions.

The outsider analog to this vision may be either a more horizontal picture of two (unequal) worlds colliding—their civilization and ours—or a world unified by a diabolical logic and run by malevolent forces. These ideas reframe a situation—in Syria, in Ukraine, in Iraq—not as the world enforcing norms on an outlier but as a clash of civilizations: Russia versus the West, Sunni versus Shiite, secular modernity versus Islamic truth. The Syrian regime of President Assad tried both strategies to counter efforts to define them as universal outsiders: presenting themselves as allied with the world against Islamic terror and as caught up in regional power dynamics between opposing alliances and interests. The Occupy movement slogan "we are the 99 percent" also merged these ideas: there are two worlds, theirs and ours—and the elites are the margin to our whole.

For many insiders, the "one world" idea arises as a defensive necessity rather than an ethical object of desire. The opponent is a "problem" whose urgency demands global action. Not every issue breaks through to this level. The distinction between truly global problems or crises and quotidian suffering is crucial. Problems must be severe, local crises must threaten the peace, and ethical violations must truly "shock the conscience." But if you can get up there, the way is clear for problem solving.

In this frame, it is ethically acceptable and only to be expected that people remain affiliated with their tribe or nation. There need be no ethical consensus:

ethical allegiances are matters of private commitment and local patriotic senti-ment. But global problems demand that we rise above those affiliations and act together in the common good. The technical and managerial professions find this frame more congenial than war against the outsider. Problem solving is their trade, while the articulation of virtue and the defense of civilization are someone else's brief. This picture comes with an implicit global architecture. Down there, people live in households, cities, and nations, with various reli-gious beliefs and political engagements. In their routine work, even managing elites may well feel they float in a sea of uncertainty and risk, buffeted by one thing after another. But when they raise their sights and look out at the world whole, the air suddenly feels thinner, beliefs are fewer, and political differences can be set aside as distractions from the work of collective problem solving. At Davos, it is easy to feel everyone should rise up onto the international plane to address the technical demands of global policy challenges.

This world picture also has—and is intended to have—distributive conse-quences. Some problems get globalized and others do not. Some become tech-nical while others remain stubbornly political. If your issue didn't make the cut, you will need to work harder to frame it as a pressing global challenge and generate an elite consensus on its amenability to technical resolution. The alternative is to resist the frame: ours is not a world of technical reason atop a quagmire of political particulars but one of clashing political interests. This is where the outsider voice can be heard. When the European Central Bank demands austerity in the name of technical wisdom to promote growth in recession, it is routinely opposed not only as bad economics—countercyclical investment the better course—but also as the mouthpiece of Germany and investor interests. When climate change pits technical response to a global problem against the national political interests of those who would pay the economic price, we can hear the clash of inside and outside perspectives. The enormous attention given to island microstates reflects not only their real peril but an effort by environmentalists to play on the boards of opposing interests and one world at the same time.

IMAGINING A WORLD WITH PROBLEMS

The idea of a "global problem" is a complex work of imagination. It runs counter to the human experience that bad things rarely happen to everyone. Pandemics or severe weather happen here and there, sparing these and deci-mating those. Some profit while others are wiped out and the costs of every solution will be unevenly distributed. To see diverse climatic changes as "climate change" or "global warming" even if your own weather is likely to be rather stable through your lifetime requires an act of imagination, of solidarity with future generations (at least of your own offspring), and of common vulnerability, humanity, or destiny with many people you will never meet. It is more common to hope that plagues, poor crops, and floods will happen to other people. And people are usually quite adept at explaining why that should be. Perhaps sickness falls harder on the unjust, the unprepared, or the unlucky. Perhaps wealth, technological superiority, and superior adaptability will be enough.

Although the list of problems people propose to see as "global" is rising—global warming, cybersecurity, pandemics, terrorism, corruption, human trafficking, drugs, migration—not everything makes the list, in part because this is a technical vocabulary of insiders. People see the "problems" their tools make tractable and people with technical and managerial tools frame things as technical and managerial problems, at least when they wish to take responsibility for their solution. The available public health tools enable us to see pandemics as a "problem" rather than simply as a "tragedy" or "act of God." For diplomats, the challenges will look diplomatic; for outsiders, they may well simply seem political. The identification of the problem and the selection of tools arise together. Is terrorism a global problem because it can be combatted with global surveillance, international police collaboration, and the military, or do we use those tools because it is a global problem? Both. And as terrorism becomes a global problem, the tools to respond migrate from local policing to national defense and global cooperation in surveillance, security, and financial control.

Insiders find it hard to frame widely shared troubles as global problems if they are unlikely to respond to the specialized competences of public administrative functionaries, the bureaucratic competences and technical knowledge of private enterprise, and the special professional expertise of global charities and nongovernmental organizations. As a result, distinctions that mark the boundaries of global governance—between public and private or local and international—also limit the problems that get to be global. The prevalence of false prophets and the spread of heresy are not global problems because they are not what governance is for. Domestic violence kills many times more people than terrorism and is far more broadly—and evenly—spread throughout the world. But the tools that seem appropriate for response are *local*: criminal law, social welfare, and a range of interventions in particular families. Loneliness, love, dignity, sexual desire, and spiritual well-being remain *personal*, while economic development, health care, education, and employment are seen as functions of *national* social, political, and economic arrangements. Even technical experts who address the suffering of human grief, anxiety, or cultural disenchantment rarely find a role in global governance: religious communities, purveyors of diets and self-help materials, comedians, fitness and yoga specialists, pharmaceutical companies, and psychotherapists. Their tools are for *private* use. We know that global policy choices and enforcement machinery affect all these things: war disinhibits sexual desire, economic development shatters families, transforms religions, and remakes gender dynamics. But it is hard to imagine using these tools deliberately for such purposes let alone developing a global program for their accomplishment.

Problems also seem global if they require a "global solution," whatever the tools to be deployed. This is not as obvious as it may seem. The idea that a problem needs a "global solution" usually says more about the tools to be used and the jurisdiction to be held responsible than about the nature of the problem itself. Many problems that are said to be global, like climate change, may actually be addressed in a perfectly suitable fashion by quite local measures. China could do a great deal on its own. A powerful technological innovation might turn the tide. A local or national rule changing the economics of energy production, a compact among leading private entities, or a side deal among governments whose nations account for the lion's share of the problem may all be far more effective than solutions hammered out globally. When people say that something demands a global solution, it is likely they are saying something about who should do what. The United Nations says this when it wants to convene a conference. National governments say this when they want the United Nations to convene a conference—and do not want to act themselves.

A problem may also seem global because "it" is understood to be happening to all mankind at once. To see multiple events as part of a larger common problem is a matter of interpretation and perspective, both often provided and managed by experts from the hard and social sciences. To argue that my poverty and your wealth are part of a common global problem requires a story. So does the claim that this storm, that flood, and this drought are effects of the same cause and might all be addressed by switching from coal to nuclear power. For more than forty years, "earth day" celebrations have promoted the idea that any damage to "the earth" affects us all, like an invasion from Mars. Science has been mobilized to show that diverse and dispersed activities generate "pollution" of "*the* environment." Experts add to the stock of available global problems by linking diverse phenomena under a common rubric, providing a kind of technical footnote for debates about what to do about "terrorism," "corruption," or "underdevelopment." For people with projects, transforming parochial interests into global problem solving requires translation. Hegemons and small Scandinavian nations, philanthropies and corporations, religious orders and professional guilds need to learn the languages of common interest and technical management. International law is one such language that has infiltrated the vocabulary of statesmen, soldiers, and civil society by promising to enable a conversation on the international plane of universal interests.

If history is any guide, common problems rarely give rise to common solutions. Even where people see the common threat, they may not be motivated to link arms in response. After an invasion from Mars, there would be all manner of strategies to be pursued. Some might become better off through collaboration, others by prolonging a futile resistance, still others by ignoring the whole thing. Those who think their professional expertise, position, and prerogatives are somehow linked to planetary defense will be more inclined to see a global problem ripe for solution. The "common problem" is less escape from conflict than tool of struggle and argument in debate about who should do what.

A WORLD OF GLOBAL PROBLEMS AS POLITICAL STRATEGY

Identifying a global problem is rulership: it distributes authority and legitimacy among actors and sets priorities for action, distinguishing what must be accepted from what must be addressed. Like any powerful framing device, naming "global problems" will be used strategically as hegemons justify interventions, advocacy groups raise funds, international institutions enlarge their mandates, and local rulers shrug off responsibility. Once a global problem has been identified, people will frame diverse concerns in these terms: suddenly everyone's political enemy or criminal gang is a "terrorist" to be engaged by the larger world. The outcome for particular interests, however, is hard to predict. Problems you care about may garner resources—or loose political focus—if they are reframed as global. The identification of a common problem may make the interests of those who will be affected first or most egregiously synonymous with the general interest. But there may also be a global strategic reason for them to be sacrificed. In the early months of the Ebola epidemic we saw a range of possibilities: did the global nature of the threat suggest the world redouble its engagement with the most affected African communities or that they be isolated to protect the larger world?

The language of "global problems" may also express a tacit agreement among people who wish someone else would do something about it. Poverty is a good example. It is very difficult for most people to experience the poverty of others as something that is also happening to them in the way they experience a faraway oil spill as degrading a shared environment. It would take a complex scientific, technical, religious, or political story to experience their poverty and our economic security as part of the same "problem." Yet poverty may arouse our empathy. To say that poverty is a global problem underlines the importance of doing something about it and the strength of our empathy. It also assigns it to others—perhaps even to institutions with no reasonable prospect of effectively responding.

Despite the distributive impact of global problem identification, insiders often feel that associating institutional mandates with global problems is a rough substitute for democratic government. If global elites stick to truly global problems, there is no need for a representative body to triage and aggregate interests. Their work is in everyone's interest. If solving these problems will improve the state of the world, it seems churlish to raise distributive issues. Even a plastic bottle manufacturer has an interest in reducing the plastic waste in the world's oceans. It is not surprising that global elites and those who pay the costs of their initiatives find themselves speaking different languages: of problem solving and global welfare, on the one hand, and of distribution and struggle on the other. Who will occupy which role in their shared language of engagement is often unclear. Just as the world's indigenous peoples have flirted both sincerely and strategically with assimilation to the inside spaces where the world is governed, so the world's elites—whether Vladimir Putin or George Bush—are able to understand and inhabit the posture of outsider to global common sense.

GLOBAL MANAGEMENT BY PREFIGURATION

Among the global policy class, it is understood that global problems are rarely "solved." At best they can be managed. Better global governance is at once a practical and an aspirational project: you can work toward it using the tools at hand, although you realize it may not easily or soon be achieved. The result is a tension in global governance projects between ideal—even utopian—images of governance to come and the practical need to root global public policy realistically in the world as it is.

One common way to manage this tension is to picture today's governance projects as prefigurative: to see in the interactions of independent states the outlines of a collaborative community or in the uncoordinated action of corporate officials and bureaucrats a kind of global administration. International lawyers see the outlines of what may one day be a fully functioning international criminal law in sporadic contemporary efforts to prosecute individuals for war crimes in national courts. To prosecute someone is to align oneself with a *future* criminal order. Adoption of this UN Protocol, the establishment of this intergovernmental actor, or the empowerment of this NGO, however partial, set precedents for further reform. Meanwhile, if people can be coaxed into settings where problems can be discussed, at some unspoken time in the future, a solution will present itself. An interminable peace process may not bring a final resolution, may be understood by all sides as the continuation of war by other means, and yet an open-ended process of problem management can also be seen *as* governance.

Strengthened habits of problem management may contribute more to the world than solving any particular problem. In this way, prefiguring may be more important than performing. When partial efforts are seen as down payments on a better future, defects in current practice seem tolerable. Today's minor players can be valorized for the role foreseen for them in later acts. Actors or interests that do not prefigure can be overlooked or stigmatized. To see a better world prefigured makes it easy to talk about what everyone might favor in the long term without mentioning whom that will actually favor between now and then.

Getting to that future requires people who can see beyond parochial interests and speak the language of technical problem solving. Just as lawyers see themselves as agents of a legal order, others must come to understand their work in government, as corporate leaders or citizen advocates, as the technical and managerial work of building and exemplifying a future order. Today's politicians, with their parochial ties to polity, are distinctly unsuitable for this role unless they come from a very small country and can reimagine themselves as citizens of the world. Corporate managers, international civil servants, technocrats, and academic policy types are closer to the mark. Just talking about oneself this way is prefigurative: thinking it, saying it, acting like it, can also make it so. It also feels good to imagine yourself as a global technocrat. You are no longer down there where problems arise but up here, part of the solution, a participant in the commanding heights. Before you came to Davos, you were just a corporate CEO, but now you see that you are part of a network and process of global leadership. Actually, anyone with an opinion and access to media can become a participant in "the international community," part of the "civil society," and an arbiter of "legitimacy" on the global stage: indigenous peoples, opponents of the death penalty, proponents of open-source software, and many more. It can be thrilling to find a voice and a lever to move a future world.

SOVEREIGNTY AS PREFIGURATION

Meanwhile, something will have to be done with the "state system" and "sovereignty." It is possible that perfecting and completing the nation-state system may itself be prefigurative. The state system began, so the story goes, as a global governance solution to empire, religious and ideological conflict. Perhaps we can see in sovereign and equal states the foundation for a normative and institutional order to secure the peace, manage the process of peaceful change, and address common issues of welfare requiring cooperation. All we need is wise leadership and vigilance against backsliding. At the same time, we might also look *through* the state, recognizing that real power today rests with smaller and more mobile players, within the state, among states or networked around states. Corporate leaders and global philanthropists, national courts and city managers are the harbingers of a future international community. To prefigure, professionals in both states and nonstates will need to align their agendas with the technical requirements of global problem solving.

Neither prefigurative tradition is particularly robust as either description or prediction. Each requires one to overlook a great deal. To see "states" as formally equivalent or analogically parallel territorial powers is to ignore a great many anomalies. Some states are complex bureaucracies while others are a few families. Nothing like parity or equality characterizes interstate bargaining and rarely do governments effectively aggregate interests or exercise anything like exclusive authority within their territory. The instruments of government have often been captured or displaced as power has leached upward to transnational and private technical bodies or downward to local and regional entities lacking the capacity to transform their priorities into effective policy. To conjure an international policy process of decentralized adjudication, administration, legislation, or ethical judgment from the dispersed interactions of nonstate actors is no less an act of imagination. The interesting point is that neither strategy needs to be compelling so long as they provide a suitable array of images and arguments to sustain a robust discussion about what to do that focuses on the benevolent work today's disappointing institutions will perform in the future. As images, they work.

Part of what makes both strategies plausible is their familiarity. If you can imagine states as a solution to the inequalities of empire and conflicts of religion or ideology, you are more than halfway to imagining the world governed. After a century of efforts to transcend sovereignty, people who dream about global governance imagine something very like sovereignty: a general being hovering over the society, oriented to problem solving in the general interest, responsible for the management of the whole. What people know as sovereignty shapes what they imagine as governance. For example, the governance they envision operates at one remove from economics. The world economy is somewhere out there to be managed or regulated. Private actors make only cameo appearances as participants in disaggregated public governance functions. Their routine decisions and the legal or commercial relationships they establish—from credit-default swaps to currency markets—are external to governance. Corporate "governance" connotes the arrangements through which shareholders and managers share authority for a corporation's economic activities rather than a constitutional arrangement of politically responsible actors. When investors misjudge the risk of lending to this or that government and withdraw funding or raise interest rates, they are not governing. The governance challenge is to address the global problems that result, perhaps by disciplining the government that has lost investor favor or bailing out those investors until they are again willing to loan funds.

Nor does global problem solving know itself as culture. Nations have culture, along with localities, civilizations, ethnic groups, or religions. To work prefiguratively is to step outside your culture to become a citizen of the world, tethered only to a shared technical and professional knowledge. The civil service of the European Commission is proud of the technical competence of its specialized staff, their multilingual capacities, rate of transnational intermarriage, and double citizenship. Somehow these go naturally together: the EU Commission has skimmed the cream, detaching people from national political or cultural affinities to distill a kind of pure "European" technical competence.

The promise of a benevolent sovereign power permits people to look past their contemporary struggles with the exhilarating feeling that today's tawdry compromises will all add up to wise rulership if we just keep at it in the right spirit. Within the world's institutional, corporate, financial, diplomatic, and government elites people can imagine themselves, their networks, and their colleagues functioning as this kind of general sovereign being. When you are at places like Davos, it is hard not to share the dream. There are all these global problems and everyone else is preoccupied with parochial things. *Some-one* should somehow provide governance at the global level—why not us?

FROM THE OUTSIDE: GLOBAL GOVERNANCE AS THE MYSTERIOUS STATUS OF FORCES

People who do not imagine themselves as prefigurative global rulers speak about global political and economic life in a different idiom. Rather than "global governance," they might speak of "the world system," "the new world order," "empire," or "global capitalism." The economic, political, and cultural arrangements they see have a structure, empowering some and disempowering others. Someone else sets economic forces in motion, transforms our culture, and makes political decisions affecting our lives. Global governance is not about elaborating or prefiguring an ideal: we are already governed. The motive for understanding governance is to change it. The intellectual project is diagnosis: how are we ruled, how is hierarchy reproduced, who benefits? The usefulness of ideas about power and government lies in their ability to help us know it when we see it. Political theory may be instructive to the extent the world is governed in its name or navigates by its light.

Where insiders talk to *one another* about where to begin, what is realistic or what goes too far, on the outside people tilt at global windmills from different directions and decry different things. They seek less to persuade one another than to mobilize those who share their interests to identify a common enemy. Their stories about how things go wrong draw on shared intellectual traditions and return to the same imponderables: Is the world order a *system* or something much more ad hoc? Is there one global order—or many? Who are the most important actors? States and corporations, or more aggregate forces: labor and capital, East and West, or center and periphery?

If the central drama for insiders is the relentless effort to transform interests that are parochial into governance that could be more universal, from the outside the central drama is a struggle among people and groups, a matter of power more than governance, of winners and losers more than common interests or shared problems. The imaginary architecture is one of top and bottom, center and periphery, rich and poor. As a result, the outsider leans toward rupture and a society remade rather than prefigurative reform. Where the global governance tradition aims to re-present the world as governable, outsider traditions aim to represent absent or subordinated interests against those who govern. People speaking in this style are not aggregating the general will: their perspective is more partial, interested. Where insiders imagine themselves as agents of the general interest, outsiders find it easier to imagine themselves in a fantasy relationship with others whose interests and viewpoints are not now ascendant. Outsider analysis is less concerned with sovereignty and less drawn to the fantasy of a capability above society, aggregating the general will and attending to the general interest. There is no benign power above the struggle of interests and the injustices of current arrangements are more salient than its capacity for management. At the center of analysis is an identification of power and structure—the structure of hierarchy, the power to dominate, distribute, and decide. Rulership—or sovereignty—is the reproduction of hierarchy: war is continuous with technical management and governance is the routinization of success. Patterns of domination, inequalities, and hierarchies are all marks by which the structure of power can be known.

To insiders, outsiders can sound like everyone else with an ax to grind. Drawing attention to hardship and hierarchy seems obtusely inattentive to the practical demands of the situation, more conducive to the nursing of grudges than the solution of problems. For much of the last century, this outsider style has been stigmatized for its association with disruptive or sectarian political movements—from communism, ethno-nationalism, and third-worldism to religious fundamentalism. In the United States, the outsider analytic tradition is most visible in media portrayals of nativists, localists, xenophobes, and people who worry that the United Nations is about to send in the black helicopters.

But, of course, sometimes and in some places, the United Nations—or the United States or the "international community"—does send in helicopters, and it is not always clear they are there to help. In fact, it is difficult to travel outside the commanding heights of the global economy or intergovernmental system—or beyond the leading European and North American nations—without finding some version of this outsider sensibility. For all it has been stigmatized, the outsider framework is also familiar. One encounters it also among people who are part of the "elites" of their own societies—among people one would have thought it easy to assimilate to the project of "rebooting" our global architecture from the inside. You can hear it in the sensibility of young international lawyers from Eastern and Central Europe encountering their generational cohort in Germany, France, or the Netherlands. At home, they may be cosmopolitans dreaming of global governance, but when they get to Brussels or Paris or London, they often feel the pull of outsider modes of analysis. The same can often be said for international lawyers in Paris or London whose racial, ethnic, or religious backgrounds place them off-center in their homeland.

Although the difference is easy to personify—the CEO at Davos, the local politician in Iran, the militia leader, and the human rights advocate—it would be more accurate to say that many, even most, people who think about global power dynamics and governance shift gears from a relatively complacent "insider" aspiration for global governance to a more critical "external" assessment of the structure of global power and influence. Many experience professional work somewhere on a continuum between Davos or Geneva, on the one hand, and Idaho or North Waziristan, on the other. There is something to both sides: global governance can be a hopeful project of establishment reform, just as it can legitimate the privileges of the few in the language of general interest. As people pursue various projects, the relationship between these perspectives remains something of an open switch, the differences a matter of degree. Corporate managers learn both to focus on their duty to shareholders and to rise up to the challenges of global citizenship. Aspiring to participate in global governance as a practical aspiration is also a role one can learn and perform, like the experience of being on the outside, speaking truth to management. The language of engagement draws on both ideal-typical positions and visions of the world depicted in table 3.1.

Expressing yourself in the language of one or the other vision also positions you as an insider or outsider. It is easy to see those more troubled about a particular global governance initiative than oneself as outsiders and those more hopeful about global problem solving as part of the establishment. The insiders seem complacent, the outsiders impractical. These are positions on a continuum. Small disagreements about particular programs or the promise of particular reforms can mark the difference between those who are "part of the solution" and those who are "part of the problem." In struggles about what to do, large pictures of the world and its future arise as alternatives, their invocation calibrated strategically. If you favor that, you must be one of those Davos elite who are running the world into the ground—if you cared about justice, you would join me in the fight. Or: when you ask me to do that, you reveal yourself to be one more parochial complainer who fails to understand what makes the world go around and where it is heading. Don't you want to solve global problems and improve the state of the world? Why won't you prefigure with me?

People everywhere struggle to reconcile these divergent sensibilities when they think about issues like climate change, poverty, or national development. The choice of perspective can cause anxiety: ought one to pitch in and try to make things better or listen to doubts that the system could ever be satisfactorily reformed to save the earth or share the wealth? People sometimes

Table 3.1. Two Postures of Engagement

Insider vocabulary	Outsider vocabulary
Global governance as aspiration/hope/solution	Global governance as reality/problem/threat
Prefiguration: current practices anticipate future solutions	Power struggle: current practices confirm past victory
Central drama: universal against the particular and law against politics	Central drama: a struggle of interests, the power of the few transformed into the law of the many opposed by resistance
Architecture: a plane of global problem solving above a world of parochial differences	Architecture: a horizontal opposition of interests, a hierarchy of winners and losers
Global problems and common values	Distribution and difference
Global governance: technical management in the general interest/the implementation of shared values	Global governance: a power practice of the powerful
Fantasy identification: commanding heights	Fantasy identification: peripheries/the dispossessed
Proposed mode of action: regulation/dispute resolution/problem solving	Proposed mode of action: conflict/power and resistance
Work on the self: rise up to think globally as an agent of the general interest	Work on the self: wake up to think globally as an agent of the periphery
Objective: reform	Objective: rupture
Sovereignty is central: global governance prefigured in the state system, completed as the emergence of an enlightened global management capability; meanwhile, parochial political sovereignty a continuing threat	Sovereignty just another form of power, another fantasy of an end to struggle; meanwhile, foreign or international authority as problem/local-national sovereignty as solution
Global governance outside, above, or after politics/economics/culture	Global governance as the dominant political, economic, and cultural order

associate these perspectives with different bureaucratic settings. Young professionals often wrestle with alternate career paths by framing them as a symbolic choice between working as an insider or an outsider: to work with an international institution as opposed to an NGO, with a global NGO as opposed to a local community organization, with one's home government rather than civil society. In the academic world, differences between disciplines or between the "mainstream" and "heterogeneous" traditions within a discipline are often marked in these terms. Where international law seems the insider work of improving global governance, political science may carry the impulse to resist. Where economics can seem the handmaiden of global economic management, "international political economy" provides a home for those analyzing the dark sides, distributional consequences and inequalities of the world economic system. Where one field privileges the voice of modest pragmatism, belief in a diabolical "world system" takes hold in another. Disciplines with self-confident analytic models and technical tools often find it easier to speak as insiders to global problem solving while those focused on the messy world of facts gravitate more naturally to an outsider voice. It is common today to associate endogeneity with outsiderness and insider status with more robust, if less capacious, analytic models.

Over time, these disciplinary and institutional contrasts are more fluid. What remains constant is the tendency to develop opposed sensibilities marked on the one side by prefigurative stories about the potential for global problem solving and on the other by stories about the power dynamics of a world in struggle. Global governance begins with the claim that this or that ongoing practice is, or could be, the operation of a global public hand. Resistance begins by the identification of interests in conflict and the interpretation of problem solving as power. The most effective players are strategic, flexible in their use of the available vernacular, finding ways to cross lines and embrace arguments from the other side to characterize projects with which they do not agree.

CHAPTER 4
EXPERTISE: THE MACHINERY OF GLOBAL REASON

Expertise is special knowledge made real as authority in struggle. My starting point for exploring expertise is the *work* experts do rather than the specialized knowledge they bring to bear. Expertise is less a form of knowledge deployed by specialized actors than a form of knowledge work undertaken by all kinds of people in their relationship with others. Expert work positions the people who do it between what is known and what must happen. The work is interpretive, translating the known into action and knitting the exercise of power back into the fabric of fact. One characteristic of this work is disagreement. Experts struggle with one another using tools of interpretation, articulation, and persuasion that are, when effective, at once words and authority.

The role of specialized knowledge *in government* has been explored for centuries in theology and political thought and has been a central preoccupation of sociology at least since Max Weber. Already in the sixteenth century, international lawyers were advising rulers to take advice to determine whether war was just.[1] Although Machiavelli had little advice for the prince on the role of advisors, his thoughts on the qualities to seek in a minister provide an early definition of expertise by role rather than knowledge. A prince must seek out men who place the interests of the prince above their own in all things, who must "never think of himself, but always of the prince, and he must never think of anything but what concerns the prince."[2] At issue is less the knowledge or wisdom of those who serve the prince than their posture of alliance and loyalty. The rise of self-confident technocratic management in the past century generated both optimism and worry about the role of experts in government.[3] Ever since, people have sought ways to harness their distinctive knowledge for rulership while limiting their authority and humbling them before the popular will to ensure their accountability.[4]

One hears two different stories about global affairs: it is a place of unrestrained politics, a war of all against all, and it is a space of technocratic rule unrestrained by politics. Expertise either predominates or is invisible. I aim to bring these stories together. The diplomatic history and international politics story of leaders expressing national interests, paradigmatically through force of arms, captures the centrality of struggle and coercion in global life. Yet it underestimates the ways in which the choices and beliefs of statesmen are shaped by background players—other than the occasional Svengali—and the everyday vocabularies they use to articulate the national interest, even in war. This underscores the importance of interest in driving the projects people pursue, but underestimates the complex interpretive process through which national "interests" are formulated and brought to bear as things like geography and ideology are taken up as drivers of national interest. After all, diplomacy is as much the paradigm for war as the reverse and the use of force has also become a matter of communication and persuasion. The technocracy story identifies the significance of professionals and specialized modes of communication in global affairs, but underestimates the brutality of struggle within and through expert work while exaggerating the difference between technical and political modes of engagement.

The role of knowledge in global power is particularly easy to see because it so often arrives as an assertion, an argument, a program of action, or a call to resistance. Although authority always comes into being as an assertion, in other contexts that can be forgotten. Other than in moments of revolutionary turmoil, people forget that the sovereign is just a person whom everyone says is king. The institutionalization of public power makes authority seem "real" just as it makes the distinction between "public" and "private" or "legislature" and "executive" seem natural, however much institutional fine-tuning may be necessary to get the boundary right. At the global level, the saying and performing are often right on the surface. Global governance must be *claimed*, through an assertion that this or that military deployment or human rights denunciation is the act of the global public hand: the "international community" in action. The rhetorical dimension of global power is equally significant for those who would resist. Identifying the global hand in local unpleasantness is also an assertion and an allegation of responsibility. Whether one aspires to bring global governance into being or fears its power, one must name it, assert it, and identify it, propose it as something to build or destroy. In a sense, "global governance" is simply the sum of what those who wish to manage and to resist globally have jointly drawn to our attention as governance.

This is on display in moments of crisis, when people who style themselves as participants in the "international community" discuss what to do about Muammar Gaddafi or Syrian chemical weapons or Burmese democracy. The situation needs to be framed—as a crisis, a conflict between the world and outlier rascals, a manageable problem, a precedent, a challenge to the credibility and ethics of the community. Military intervention, should it occur, is at once confirmation and consequence of the frame. Although we might come to see the situation as driven by power politics, geostrategic interests, regional rivalries, or historic grievance, these also need to be articulated. They are also made real—or not—through practices that confirm the analytics. Such modes of interpretation and methods of engagement are developed, deployed, and defended in specialized terms. Those terms are often rooted in law, but may as well be rooted in political theory, political science, history, religion, morality, national identity, and much more. In each case, they will have been honed by specialists before and as they are used.

Although less visible, expert practices of knowledge and power are more significant in routine situations. The structures of global political economy, the channels for diplomatic struggle, and the tools for the allocation, consolidation, and contestation of economic privilege require interpretation and framing as much as implementation or enforcement. Vernaculars developed by specialists—again often lawyers—are crucial here as well. We know, for example, that if everyone thinks the stability of the euro is at stake—well, the stability of the euro *is* at stake. But this is equally true of arrangements everyone thinks are stable: so it was, for example, with slavery or empire. And so it is for a territorial politics and a global economy in the form I explored in chapter 1. In this sense, the constitution of a world is ongoing: a technical and institutional practice as well as a communicative and performative work of the imagination.

EXPERT WORK: THE BACKGROUND BETWEEN FOREGROUND AND CONTEXT

I associate the term "expertise" with a type of intellectual and practical work that links analysis of the context for a decision with people and places marked out as the locus for decision. I call this activity and the style, posture, and role associated with it "background practice" or "background work." Specialized professionals do this when they explain to laypeople and leaders what is going on in a crisis, interpret public opinion, outline the options for action, and

Figure 4.1 Expertise as Background Practice

explain what history and precedent require. After the people or the leaders have taken a decision, background work moves in the other direction, interpreting and implementing, giving effect to the general or sovereign will.

Background work linking context and decision is undertaken by all kinds of people, although people often draw upon more or less vulgate versions of ideas developed by specialists. The expertise and professional practices of specialists warrant attention not because they exercise disproportionate influence over princes and popular opinion as a kind of Rasputin/Riefenstahl monster, but because their interpretive background work is so characteristic of global struggles, whether undertaken by experts, princes, or populations. When people work in the "background," they situate themselves between two kinds of imaginary space that I term the "foreground" and the "context."

If foreground deciders seem empowered to decide in the context of forces and facts that have no agency, the experience of experts working in the background is different. They are people with projects, projects of affiliation and disaffiliation, commitment and aversion, and with wills to power and to submission, just like the foreground folks. Yet their practice is oriented to replace the experience of agency with something like the felt necessity of deference to contextual forces and facts and the experience that someone else will act. Background experts stand between the objective observation of facts and the subjective exercise of discretion. They advise and interpret by inhabiting modes of knowledge and communication through which they can pursue projects with some plausible deniability of agency.

Experts know in a general sense that they are not simply channeling the necessities of context. They approach one another's assessments and arguments with suspicion that interest or ideology might have gotten into the clean room.[5]

But they also know that they are adding something—professional judgment—where contextual forces may have supported a range of interpretations. Their agency in doing so is deniable so long as what they add is *plausible* given the conventions of their expertise and the practices of their profession. This is only possible, in turn, if there is a community and a discursive field that disciplines the plausibility of their interventions. The community and field need not be a recognized profession or academic discipline, but the work of specialized professionals like lawyers or economists provides examples of how this kind of plausibility is created, sustained, or undermined.

The *context* for decision consists in the facts and forces that are understood to impinge on a decision or that need to be taken into account. In chapter 1, I distinguished matters of technical or more general debate from the shared commonsense images and outcomes of earlier technical struggle that were taken as fact and not available for contestation. The first is background, the second context. But it is background work that draws the line between them. To raise issues up for debate is to bring them into the background. Context would include the "drivers" that decision makers are said to ignore at their peril: technological, historical, social, economic, or political "realities." People speak about "national interest" this way: as a fact about the nation determined by its geographical position, history, economic structure, cultural identity, or objective place in the world. Trade economists often speak about a nation's comparative advantage or factor endowment in these terms. People sometimes speak about the "productivity" of factors and the "competitiveness" of outputs as facts to be taken into account rather than reflections of decisions that could be reconsidered. Context provides the constraint within which allocations may be more or less efficient, business more or less profitable, nations more or less productive. This is what social scientists speak of as "structure": the arrangements that shape and constrain the decisions of agents. Here we find the impersonal forces of the material world and the social system as well as the immutable beliefs of ideology or religion. The context is not a black box of subjective preference, nor the brute force of objective necessity. It is the settled outcome of background work. Interests and facts relevant for decision are socially constructed. The place where that happens—and could happen differently—is the "background."

In the *foreground* are people identified as actors making decisions that affect the distribution of power, wealth, and status in the world. This is the space of world leaders, particularly at moments of crisis: perhaps Kennedy and Khrushchev in 1962 provide the model. This is how George Bush presented himself when he claimed to be "the decider." These, in social scientific terms, are the "agents." Political leaders, statesmen, sovereigns, and the institutions of public law are all overrepresented here. This is how people sometimes view the commanding heights of finance and interpret what goes on at places like Davos. The defining characteristic of the foreground is the attribution of discretion and decision-making power: these people could take one road or another and decide which way to go on the basis of their interests, preferences, or political views.

Attributing this kind of power to decision makers misses the process by which constraints are made real to them and overestimates their own experience of discretion. Although government ministers and the heads of administrative agencies spend all day making decisions, briefed by staff, lobbied by constituents, urged on by allies, opposed by a wide variety of forces, such people are constrained and experience themselves as constrained by their institutions, their legal obligations, their political beliefs, their access to information, their assessment of colleagues, rivals, and opponents, and their own sense of role. To identify and understand those constraints, those drivers, and those interests, they must engage in background work.

Early in my career, I spent some time in the cabinet of a commissioner of the European Union, the rough equivalent of a national minister or, in the American system, a cabinet secretary. The one thing my commissioner rarely seemed to have was the feeling of "freedom to decide." Or rather, he experienced this only fleetingly and often in moments of clarity about what his prior political commitments or the strategic situation *demanded* that he decide. More often, the situation was muddy, decision a matter of small steps and trial balloons. The essence of political decision is confusion and constraint, even in the White House in October 1962.

Being "the decider" is not only an experience, if a rare one. More often it is an assertion or attribution made in a retrospective interpretation. The president claims to be the decider as an assertion of authority and responsibility, just as holding the president responsible begins with an allegation that he decided. To identify someone as responsible—like the identification of a force as contextual—is a claim. The claim comes to seem true when the background work of those who made it fades into the background. People speak about the "forces of globalization" or the "needs of the market" or "global warming" as if they were facts demanding responses rather than interpretations rooted in human decision. They speak about Davos or the CIA running the world as an accusation. If they come to be held accountable, the work of attribution will be completed and can disappear. A focus on decisions obscures the knowledge work of those who attribute decision-making responsibility. Once taken, decisions are available for reinterpretation, review, reversal, or simple erosion as they are implemented and remembered, and the work of the background recommences.

The continuing presence of expert calculation, assessment, and interpretation in high politics is often overlooked because the vocabularies associated with high politics can seem markedly different from those more customarily associated with background advising. Leaders speak the language of politics, of with us and against us, of clashing civilizations, ideologies, and interests: the West versus the Rest, left-center-right, labor versus capital, South versus North, industry versus agriculture, the United States versus Europe, Sunni versus Shiite, secular versus religious, liberal versus conservative. We expect leaders to speak this way and routinely attribute agency and discretion to people who do. Experts who work in background spaces typically refrain from the language of interests or ideologies. They speak professional vernaculars of best practice, analytic rigor, empirical necessity, good sense, and consensus values. They may speak about the national interest and what it requires, but to decide on the national interest or to act in its name is above their pay grade.

The distinction, however, is rarely sharp. Whether making war or pursuing economic development, politicians also speak in languages of technical expertise. The media have become adept at educating their audience about the nuances of what had been technical disputes. Perhaps the most significant example was the strategic studies profession's work transforming their computer models of prisoners in reiterated dilemmas into massive defense funding—in Moscow no less than Washington. Experts are also required to develop and apply the language of politics and ideology. This is where spin doctors and media consultants and all the intellectuals who write op-eds come in: working out what it means to be "liberal" or "Islamic" or "European."

The difference between foreground and background is itself a product of fluid expert analysis. One way to think about it would be to say that the *background* is the space where people argue about and make real the claim that something or someone is foreground or context. Foreground political decision can often be reframed as a question of technical management, a mopping-up operation for a decision taken elsewhere, just as the technical debates of experts can often readily be assimilated to the left-center-right structures of public political discussion. People in the governing professions deploy the distinction strategically as they locate responsibility for decisions with which they agree or disagree. It is striking how often people in government locate the moment of political decision elsewhere—yesterday, in the Council, in the Oval Office, in Congress, in precedent, by the member states, at our last meeting—or deny the possibility of decision: the context determined the outcome, the bean counters just wouldn't go for it.

In national systems, this potential is dampened by the convention to treat particular institutions or role occupants as avatars of the political— the president, the king, parliament—and others as the space of expertise— administration, adjudication, the academy. At the global level, rulership is far less the monopoly of identifiable institutions. The colonization of foreground institutions by background vernaculars and the strategy of attributing respon- sibility elsewhere are far more pronounced. State power is everywhere spoken and exercised in the vocabulary of international relations, political science, in- ternational law, military science. Wars and the machinery of war are ordered, purchased, launched, and pursued in professional vocabularies, whether the computer-modeled rationality of nuclear deterrence, the justificatory language of humanitarian intervention, self-defense, and rights enforcement, or the gaming vernacular of dispute resolution and grand strategy. International eco- nomic life is organized in the vocabulary of professions committed to growth and development. Markets are structured to reflect professional notions of "best practice," and defended in the professional language of efficiency. Like- wise, when state power takes the form of public or private law, it is conceived and exercised in the vocabulary of law and lawyers.

The background work linking context to decision is a commonplace way to imagine deciding what to do. I have needs and desires I would like to realize. There are limits, pressures, and constituencies I must heed. As I contemplate what to do, argue with myself about the direction to take, I consult my de- sires, assess my needs, and evaluate the forces arrayed around me before ad- vising myself on a course of action. I also want to look ahead to evaluate the likely impact my decision will have and how it will be interpreted. People have something like this in mind when they say they want to "think it through." Interpreting this from the outside, it is easy to focus on the needs, desires, and impinging forces—and on the decision. By attending to the "background practices," my intention is to focus rather on the ways people individually and collectively "think things through." Background work lies behind the large- scale decisions of businesspeople and investors allocating and conditioning the use of vast resources, made in the vocabularies of economists, accountants, and policy analysts seeking to maximize return or corner markets as well as the decisions within families distributing resources among members in terms developed by priests, therapists, the advice givers of the media or the sages within each family network. People doing background work in all these sites routinely imagine that, in their own special way, they are figuring things out and thinking things through.

MAKING THE BACKGROUND VISIBLE

When background work has been most successful, it is very difficult to see. It just seems obvious: he's the president, that's the situation. Or, as in chapter 3, this is the world and these are its problems. It takes effort to reverse engineer the expert work embedded in this kind of common sense and open it to contestation. To say that wages reflect the "productivity of labor" is to condense the background distributive work described in chapter 1 into the context. This harsh contextual necessity brands the outcomes of the struggles that shape relative labor productivity or competitiveness as "facts," although wage rates in a given factory may be affected by the background work of public and private administrative or regulatory players across the globe who struggle over what to interpret as a fact of economic life and to whom to attribute regulatory capacity.

For years, people wishing to influence global labor conditions focused attention on the World Trade Organization and the International Labor Organization. The ILO for its obvious subject matter competence, the WTO because it seemed more capable of compelling compliance with whatever labor standards might be adopted. The weaknesses of global legislation by either institution were well known: national actors have not been willing to adopt rules that would threaten their national economic strategies. The result has been vague compromise standards, unenforced agreements, standards that legitimate more than they restrain. But where else can one turn but to the available foreground institutions? In this situation, the possibility for background struggle disappears. Everything that is not within the decision space of the WTO is context. As a result, it is easy to overlook the impact of decisions by entrepreneurs, workers, consumers, and investors made in the shadow of background rules and expectations about the uses of property, the conditions for labor organization, the transport and trade of industrial inputs and outputs, patterns of credit and payment, immigration. The world of background norms—private law, corporate standards, transnational administrative arrangements, rules of corporate governance and liability—seems less open to struggle. They are either aligned with "best practice" or shaped by the inexorable forces of competition across open markets.

The WTO might play a larger role in global wage regulation were the background work it undertakes as an interface between diverging national background regulations reinterpreted as a foreground decision affecting global wages. We have long known that in some sense, as the saying goes, "fair trade is free trade's destiny." As tariffs came down, industrial nations began to challenge all sorts of diverse pieces of one another's regulatory environment as "non-tariff barriers to trade." In doing so, they were identifying something that had been seen as the context for national market activity and opening it to technical reassessment and political struggle. The "non-tariff barrier" is context made background through expert identification and naming. Once begun, there seems no natural limit to this practice—as the European Union's legal order has amply demonstrated. The WTO provides a context for struggle over these rule systems, including, potentially, those that affect wages. In principle, for example, the United States could challenge Mexico's or China's low effective minimum wage as an unfair subsidy of their exports and impose a tariff at the border to compensate. Or perhaps the lax enforcement of local law might be seen as "dumping" and warrant a response. On the other side, Mexico or China could find a US demand for higher labor standards to be an unfair or unreasonable extraterritorial reach of American law and a barrier to trade.

The result would be a dispute undertaken in the language of trade law. It would have highly technical components: the legal definition of "non-tariff barrier," "dumping," and "injury," the calculation of gains and losses, the rules for accessing the WTO or other decision-making processes. It would also have elements that may have been given professional meaning, but shade off into popular discussion: ideas like "unfair trade" or "level playing field." It is common to assume that such disputes will be either settled by political decision or resolved by technical expertise. The resolution may be either a foreground decision to end the "trade war" or a technical resolution by trade lawyers determining what is and what is not a "subsidy."

Resolution by the political leadership will be shaped by the technical vernacular through which the dispute arose and may be more constrained than one might expect. The technical resolution will be pursued in the shadow of the political stakes and typically has more room for discretion than might initially be visible. In this situation, for example, it turns out there is no objective intellectual instrument to determine whether the Mexican wage law is a subsidy or the American wage requirement is a non-tariff barrier. Each rule, if permitted, could have an extraterritorial impact on the economy of the other nation. Nor does international law have an objective professional method for determining which extraterritorial impact is the exercise of a legitimate sovereign privilege. Ultimately, it seems to depend on an assumption about which legal scheme is "normal" and which is not. If the difference between American and Mexican wages is "normal," American efforts to raise Mexican standards will seem an abnormal non-tariff barrier. As it processes routine trade disputes, the WTO system generates a string of decisions about globally tolerated levels of differentiation among labor and other regulatory standards—about the range of "normal" background regulation.

Deciding what is "normal" and what is not is rulership: a decision about the allocation of costs. Although the WTO provides a mechanism for settling disputes between nations asserting that *their* rule is normal, the WTO's work is not generally understood in this way. People seeking to alter wages and working conditions focus on national legislatures: that is the foreground where labor policy is made. International institutions like the WTO are significant if they can encourage changes in national labor policy—by studies promoting labor flexibility or by adoption of a "social charter" advocating stronger worker protections. Progressive interests bemoan the fact that the international legal order is not powerful enough to do much about the conditions of work, yet the WTO is deciding what is and is not a "normal" background legal regime on a routine basis. The difficulty is finding opportunities to contest the wide range of low-wage industrial strategies that result. They seem the inexorable result of economic forces that cannot be challenged in the foreground of political life.

Something similar goes on in thinking about war and peace. When people focus on summit meetings and late-night telephone calls between heads of state—or speeches in the Security Council—they underestimate the discretion and the significance of people in the background of these public deliberations. The power of *expert consensus* is real: consensus that Iraq had weapons of mass destruction, that American credibility is on the line, that something must be done, that dominos would surely fall. We now know that although 9/11 opened a window of plausibility for the invasion of Iraq, the campaign had already long been under way—and not simply because the leadership, the Bush family, say, was "obsessed" with Iraq, but also, and more importantly, because an entire administrative machine had been set in motion, with its own timetables and credibility requirements. The invasion incubated there, in the background, built momentum through hundreds of small decisions, budgetary, administrative, political, rhetorical, public and private. In some sense, of course, Bush could have called the whole thing off, and without his enthusiasm all that momentum may never have built. The interesting point, however, is that by the time people focused on "the president deciding," it was not at all clear how much room to maneuver he still had. "The United States" had made a commitment to overthrow Saddam Hussein—a commitment whose political and bureaucratic momentum could not easily have been stopped without incurring all manner of further costs—long before the decision came to the president, let alone the Security Council, for explicit decision.

A decade later, the question of what, if anything, to do about the conflict in Syria seemed to be a classic foreground issue of high politics. People debated how to understand the conflict: was this a struggle between the "international community" and an outlaw regime, or was it a more horizontal struggle between Russia and the West, among regional powers and religious/ethnic traditions? In the summer of 2013, President Obama set out to "decide" whether the United States should respond with a military strike to the use of chemical weapons in the conflict. At stake was the credibility of the international legal regime, the determination of the United States to enforce the line against use of "weapons of mass destruction" in the Middle East, the American commitment to Israel vis-à-vis Iran, the personal credibility and power of the president, at home and abroad. All these were claims made by experts in strategic thinking and political calculation who battled for attention with experts in public opinion on war weariness, experts in military tactics on likely effects and consequences, experts on political strategy on relations with Congress and electoral impact, and so on. The impact of a set of explosions in Syria—or the absence of explosions—was also a matter for interpretation, to be undertaken by laypeople and politicians, media experts and military planners, in the same vernaculars. Claims were being made on numerous boards simultaneously: about the president's war powers, the legal/political/strategic reasons for engaging Congress or pursuing diplomacy, and more. The summer passed into fall and the US did not strike. That became another fact to interpret, for diplomats and politicians, soldiers and insurgents, in Syria and beyond.

In short, the work of the background has colonized the foreground and the context. Whenever something is labeled "the decision" or taken as a force or fact of context, somewhere there is the person who argued persuasively that this was so. Argued within the constraints of plausibility recognized by his or her discipline, field, and professional community. We should understand the foreground and context to which people attribute facticity and necessity, agency and political significance, as the spectacle-like effects of background performances.

MAPPING THE KNOWLEDGE PRACTICES OF BACKGROUND PROFESSIONALS

Background work is a plural and contested activity. To map the background work of expertise in global economic and political life requires attention to the professional communities where expertise arises, the roles people in those communities imagine for themselves, the boundary work they do to maintain those roles, and the more and less conscious knowledge they draw upon. Background work is a plural and contested activity. There is no master vocabulary, whether from law, economics, or political science, for understanding global affairs, and no discipline is first among equals in the management of the world. Different modes of expertise jostle with one another to define and manage aspects of global life: the public analytics of government and the private logics of commercial activity; the political vernacular of international relations and the economic models of global markets and finance. The ubiquity of law as a medium of struggle across many domains makes it a good place to begin, but the same could be said for economics or science and technology and many other domains of expert work. To understand *how* experts govern—how they develop and deploy their expertise, how they struggle and reason with one another, and how their knowledge comes to be taken up by others—we need field- and site-specific studies alongside work on patterns of struggle among experts and expert communities.

GETTING STARTED: IDENTIFYING AN EXPERT COMMUNITY

A first step is to identify a group of people in a particular time and place whose projects generate materials one can study. I have begun with specific professional disciplines: public international lawyers in the United States after the Second World War, human rights advocates in the West after 1980, specialists in "development policy" who draw on legal and economic materials. The fields I have studied are self-consciously oriented to interpreting and advising foreground actors, at least in fantasy. People working within them weigh in on issues of the day in terms that may be practical or polemical. They also write texts we might call "academic" or "theoretical" about how the world works and the (appropriate) role or significance of their field. One can identify thought leaders who would be recognized as such by people in the field and outside and whose arguments are taken up, transformed, and distorted by people pursuing projects. People in these fields manage the boundaries of their discipline to maintain the field's autonomy and integrity while borrowing avidly from neighboring disciplines. In each field, there is a self-conscious feedback loop through which perceptions of the field's uptake among policy makers, commercial or public actors, and citizens influence ongoing work.

Having identified a field, it takes some interpretive work to understand the role and significance of their expertise and professional work. What is their context? What forces and facts do they interpret and for whom? Whom do they credit with foreground agency? As they work between contextual forces and foreground deciders, with whom are they in conversation, at what institutional sites? Experts speak and write about these things all the time. What they say is an important clue to the workings of their expertise, but one cannot take their word for it. Much of their shared knowledge lies beneath the surface of their performances in training and acquired common sense. Experts—and their lay audiences—often underestimate the blind spots and biases common in expert communities and overestimate expert capacity: imagining that development economists *know* how to bring about development or lawyers *know* how to build an institution or draft a statute to bring about a desired result. And much of what experts say about their role is argument. Professionals routinely disagree about things like the status and significance of law, the priority of economic analysis in policy, or the importance of cultural knowledge. This makes sense: if they agreed there would be no need for articulation. Things they all take as facts slip into common sense and settled field boundaries need not be defended. If law always already binds, there is no reason to assert law's binding force: people will have complied.

Experts make arguments about such things for a reason: their assertions are motivated. Often, the motivation is their role in a distributive struggle. Someone wants to do one thing, someone else another, and the expert makes assertions about what law or economics requires, what the facts are, who the decider is, to tip the balance one way or the other. If law is this or law binds this way, then this assertion of power is legitimate and that one is not. As a result, it is difficult to grasp what expert work is about without identifying its oppositional animus. Against whom have they bestirred themselves to argument or action? What is their strategy? How do they imagine their work will affect the status of forces? People deploy expertise in struggle to influence outcomes, whether by enlisting someone's discretion or persuading him or her that they have no discretion.

In assessing the significance of expert work for governance, there is an enormous temptation to resolve expert disputes about their respective significance. It is difficult, for example, to write about the US Supreme Court without opining on whether and when the justices overstepped their proper role or strayed beyond the text of the Constitution. These, of course, are likely to be questions disputed by the justices themselves. The scholar need not adjudicate that dispute, although much legal scholarship tries. Scholars often nominate themselves a kind of tenth justice, more well informed by history or theory or ethics than those on the bench, restrained by a scholarly rather than a judicial role. Their scholarship continues the ongoing background work of judicial expertise. Focusing here, however, much can be overlooked: knowledge and role constraints for both judges and scholars that are outside explicit dispute, shared biases and blind spots of the legal community, and the larger sociopolitical function of an endless debate about judicial function that remains unresolved.

At the global level, international lawyers make many disputed assertions about the importance of international law, about who breaks and who complies with law and how law does or ought to shape political or economic activity. To understand the significance of international legal expertise, it is tempting to try to adjudicate these claims. Was Germany or England the more law-abiding nation in World War I? Which nation had the correct theory about what "law" is all about?[6] Do states comply with treaties because they are legally binding or for other reasons? Historical and empirical studies have been undertaken to resolve such questions, continuing the background work of international legal expertise. When published, they may—or may not—effectively end debate on one or another such point. But the significance of international legal expertise in global life is not exhausted by resolving these salient queries. International legal expertise is also important—may be more important—when such questions are unresolved or when their resolution rests dormant awaiting its reemergence as something to be debated.

As a result, in studying the background work of experts, it is important not to take their own assertions about the boundaries and content of their field too seriously. Arguments about who is and is not within the discipline, whose arguments are and are not plausible, or what expert work has what consequences in the world are all part of expert practice. To understand how struggle over such things is undertaken—or avoided—and what its consequences might be, it is important not to prejudge the outcome and to understand the oppositional posture that animates these articulations.

At the same time, it is not possible to escape the tendentious nature of inquiry into the significance of expert performance in global political and economic affairs. You are also exploring their activities for a reason. You have an intuition about the significance of their activity; a hypothesis about how their role has been over- or underestimated and why we should be concerned. Presumably, your intuition differs from the field's direct engagements with their own power. To say that framing an issue in legal rather than religious terms may affect the outcome of distributional struggle, for example, is different from identifying and interpreting the legal norm that controls. Nor does the routine boundary work undertaken by legal experts managing relations between "legal" and "political" questions exhaust inquiry into the political significance of legal ideas, practices, and institutional arrangements that frame political strategies or objectives. To keep this distinction between routine expert work and your own investigation in view, it is helpful to begin with some working hypotheses about how you imagine expert work in a field to be significant. Who gets persuaded, what do they do differently, what might have happened had these experts not been involved in this way? Developing a sense for the possible social pathways through which one expert performance or idea or activity rather than another might matter is helpful in avoiding the temptation to imagine that once an expert community's unfortunate ideas are exposed it will be clear to all why they matter. Working hypotheses about the impact of expert work need not be unduly specific: they speak to the avenues by which the ideas of an expert community, conscious and unconscious, the victories won and lost in expert struggle, and the terrain defined by expert work may affect the distribution of power and resources in society. For example:

- Although development specialists have oscillated wildly in their ideas about what the state should do to promote "development," their advice, when taken, has shaped government policy. Their vocabulary has been used to defend and attack policies and has become a mark of legitimacy, even where the analytic link to specialized knowledge is weak. Their shared ideas about what an economy is and what development could be have constrained political choices as people in public life, whether politicians or citizens, interpret their world in terms they have absorbed from these professional communities.
- International lawyers are sometimes able to assert the authority to say what is and is not "legal." Where their assertions are effective, they may affect the outcome of struggles, limiting or enabling action by different public or private actors. Their doctrinal tools have constructed and empowered actors in global economic and political life—states, citizens, international institutions, corporations. Their vocabulary has been used to legitimate and delegitimate military campaigns, state policies, and the

governments of particular states. And they have contributed to the common sense of the global policy class about what governance is and what "sovereignty" does.

- Human rights professionals and many others have used their vocabulary to denounce and defend government practices. Their work has shaped government and corporate policy, altering the practices that seem normal and abnormal, defining what it means to be a "legitimate" government or a "socially responsible" corporate citizen. Their commonsense ideas about what justice requires, what it means to be a citizen or a state, and what should and should not be evaluated in cost-benefit terms have affected the balance of power among interests by affecting the perceptions of people taking action and evaluating the actions of others.

The purpose of such hypotheses is to understand and distinguish one's own animus—why do I care about these people?—from the desires and projects of the experts one studies. My belief in the significance of international law as an expert framing device and tool of battle may animate my study, but to say so is not to carry a brief for the binding force or meaning of international law whenever it is asserted by international lawyers. International law may be meaningful, for example, precisely because it *cannot* cleanly resolve disputes about what is and is not legal. As I imagine these possible effects of expert work, they do not depend on the analytic rigor or clarity of the expert vocabularies involved. Sloppy reasoning and contradictory materials may be important. Unresolved arguments can shape outcomes. So can unspoken or unconscious commitments.

Nor is my objective to formulate hypotheses that could be proven in the social scientific sense of demonstrating cause and effect. It is very unlikely that one could prove the impact of professional ideas in this sense. Efforts to do so risk narrowing the inquiry too sharply to be of much explanatory power. Moreover, arguing about effect is one of the most prevalent activities through which experts pursue their projects. The objective is to evoke the world as they see and create it and articulate pathways through which this work could be impactful without adjudicating their own claims to influence in one or another situation.

BOUNDARIES: PROFESSIONAL ROLE AND POSITION

My own next step has usually been to spend time with these people, observing their modes of work, listening to their styles of argument, and reading the materials they produce. There are some practical things to understand: How were they trained, what did they learn and what did they not learn, what jobs do they have and what institutional opportunities to use their expertise? How do they imagine themselves in the world, and how do they differentiate their expertise and professional practice from others? With which other expertise do they compete, what adjacent fields make them feel insecure or self-confident?

International lawyers, for example, will typically tell young students seeking to join the profession that it is crucial to "become a good lawyer first." This is partly about training—the first years of law school are largely devoted to national law—and partly a shared sensibility about what "being a lawyer" means: an attitude toward legal materials and legal reasoning, pride in technical competence and in professional alternatives and opportunities available alongside whatever "international" work comes along, and a sense for the leverage and authority that comes from being a lawyer in the locations where professional projects are undertaken. It also says something about not being a political scientist or specialist in international relations and foreign policy: having something more rigorous, technical, and professional to offer. The professional focus on the legality of international law speaks also to the international lawyer's confidence and ambivalence about her role.

Expertise about economic development policy, by contrast, self-consciously lies at the intersection of at least three different realms of knowledge. The professional role of "development policy" expert is linked not to a particular academic field, but to a posture toward several fields of knowledge and to the work of politics. Although economics has often been treated as the "queen of the sciences" by development policy experts, the discipline also draws upon ideas about society from the fields of history, sociology, anthropology, or philosophy and ideas about institutions, governance, and law, often from political or legal science. Ideas from these fields filter into the expertise of the development professional in ways that blend highly technical knowledge, both empirical and analytical, with lay versions of ideas about the economy, the society, and the legal tools of governance.

- *Economics*: Are there many national economies, or one global economy? If we might choose, which is better for development? Should we think of an economy as something to manage, or as something best left to its own devices? Should we imagine the economy as an input-output cycle responsive to government stimulation, or as a market of private actors responsive to price signals? Should we aim to "get distribution right" or to "get prices right"? How different are the economies of developed and underdeveloped societies? What does it mean, economically speaking, for a nation to be a "latecomer" to development? Might there be more than one equally stable or efficient economic modes of development in a given society? How important are institutions, path dependence, or local culture in economic life?

• *Law, governance, and institutions*: Is law an instrument for the development state or a limit on the economic powers of the state? Should the state be large or small? Which legal institutions are most important for economic development? Should we strengthen public law and administration? Private law and courts? Is it better to rely on formal rules or discretionary standards? Should we seek to legalize the informal sector—and what would that mean? How appropriate is it for legal professionals to engage in policy analysis? How effective an instrument of policy is law? How autonomous are legal doctrines and institutions from a nation's economic and political life? How significant are "rights" in a legal order? What is the relationship between "rights" and law's role as an instrument of public power or a strategy for development? What legal rules are necessary to establish a market? To regulate one? To ensure that a nation's economic market contributes to national development? Is there one "rule of law" or many?

• *Sociology, anthropology, and history*: Are all societies functionally rather similar, or do they differ? Are the important differences matters of culture, or stages of economic life? How do "modern" and "traditional" societies differ? Are they linked by natural stages of progress? Is development something that happens once in the life of a nation? Is the industrial revolution in the North Atlantic nations the model? How large, how decentralized, how democratic, how active should a state be for development? What social bonds and divisions accompany, facilitate, or impede a market? How was development linked to the Enlightenment, the Protestant Reformation, to pragmatism or "entrepreneurialism"? What was colonialism, and how is it relevant to cultural and economic progress today? What is "capitalism," and what might it become? What drives "globalization"? How is inequality between rural and urban, male and female, or rich and poor reproduced? Is there a "world system"? Are the interests of the "center" and the "periphery" complementary or antagonistic? Are families the building blocks for development or obstacles to modernization? What about ethnic groups, cities, or nations?

Development professionals debate one another both by pitting economics against sociology or law against political science, and by drawing on professional

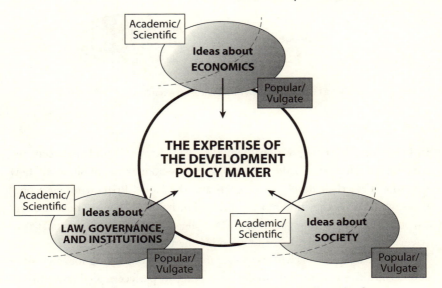

Figure 4.2 The Economic Development Policy Maker: Intellectual Influences

debates already swirling within each of these fields. As they do, they ride the waves of fashion that move all academic disciplines. Economics may seem prestigious for a period, and then fall out of fashion, to be replaced by law or sociology. Macroeconomics was dominant for a generation, only to be displaced by microeconomics within a few short years. Institutional economics rises and falls. It would be tempting to picture the development professional as a consumer, picking and choosing from the ideas of various disciplines as they suited his purposes. That is surely part of it. But the tail of disciplinary knowledge also wags the dog of professional work.

Professionals in different fields approach the boundaries of their special knowledge in different ways. An international lawyer's sense for the distinctly "legal" nature of his field contrasts with the development policy professional's openly parasitic relationship to the knowledge of these adjacent fields. Their attitudes toward amateurism and laicism are also different. International lawyers may be pleased when others pick up their arguments and use their institutions, but they imagine themselves having professional custody of the tools of validation, persuasion, and legitimacy. They are "legal practitioners" whose work is "lawyering." The development policy professional, by contrast, is an amateur economist, lawyer, and sociologist all rolled into one. Their work is "policy making." Policy is defined more readily by what it is not than what it

Figure 4.3 The Policy Maker: Suspended between Science and Politics

is. Policy professionals position themselves in their own minds between two ideal-typical alternatives: the national leaders whom they advise about how best to achieve their development goals and the Nobel Prize–winning economists whose ideas they find most influential or helpful. They are neither scientists nor politicians. Policy is an applied amalgam of both, more practical than science, more knowledgeable and reasoned than politics.

Unlike academics or scientists, policy makers are not looking for interesting counterintuitive experiments to try or seeking to perfect a predictive model. They are not experimenting on their society—they are doing their best to do what makes the most sense. Their authority is rooted not in a school of thought—or in a political constituency—but in the consensus wisdom, the apparent "reasonableness," and even necessity of what they propose. Against scientists, their most potent argument is that this will simply not fly politically—against politicians, that it contravenes the clear consensus of the scientific community. In the world of policy, a consensus scientific view, like the safe political center, will have a strong appeal. The work of policy proceeds most smoothly in moments of relative consensus within both scientific and political communities, and policy work can adjust scientific and political consensus to one another. This is a work of translation as political and scientific differences fade into policy. But sharp differences in either community can also be heightened as they are harnessed to disputes about policy differences. Policy work then becomes a mode of battle that threatens the carefully neither-nor posture of the policy maker with collapse into either scientific truth or public preference.

Politicians thinking about development are also straddling two stools. On the one hand, politicians are also trying to get something to happen rather than figure out what is true. But politicians come to debate about what "makes the most sense" from a position, with allies and enemies, with a constituency, with particular interests to protect and further. The political world, like the scientific community, is split into factions. Political work may be the smooth translation of factional preference into scientific truth and political fact, or it may be a battle in which politicians find it advantageous to exaggerate the degree of consensus in the policy or scientific community to buttress their preferences or to overstate the professional disagreement to garner a free hand. There are analogs in scientific communities that are also home to factions with interests that may be served by their affiliation with politics or policy. The relative hegemony of various methods within economics owes a great deal to the prestige and funding that accompany positions for thought leaders in governance.

The differences within these various professional communities do not arise independently of the differences between them. Politicians interested in development frame their policy differences in the shadow of differences in the scientific and policy community. Not because they are "followers" of different economic schools of thought or believers in one or another economic theory, although they may be. Differences within these communities come into alignment as positions in one are associated with positions in another in struggle.

A great deal will depend upon how the expert languages of science and policy have already been assimilated by the political class. Differences between scientific theories or policy alternatives may have come to define the nation's political vernacular. Where the political elite share in an expert consensus about the range of alternatives, things that seem either obvious or inconceivable to the experts may disappear from the politically contestable, whether politicians are motivated to exaggerate or understate differences. On the other hand, a politician may fasten on a difference that is relatively insignificant in the scientific or policy world to differentiate his or her own political position.

As a result, the "degree of difference" or the felt passion of quite similar debates may differ wildly between the worlds of science and policy or politics. The hot passions of normal science are often reserved for quite narrow differences within a well-accepted general approach. These may, in the end, make little difference for policy and may be glossed over by policy makers or ignored by politicians. On the other hand, politicians may transform small scientific or policy differences into sharp tests of political affinity, just as they may blur ideas that are considered incompatible by the scientific world. It is common, of course, for politicians to associate their opponent's position with what seems "extreme" and their own with what seems "appropriate" or "reasonable." As political debate goes forward, narrow scientific differences can become exaggerated, even in periods of great scientific consensus. For the policy maker, the tendency of both the scientific and the political communities to exaggerate their differences poses a real challenge. Efforts to design politically acceptable proposals that seem to reflect a scientific consensus will need to be redoubled, driving policy analysis to an ever narrower range of alternatives or to mixing and matching bits from various scientific and political programs.

The same idea may well sound quite different depending upon who articulates it, and it is often helpful to think of the scientist, the policy maker, and the politician as speaking dialects of the same language. They may value nuance, for example, quite differently. It is often the very work of policy to simplify, and it is common to find ideas expressed more crudely in politics than in science. For the scientific expert, assumptions stay assumptions, qualifications stay qualifications—no one is trying to *do anything* with the results other than refine them, improve them, reproduce them. An argument may be a sensation within a scientific paradigm, regardless of whether the paradigm corresponds particularly well to any particular society. That is in the nature of basic research, in economics no less than biology or math or physics. The world—or the "market"—to which the scientist refers could well be a fully imaginary one, sketched in a few crucial assumptions. The real world to which a policy maker refers may be that imagined by scientists or politicians, or that pressed upon the policy process by the short-term administrative requirements of implementation. For the politician, the real world may be an ideological construct, or a place peopled only by constituents and their enemies.

EXPERTISE: MAPPING PROFESSIONAL KNOWLEDGE

After identifying the field of expertise, developing some hypotheses about how background work by these experts might matter, and understanding their sense of role and field boundaries, one can turn to the *knowledge* an expert community brings to their work. In chapter 1, I proposed that the intellectual content drawn upon in expert practice consisted of disputed material, either technical questions or broader thematic disagreements that had not been resolved in earlier disputes to the point that they had sunken back into commonsense matters of fact. In the next chapter, I focus on the structure of expert dispute: how knowledge is mobilized by opposing experts in struggle. A preliminary map of expert knowledge in a field aims to identify the knowledge that will affect the attitudes, ambitions, and strategies of these experts in their background struggles. Although some elements of a discipline's expertise will be visible on the surface of expert work, many will lie forgotten in common sense and in the semiconscious space of shared disciplinary consciousness or sensibility about how things are and will need to be reconstructed by empathetic interpretation.

What do you need to know to be a competent international lawyer, development professional, or human rights activist? The degree of complexity will differ: the human rights movement has defined their basic materials with a view to ease of entry. One does not need much detailed knowledge to begin naming and shaming: there is a catalog of rights, a rather basic historical narrative about their history and a simple model of their applicability. Amnesty International set the frame: individual citizens could write letters to statesmen as human rights experts after reading a simple set of materials. Development policy expertise is at the opposite pole—even a moderately competent player needs a fair amount of economics and sociohistorical knowledge. Different expert communities will value analytic and empirical, counterintuitive and commonsensical, historical and contemporary knowledge in different ways.

It is useful to distinguish knowledge that is widely shared or taken for granted from points about which people in the field disagree when they argue about what is legal, what policy to adopt, or who should do what. The line between them is not firm. Commonsense matters can be brought into more conscious focus by dispute. As disputes are resolved, an outcome may, after a time, begin to disappear from a field's consciously shared knowledge into common sense. The as-yet undisputed material is important for understanding the biases and blind spots experts bring to their background work and can usually be seen only in moments of transition or by empathetic reconstruction. Experts may share many things not immediately relevant to their supposed substantive expertise. International lawyers share desires, fears, and hopes for the world community that are only loosely linked to international law. They have ideas about what progress means, how it occurs, what problem-solving requires, the horizon of possibility for their profession, perhaps also for mankind. They share a sense for the limits of things: of theory, of politics, perhaps even of human achievement.

Even within the legal field, neighboring subspecialties see the world differently. Public international lawyers share a picture of the history of their field and of the interstate system, which they see developing in parallel. There are crucial dates associated with postwar settlements: 1648, 1918, 1945. Other dates are less relevant: 1789 or 1815 or 1929. They see a world of nation-states and worry about war. They remember the trauma of the Holocaust, fear totalitarianism, and are averse to ideology. They understand legal arrangements as fragile human constructions seeking to tame a sea of political conflict. International economic lawyers remember different events: more the Smoot-Hawley Tariff Act than Verdun, more Bretton Woods than the United Nations. Trade lawyers

Table 4.1. Mapping Expertise: Disciplinary Sensibilities

	Public international law	International economic law	Comparative law
	International / National — Triangles in a void	Buyer State A / Seller State B — The trade law banana	Cultures / Functional stages of development — Eggs in a row
What they see:	States	Buyers and sellers	Cultures and economic systems or technical levels of development
Desire:	Governance	Trade	Understanding
Worry:	Is law possible?	Is trade free?	Is understanding possible?
Traumatic memory:	War and holocaust	Depression and collectivism	Parochialism, imperialism, and national extremism
Program:	Progress from autonomy to community through progress from formal to antiformal law	Reduce tariffs and nontariff barriers through multilateralization of bilateral commitments	Improve knowledge of each other
Allied discipline:	Political science	Economics	Anthropology and sociology

see a world of commerce and remember the trauma of the Depression. Their attitude toward legal arrangements is more straightforward, rarely pausing to doubt the "binding" or legal nature of the private law, public regulations, treaties, and global institutional arrangements affecting trade. Comparative law experts, in turn, have a different project and worry about different things. The world they seek to understand is one of diverse cultures crisscrossed by varying stages of economic and social development. All these ideas affect what each profession feels able—or willing—to do.[7]

The central preoccupations and worldview of a discipline change over time. Ideas come in and out of fashion in each discipline on different schedules. Economics can seem more important than political science for a time, and then the reverse. Some economic ideas can seem more significant than others. When international lawyers think of "the economy," for example, they no longer imagine a national input-output cycle responsive to government stimulation, but a global market of private actors responsive to price signals. In different periods, the tools they find most attractive, the modes of argument they find most compelling, the disciplines they find most useful and most threatening all differ in ways that affect their interpretation of the world and the governance strategies they adopt. One way to map changes in the sensibility of public international lawyers over the twentieth century would be as depicted in table 4.2.

This mapping exercise could be continued in a variety of ways. The goal for this kind of preliminary map is to catalog elements in the shared vision of experts that may affect their governance work, either by sinking into common sense in ways that make some problems easy to address and others to ignore, or by becoming overtly thematized in the arguments experts make with one another: this is the way the world is and we should therefore do this. The next step, to which I turn in the next chapter, is to understand the ways in which points of difference that arise within the field become grist for the mill of struggle over what the context requires and what deciders should decide. These points of potential contestation are often marked by divisions among schools of thought, national traditions, or methodological preferences.

Table 4.2. Mapping Expertise: Public International Law

					An intellectual history of public international law				
	Trauma	Doctrinal focus	Preoccupation	Mode of action	Mode of organization	Heroic figure	World map	Mode of thought	Inter-disciplinary resource
1900–1950	War Hague League failure	Sources: Treaties Customs	Minority rights Colonial management Collective security Nationalism Self-determination	Codification	International organization	Jurist and international judge	Civilization and mandatories Progress Paternalism	Antiformal Social reform Positivism	Politics
1950–1989	War Cold War Totalitarianism Depression	Process: Jurisdiction State responsibility Claims	Decolonization Development Disarmament/security Social welfare Expropriation NIEO Human rights	Administration Policy management	International institutions	Managers/statesmen	East/West and third world Coexistence and cooperation	Functional problem solving World order building	Economics and social science
1990–2000	Thatcher/Reagan/Bush Neoliberalism Vietnam American empire	Substance: Environment Human rights Terrorism International crimes	Trade and economic management "Globalization" Humanitarianism Intervention Environment	Debate and adjudication Principles and standards	National and international NGOs National and international courts Networks	Citizen/NGO advocate National judge	Democratic liberalism and the nondemocratic world Globalization	Pragmatism Legitimacy Humanism Ethics	International relations Cultural and human sciences

CHAPTER 5
EXPERTISE IN ACTION: RULE BY ARTICULATION

Experts rule by argument and assertion. In whatever settings they work—advising diplomats, advocating development loans, or denouncing governments—experts bring their expertise to bear by articulation: this is how it is, this is what should be done, this is what has been decided. Expertise is most visible when experts differ and their arguments are engaged. In this chapter, I develop a tentative model for exploring the process of expert argument and assertion rooted in my studies of international lawyers, human rights activists, and economic development practitioners.

The centrality of articulation to expertise is familiar in law. Although people routinely speak of "law" constituting actors, allocating powers, or distributing resources, strictly speaking law does not do these things: people *argue* and *assert* that legal materials, properly understood, indicate this is legitimate and this is not, coercion should be brought to bear here and not there, this is an entitlement and that is not or the ax should be brought down on that neck. These articulations are sometimes contested, sometimes ignored and sometimes simply followed through. This is as true for the sovereign as for the legal experts who advise him. When the prince decides, his decision is also an argument and assertion, to himself and others: an argument for his own authority, for its meaning, and for the consequences that ought to flow from it. The old adage that to a man with a hammer everything looks like a nail is instructive here. For him, the hammer functions as an assertion—I am your tool—that brings into view a world of nails and an identity as carpenter. Should the man begin to pound, he is also affirming: I am the man with the hammer, see me (myself) pound.

Arguments and assertions become effective—become acts of power—when someone does something as a result. When someone says "off with his head" and someone else picks up an ax, or when someone says "I am sovereign" or "I am entitled" and no one contests the claim. But the blow of the ax is not outside or after articulation. When the ax strikes the neck, we can read beneath it a subtitle: this is what was commanded. The reception of expertise is also an argument: so let it be written, so let it be done, so let it be understood. In one sense, of course, when the blow strikes, a struggle has concluded, an argument and an assertion have prevailed as performative. Be deterred. Know the authority of the state. Opponents of the death penalty, purveyors of heresy or opponents of state power have been defeated. But their struggle may also continue, this ax blow appropriated as an argument to reshuffle authority or recalibrate state power.

Focusing on argument may be misleading. Although ongoing struggles are carried on by argument and contending assertion, most struggles have already been won or lost—or not yet joined. When a struggle has been won, there is no need for argument. The work of expertise is to carry the decision forward as fact. Expert articulation is straightforwardly performative: this is how things are. In this sense, expert argument is the tip of a large iceberg of expert effect. The process by which an assertion that began as an argument passes over to performative articulation is difficult to unravel. It is easy to underestimate the role of coercion or social hegemony, to overestimate the role of persuasion, or to imagine persuasion as a matter of good arguments driving out bad. In every field, relations with the material world of force and the social world of prestige and legitimacy will be different.

The striking thing is how often articulations that have become performative began as matters of dispute and can be reopened for argument by determined experts. I focus on argument both as a window on expert struggle and to highlight the possibility to reopen matters of contextual fact and foreground authority for disputation. Focusing on argument foregrounds the plasticity or malleability of expertise and opens a window onto the discretion of experts—their freedom to argue and decide one thing rather than another—and the potential to interpret theirs as the work of decision.

In the first three chapters, I explored the world-making effects of expertise by situating coercive struggles in the context of shared commonsense pictures of the world and matters of technical or more general dispute that experts bring to their work. I imagined the knowledge experts brought to bear as a stack of technical and more general understandings, some of which were in active dispute, others of which had been settled.

Experts, I argued, influence the world through the outcomes of their active debates as well as through their shared common sense about the world: about

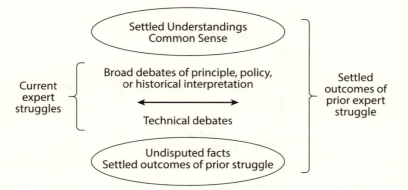

Figure 5.1 Expertise: The Elements

who the deciders are, in what context they decide, and what needs to be decided. These imaginings change what people do and what they consider doing. As I turn to the structure of expert debate, it is important to remember that the shared imaginary of undisputed facts and common sense sets the terrain for articulation, and yet both undisputed facts and common sense are themselves performative assertions that have settled back into knowledge.

In the last chapter, I figured the background work of experts as an interpretive link between foreground decision makers and the context for their decisions. I defined "expertise" as "background work" interpreting the context for a decider and decisions for implementation in a context. Background work is an articulative practice, undertaken by *saying* what these things mean and what they require.

I proposed that we think of the foreground and the context as effective attributions of background work. We might also think of the content of the context as a work of expertise that has sunk back into common sense, the work of decision a kind of parallel expertise undertaken in dialog with background experts. Although foreground players might be thought to specialize in "broad debates" while background experts tended to "technical argument," in contemporary global economic and political life everyone makes arguments and accepts assertions of both types.

It would be better to imagine expert "deciders" and expert "advisors" in dialog with one another, their positions marked by their use of different fields of knowledge or different styles of argument. The advisor might, for example, speak the language of development policy, the leader a language of political ideology or interest. One may speak the language of modest accommodation,

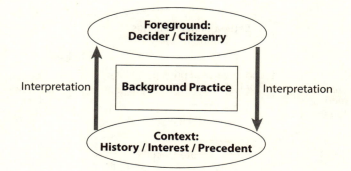

Figure 5.2 Expertise: The Work

the other of hyperbole; the one of pragmatism, the other of ethics. At the same time, to express yourself in one vocabulary rather than another is also to position yourself *as* an "advisor" or "leader." Within each vocabulary, there will be settled matters of consensus that do not need expression, matters of consensus that seem nevertheless to require articulation or affirmation and active debates. What does ideology or interest require; what does good policy demand? Discussions of each will be framed by what need not be articulated and will combine matters of shared ground and active disagreement. In this chapter, I reframe the work of experts by focusing on these arguments.

This makes visible the often surprising variety of possible associations between political positions and policy alternatives within a field. In development policy, for example, people often argue about what to do by associating particular development policies with ideological positions. Someone might say that a regime's decision to "privatize state-owned enterprises" is or was "neoliberal" and therefore wise or foolish. This way of speaking can make the translation of ideological commitments—neoliberalism—into legal and institutional outcomes—privatize the state-owned enterprises—seem straightforward. These people *are* neoliberals and their choice of privatization flowed naturally. Experts are thought to influence events either by persuading the politician to be a neoliberal in the first place, or by explaining the legal or institutional entailments of his neoliberal commitments. Political advisors—or the politician's internal expertise—explain neoliberalism and policy advisors explain its entailments.

At each point, there is also likely to be an argument or dispute. Although ideological labels like "neoliberalism" suggest coherence among a range of different ideas, arguments, default judgments, and favorite policies, these are also matters of dispute both among neoliberals and with those who have other

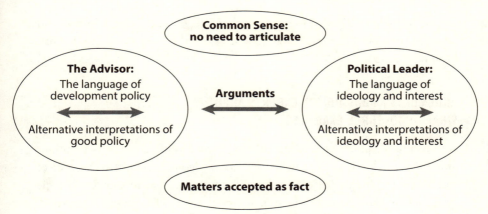

Figure 5.3 Expertise: The Zone of Argument

commitments. How the elements—small state, monetary stability, free trade, strong property rights—are defined and combined needs to be worked out. Moreover, "privatizing the SOEs" is not a simple decision—it requires a regime, composed of many details. One might privatize more or less, to these or those people, paying or not paying compensation, allowing more or less monopoly power, before or after implementing a regulatory regime, and so forth. Nor is the link between neoliberalism and SOE privatization in any of these forms obvious: privatization to worker cooperatives rather than foreign investors might be worse, from a neoliberal perspective, than retaining state ownership to force reorganization.

Rather than the smooth translation of ideological positions—or interests—into policy, the interaction between policy and politics is more of a conversation to be played strategically among people with different roles and overlapping modes of expertise. A politician might "decide" to privatize to reap the political benefit of identification as a "neoliberal" and then find a policy maker able to design a privatization regime that was quite hard to distinguish from the regime of state ownership it replaced. The next government may claim that privatization was a mistake—of just the sort to be expected of those neoliberals—and that it was time to "bring the state back in." This might—or might not—lead to a new legal and institutional regime, depending on how disputes about the details of ownership, management, and so on are resolved. Bringing the state back in might turn out to mean exactly the same regime—or something more fully private but regulated. Or the new government might affirm the neoliberal commitment to privatization but feel the regime had been a disaster: the reforms that follow in the name of a new and improved neoliberalism might well look a lot like the state ownership that had been dismantled.

ARGUMENTS AMONG POLICY EXPERTS ABOUT WHAT TO DO: THREE EXAMPLES

Argumentative practices in different fields reflect different role conceptions and affect the kinds of arguments that get made and the relative salience of method, tone or style, or content in the differences that matter for struggle about who should do what. Argument among development policy experts illustrates the way diverse technical and ideological materials can be harnessed in the struggle over how to define and achieve a common objective. The argumentative practices of international lawyers bringing law to bear in war highlight rather the oppositional nature of expert argument with common materials. Human rights professionals typically draw on a range of materials and aim for a common objective. Their battles illustrate the significance of struggle over strategic differences. In my experience, expert argument in each of these fields, and others I have observed, exhibits each of these facets.

In the world of economic development policy there is a great deal of argument about the way academic or scientific ideas from different fields—economic theories about what development is and how it happens or legal theories about what law is and can accomplish—are linked to policy goals and policy instruments. The work of development experts is to translate ideas from economic theory or empirical study into arguments for particular policy objectives, and translate those in turn into arguments for the use of particular policy instruments. For example, import substitution industrialization as a development model suggests insulating domestic prices from international pressure. That objective, in turn, could suggest the use of a tariff. The links between theories, objectives, and instruments might be disputed or may be regarded as obvious. The links may be argued with rigorous analytic proof or empirical evidence, or they may be rules of thumb, depending in part on whether the vocabulary of expertise in habitual use has a more academic or vulgate form. The "theory" can itself be a tight analytic or the loose invocation of rules of thumb, perhaps associated with the name of a famous economist. Sometimes people argue about which "theory" is right—at other times there is consensus at that level and discussion only about what theory requires. In some periods, empirical or historical data are more common than arguments from theory, at others, the reverse.

Similarly at the level of objectives and instruments: links to either may be a matter of consensus or intense debate. Because development expertise lies, as I noted in chapter 4, at the intersection of several disciplines, people argue about instruments and objectives from those fields as well. Expertise in law, for example, may suggest arguments about the structure, uses, and limits of instruments like tariffs, which may suggest modifications in the objective or even of the economic theory of development itself. Legal ideas may themselves become theories of development. Human rights or strong property rights, for example, may be seen as instrumental to development or as its very definition. Like economic ideas, legal ideas, and their links to instruments and objectives may be matters of consensus or dispute.

People argue affirmatively about what theories require be done, what instruments to use, how to weigh various objectives. They also criticize the links that others have proposed, interpreting the same theoretical materials differently, drawing on ideas from neighboring disciplines, or pushing back against theory by articulating the limitations that instruments place on the objectives to be sought, or that possible objectives place on theories of development. All of these things change over time: the dominant theories, priority objectives, and fashionable instruments. With this in mind, it is possible to imagine development policy experts in a particular period working back and forth across a set of choices like those in figure 5.4, making and unmaking connections between them, all in the shadow of their understanding of the arguments about ideology and interest being undertaken in parallel among politicians.[1]

The expert work of international lawyers aiming to strengthen and limit the use of force in war suggests a different map highlighting the oppositional character of expert argument whatever the mix of materials it draws upon.[2] Although there are some who oppose development or define it in radically different ways, among mainstream economic development professionals at any given moment, everyone is trying to bring about development: the question is how. Expert struggle unfolds as people advance alternative proposals about what to do to bring about development supported by arguments about why this would be a good idea and would work. When international legal expertise is drawn upon in war, by contrast, experts softening and rearranging or strengthening legal limitations are deployed in two opposed directions: to advance military objectives and to limit the use of force. Expert work is like war itself: an

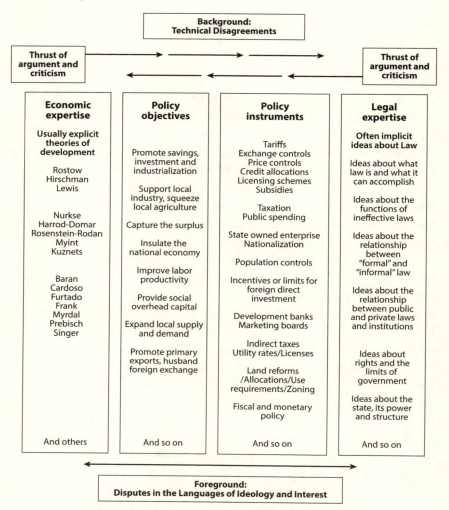

Figure 5.4 The Work of Argument in Economic Development Policy: 1945–1965

opposition of forces working to use the available tools to achieve opposite ends. The two "sides" could be within the military between lawyers with different strategies, between lawyers and operational commanders, between military representatives and humanitarian voices from outside, or among people seeking in different ways to limit the use of force by the military. This kind of argumentative work also characterizes the two sides in military conflict as people argue for the legitimacy of their tactics and the perfidy of the enemy. In each

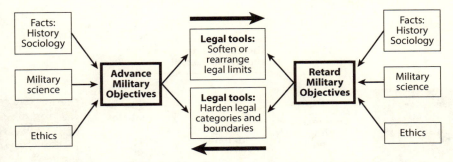

Figure 5.5 Expert Strategy and Posture: International Law in War

exchange, experts on both sides draw on historical and sociological knowledge, ethics and military science to harness arguments about legal norms and institutions to their political objectives.

The terrain for argument by human rights activists can be sharply oppositional and may draw on various materials from international law, ethics, history, political science, and more. Like development professionals, human rights activists are generally oriented to the same objective: more and better human rights compliance. The materials upon which they draw generally lack the analytic complexity and field diversity of those drawn upon by development policy professionals. Although there are different theories about which human rights are most important or how best to promote compliance, the most salient axis along which differences emerge is between two professional voices, styles or modes of engagement, one pragmatic and one denunciatory. The most salient axis of argument is strategic or tactical. Human rights professionals argue in two vocabularies, a more absolute insistence on speaking truth to power, and a more practical effort to work together with authorities toward common ends.[3] These styles of engagement face opposing dangers, the one prone to idolatry, the other to instrumentalization by power. The difference between these voices can divide institutions from one another: the International Committee of the Red Cross is known for its practical engagement with governments, Human Rights Watch for its sharp external advocacy. Although human rights professionals sometimes deploy these ideal-typical styles together, more typically they favor a more absolute language from headquarters when speaking to donors, to the media, or to their constituencies and members, and a more practical language in the field and among themselves. In both styles, they speak in the shadow of, evoke, and imagine themselves contributing to the requirements of universal ethics.

Figure 5.6 Expert Modes of Engagement: Human Rights

ACTING BY ARTICULATION: A SHARED TEMPLATE?

For all these differences in the role, style, and content of expert knowledge, experts in each of these fields act by argument and assertion, raising the question whether there might be common patterns in the iterative and interactive process of doing things with words. Perhaps expertise is analogous to language: given a vocabulary, many things can be said on the foundation of grammar. One approach to the semiotics of expert argument, developed by Duncan Kennedy to analyze legal argument, begins by assembling a vocabulary of arguments, and then examining the patterns that emerge in their use.[4] Which arguments typically oppose which others? How are arguments transformed or rearranged to support different positions? The result is a map of the "grammar" of arguments specific to lawyers in a particular culture and historical moment. It seems possible to imagine a parallel in arguments made by other kinds of experts. In each of the fields I have studied, arguments recur and are used in relation to one another in ways that can be mapped. Many of the grammatical forms and moves identified in legal argument recur, including the transformation of differences in kind into differences of degree, the resolution of an identified difference by movement to an analogous difference at another level of abstraction where a middle position seems plausible or the recurrent identification of elements from opposing arguments within one another as a tactic of criticism or affiliation.

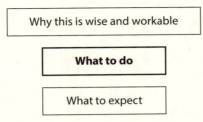

Figure 5.7 Policy Expertise: The Basic Unit

Across the fields of expertise I have studied, disputes take place in more or less stable types of argument, which can be pictured in series of "levels." The basic unit of expert assertion is a link between a proposal about what to do, a reason, and an outcome.

There are two steps here: an argument about what a foundational fact, theory, interest, or ideological commitment suggests ought to be done and an argument about the outcome that can be expected to be achieved. When I trained military commanders in Africa for the US Navy, we made lots of arguments in this form. In kinetic operations, you must ensure your use of force is proportional to its objective: in this situation, that means this bomb rather than that one. Why? Because international humanitarian laws—and your coalition partners if you want to play in the big leagues—require it. What to expect? If you do this, your campaign will be ethical, legitimate, and more effective and your military will be able to interoperate with ours. Compliance is a force multiplier.

Background policy work asserts a link between these levels: this theory requires that policy to generate this outcome. If there is a great deal of consensus in a field, these links may be clear and undisputed. There may be no argument: all the arguments have been won. People may know what to do, why it makes sense, and what it will achieve without thinking it through. Expert assertion in such a situation may be performative—the expression of a kind of obvious logic—or may not even be necessary.

Although perfect consensus is rare, something like this level of clarity is common among human rights activists: they articulate what needs no articulation. They may be ignored, but rejoinder is less common. International lawyers arguing about war have the reverse experience: people on all sides of today's conflicts make an extraordinary range of diverse arguments about what the vague and malleable legal materials require and prohibit. Over the past half century, mainstream economic development professionals have gone through moments of each. In the 1950s and early 1960s, and again in the 1980s, they shared a quite strong and conscious consensus about what development is and how to bring it about. Each time, there was broad agreement on the relevant economic theory, the policies it suggested, and the outcomes to be expected. Those with alternative views were absent from the profession.

Not all of what they shared was fully conscious. Many of the orienting assumptions that held the field together remained tacit or unstated. When development experts agreed that "import substitution industrialization" was necessary to "catch up" with the industrialized world, this was a conscious and well-formulated part of what development practitioners saw as their shared economic and historical knowledge. It was a fully conscious "theory" of development. If you didn't accept it, you were outside the field. At the same time, they shared other ideas—about the significance of industrialization to development, about the historical meaning of the "industrial revolution," and about the relationship between what third world societies would need to do and what the first world had already done—that were less conscious. Other ideas were less conscious still: that each *nation* has *an* economy, rather than there being a global economy or many small, local economies; that macroeconomic management is the most significant tool of national development policy, rather than building institutions to support the microeconomic market decision making of private parties; that public lawmaking could be effective in third world settings, rather than there being an almost unbridgeable gap between law in the books and law in action. Not to share these assumptions was also to be an outsider to the field.

In such a situation, we can expect less argument than explanation. Reception is smooth: the people making and receiving an argument think things through in similar ways. Articulation may nevertheless be necessary: just what is "modernization" or the Washington Consensus, what policies do they entail, and how can they be expected to achieve development? Where there is strong consensus, we can organize the policy language on a vertical axis from ideas about politics, economics, or history, through policy initiatives, to desired outcomes, as in figure 5.8.

Even in moments of great consensus, it is rarely this simple. Normally, there are competing ideas about each of these things. Experts argue with one another about the outcomes to be achieved, the choices necessary to bring a particular outcome about, and the reasons for thinking that choice is wise and workable. As experts differ in their views about what to do—as they struggle on behalf of policies with different winners and losers—they have an incentive to develop alternatives at each phase. People who want to pursue other policies have an incentive to find experts around the margins of the mainstream consensus.

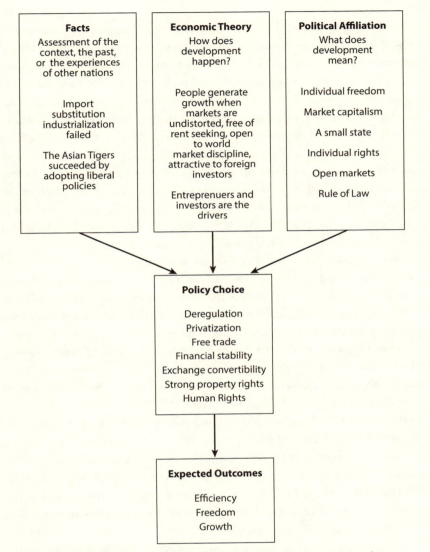

Facts

Assessment of the
context, the past,
or the experiences
of other nations

Import
substitution
industrialization
failed

The Asian Tigers
succeeded by
adopting liberal
policies

Economic Theory

How does
development
happen?

People generate
growth when
markets are
undistorted, free of
rent seeking, open
to world
market discipline,
attractive to foreign
investors

Entreprenuers and
investors are the
drivers

Political Affiliation

What does
development
mean?

Individual freedom

Market capitalism

A small state

Individual rights

Open markets

Rule of Law

Policy Choice

Deregulation
Privatization
Free trade
Financial stability
Exchange convertibility
Strong property rights
Human Rights

Expected Outcomes

Efficiency
Freedom
Growth

Figure 5.8 Neoliberal Economic Development Expertise: A Basic Template

In the development field, the expert consensus of the 1980s (like that of the
1950s and 1960s before it) broke down rapidly. People revisited the history of development policy: perhaps import substitution industrialization was more successful than we thought. When countries tried the neoliberal recipe, the results
were often disappointing. Russia did much less well than China. Perhaps the
Asian Tigers did not adopt "liberal" policies after all, but something altogether

different. New economic theories of development and important qualifications of Washington Consensus theories emerged. People came to have other political commitments or to interpret a commitment to capitalism and individual rights differently. New theories became associated with new examples. New policy sets became fashionable. These policies came in different forms—alternative strategies for insertion in the global economy, for the institutional arrangements of privatization—and were juxtaposed to alternatives. Policies that may have been bundled in a package needed to be defended one by one. Links between policies and outcomes were disputed: a one-time efficiency gain may have no link to more rapid growth or may set the economy on a trajectory of development that will yield slower growth or greater inequality or both. As these differences arose, the policy alternatives themselves became more nuanced and specific: privatize, but this way, to these people, using these instruments.

Over a decade or so, the vocabulary for arguing about what to do became more complex and diverse as new theories were developed and old theories were chastened or qualified and as the range of empirical evidence and historical experience available for argument expanded. As the consensus disintegrated, sometimes experts crossed swords directly, presenting their alternative as a direct response to the analytic or empirical limitations of other theories. More often, people blended arguments of various types, perhaps dismissing neoliberalism with a contextual example and reframing a familiar policy as an "alternative" by reference to a different analytic.

The expert field became a series of disagreements about what to do, why this would be sensible, and what it would achieve. The field was characterized by horizontal arguments between alternative theories, policy choices, and outcomes, as well as vertical argument about how these could be linked. In fields like this, the armature for argument will have as many horizontal axes of disagreement as it has vertical assertions about the links between ideas, policies, and outcomes, as illustrated in figure 5.9.

In periods of dissensus, the basic work of economic development professionals is to make and defend horizontal distinctions and vertical associations on this general map. They identify a position on a horizontal axis—a theory of development, the relevant factual drivers for their decision, the ideological position or interest group they favor—and make assertions about what this entails. One might argue, for example, that economist Joseph Stiglitz is right to focus on the importance of information and coordination costs in developing countries. His theory suggests a policy choice: when we privatize, we should shorten agency chains to ensure those with knowledge of the business are in

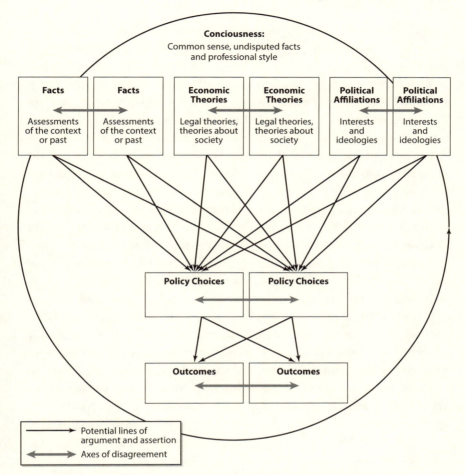

Figure 5.9 Policy Expertise: A Template for Assertion and Argument

control through worker ownership rather than sale to a foreign investor. If we take that route, the outcome will be a more productive use of the social and physical capital in the firm, stronger growth and development. Moreover, if Stiglitz is right, the alternative policy—privatize to foreign investors—will idle the assets altogether, reducing productivity. From the other side, a different theory: economic development requires that assets be shifted to their most productive use quickly by ensuring they trade at market prices, for which world prices offer a close proxy. This suggests a different policy: privatization immediately to foreign investors. Only in that way can the inefficiencies of the current productive system be eliminated rapidly and effectively.

The crucial point is that this argumentative practice is situated in a terrain of struggle as described in chapter 2. Expert argument is *motivated*. People make arguments in pursuit of projects, in struggles with stakes. They have a reason to disagree, to search for chinks in a consensus or to defend it. As a result, it would be surprising if expert consensus running smoothly from theory to policy to outcome were the norm. It is far more likely that argumentative fields would develop, over time, toward the more sophisticated template of figure 5.9.

In a given moment, the range of positions on a horizontal axis may be large or small: a consensus or sharp disagreement about the theory, policy design, or expected outcome. Over time, as argument is joined, it often becomes possible to identify a range of positions on a continuum between extremes. Cracks open as strong positions are seen, on reflection, to be complex amalgams with components that might be associated with alternative commitments or policy preferences. Perhaps these subordinate elements could be emphasized. How prevalent are market failures and information costs? At the policy level, as we privatize to the workers, how should we incentivize them to move toward world prices? Policy differences can be arrayed along a continuum from those most worried about information costs and market failures to those most ready to rely on the discipline of world prices. When this happens, the difference between two points on the continuum, whether large or small, may be said to implicate the starker choice between visions. To force the new worker managers to meet export targets after only a year is no different than handing the assets over to a foreign bank: the nation's social and human capital will be wasted. A small difference on the policy axis puts the discussion back at the level of economic theory: do you agree with Stiglitz or not?

As they engage, professionals transform the vocabulary. Sometimes, debate polarizes around extremes. The broadest issues of principle will seem to be at stake in the choice between quite fine-grained alternatives. Experts develop skill in associating other people's position on a continuum with extreme positions on an adjacent horizontal axis—to raise the tariff even slightly *is* to reject free trade and choose protectionism, with all the associated political, economic, and practical ramifications. At other times, the details dominate and it is difficult to convince development experts that any large issues of principle are at stake in their work.

It often happens that even the policies most associated with one extreme can be said to offer the best way to satisfy the concerns of the alternative theories. A shift to world market prices through quick privatization can also be said to offer the most effective remedy for information and market failures.

Worker-managers would be too far from the needed information to make wise decisions, whereas foreign investors will have the resources and experience to ensure effective management or to shift the assets to more productive uses. In a sophisticated field, the range of policies that can be squared with various theories expands as each theory learns to have something to say about the concerns of the others. Although a given privatization scheme may take on a different political or theoretical hue depending on whether the scheme to which it is being contrasted shortens or lengthens the time new owners have to meet export quotas before their access to credit is cut off, experts continue to assert that a particular timeline is compelled by a commitment to the left or to Stiglitz, or by an analysis of the development context.

In the development policy field today, the range of alternatives along each horizontal axis is broad and open to debate. Experts have elaborated the alternatives with more detail, expanding the number of points on the continuum between positions and strengthening the range of arguments that might be made for and against the extreme positions with which each point may be associated. People in the field rarely have the experience that there is a clear road from an economic theory to a choice of policy and a desired outcome. At each stage, there are a range of alternatives that invoke stark differences of vision between people with different political, theoretical, or sociological commitments.

THE SOPHISTICATION OF DISENCHANTMENT

There is no expert consensus about what development is or how to bring it about. The number of possible theories, each with its own committed acolytes, has increased. More crucially, everyone has become adept at arguing across a range of theories and deploying a range of historical evidence with little confidence in any of it. The loss of faith in theories and analytics has led specialists to reach for more rigorous, if small-scale, empirical work, for ideas from other fields, including law, and for approaches to policy rooted in contextual muddling through under the guiding hand of a chastened expertise: identifying bottlenecks, trying to remove them, see if it works, try again. But all this has not ended arguments about what theories and empirical studies imply for policy. Rather the opposite. People have kept going, becoming ever more nuanced and sophisticated in their expert work. To be a development policy maven today, it is necessary to understand and work across a range of unsatisfactory theories and historical references to identify and justify policy choices.

Development policy is not the only field that exhibits this combination of internal proliferation and loss of faith. As expertise has become ever more ubiquitous in global political and economic life, it has come to function less as the performative assertion of the outcome of a past struggle and more as an argument in current struggles. The fragmentation and legalization of so many things and the use of legal language for so many purposes have generated a larger range of professional arguments to master and a broader range of professionals trained to do so, but ever less confidence in their decisiveness or clarity. In one after another area, international lawyers have generated a wide range of positions along one horizontal axis and developed the ability to associate them with very sharp differences on another: small doctrinal differences suggest completely different theoretical or political orientations, or the reverse. Indeed, even in the human rights field, one sees the chastening effects of becoming a discourse of governance: internal pluralization and the loss of both ethical and analytic self-confidence, alongside an increasingly sophisticated professional practice shifting easily among claims and styles. People have learned to associate broad positions—the priority of national sovereignty or of the international community—with a wide range of doctrines that might once have seemed to imply the opposite.

There is something useful about a vocabulary of debate that is able to draw fine distinctions on the basis of an undecidable difference between indefensible extremes. In a way that may be typical for such situations, however, development professionals have a tendency to overstate the solidity of vertical associations on the map while recognizing that the horizontal differences that seem to differentiate positions from one another are undecidable or matters of degree. Experts speak as if the links between doctrines and outcomes, methods and doctrines are firm and predictable, although they know—at some level—that *other* experts will argue for alternative associations in terms equally consistent with their common expertise. As a result, it is a common experience to find that an association between a general theory and a specific policy once asserted with vigor—say that import substitution requires nationalization—on further reflection and under the pressure of criticism seems far less compelling. At the same time, horizontal distinctions—between two doctrines or theories or methods— seem to loom far larger in the minds of experts than one would suppose, given the quite common experience of instability along the vertical axis. Part of what experts do is define *choices* along the horizontal axis by stressing their association with different outcomes. The exaggeration of horizontal differences brings with it the common experience that experts are making mountains out of molehills.

These two tendencies—to overstate the drama of horizontal differences and the stability of vertical associations—seem to characterize expert fields that have otherwise lost their substantive coherence and stability.

One would expect a field to fall out of use as it loses decisive clarity: if you can't tell us what is and is not legal or how to bring about development, then we don't need your expertise. Instead, the more complex and indecisive the expertise, the more useful it has become. I use the term "sophisticated" to connote fields of expertise with this kind of complexity and fragmented loss of decisiveness. The eclectic diversity of such fields has something to do with their staying power. More people find ways of expressing their projects in languages that have lost their coherence and are less clearly experienced as logic or necessity. In the legal field, the correlation between proliferation and contradiction is particularly striking: professional materials that support contradictory arguments seem particularly useful and spread easily.

The expert practices for distinguishing appropriate from inappropriate political interference in economic markets discussed in chapter 1 were useful because they are indecisive and chiasmatic in structure. Although there is no persuasive analytic for identifying "market failures" and their remedies or for separating "market-supporting" from "market-distorting" regulations, arguments developed in these terms can embrace a wide range of choices about just where to draw the line. Small differences can stand in for large choices in a way that permits people to balance otherwise irreconcilable or undecidable alternatives and makes it possible to both argue hyperbolically and reach resolutions practically. Working with these tools, experts generate the experience of reasoning together without the experience of either responsibility for deciding or the necessity to decide one thing or another. Their work is a kind of shared exercise in between, neither determined nor decided.

COMMON SENSE AND STYLE: THE PLAUSIBLE AND THE UNTHINKABLE, INSIDER AND OUTSIDER

The coherence and plausibility of disenchanted fields remain a puzzle. One possible explanation would focus on a shared foundation of common sense and a shared professional style of engagement. Disciplinary common sense sets boundaries to what can and cannot be argued, even as the decisiveness of those arguments diminishes, while a shared style marks the line between insiders and outsiders to the profession itself. As the materials of the field proliferate to embrace so many positions that decisive resolution seems unlikely, the field boundaries become more important. You can argue many things, but you cannot argue in that way.

The common assumptions that set boundaries are rarely fully conscious. There is an intuitive sense for professional competence and engagement in a common enterprise, vague ideas about what societies or economies or people are like and about the appropriate role for experts, shared historical narratives, focal points for discussion, problems that seem salient, and issues that seem outside their disciplinary domain. This amalgam of considerations is compatible with the range of available theories, methods, or political commitments about which those in the field may disagree at a given time. General ideas about what makes a problem "global" of the sort I explored in chapter 3 can give people a sense that they are all contributing to better global governance, working with the same tools, aiming for the same horizon, across lots of diverse issues and positions. The boundary is implicitly set by the alternative: an "outsider" posture that fails to share the common sense that we now live in "one world."

People working in the fields of international law, human rights, and development policy have shared assumptions that provide a frame within which argument takes place: assumptions about things like what economic development means, how wars break out or how law shapes state behavior, what human rights are and why they are important. They also share what might be called a style or sensibility: a way of approaching their role, a sense of audience and tone, which gives a sense of coherence to divergent engagements.

In the human rights field, for example, people readily understand the difference between publicly denouncing a government and working pragmatically with government officials to resolve an issue: they know where to stand, how to articulate their normative commitments, in these two quite different styles. Both styles share a set of commonsense ideas about what human rights are, why they are important, and what the role of the human rights professional ought to be. Human rights professionals also understand that each of these modes of argument can be "taken too far" in ways that draw into question not only the practical wisdom of the argument, but also one's professional credentials. One can denounce firmly and clearly, but it is important not to be perceived to be shrill or altogether insensitive to practical considerations and competing harms. It is important to be able, at least in private, to step back from ethical self-confidence to more pragmatic assessment of strategy. On the other side, one can partner with governments and corporations, but it is important to retain the space for ethical pronouncement, whether in public or private, to avoid being perceived as a pawn of those one would bend to humane ends.

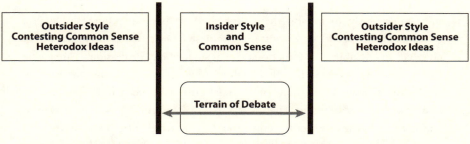

Figure 5.10 Professional Argument: Boundary Work Establishes a Terrain of Debate

As a field evolves, the boundary between common sense and contested assumption—and between insiders and outsiders—can shift. Ideas that are consciously held may sink back into common sense, while ideas that had been taken for granted may be disputed as new people, ideas, or experiences break into the field. "Facts" from other fields or from common sense can also be brought in as trumps when analytics run out—or simply be assumed as a rudder for choosing among alternatives. The sophistication of a field is partly a function of how often new ideas have been made available for contested engagement. As the range of possible contestations rises, it is all the more important to cultivate a professional sense of "how far to go." Style of engagement and positioning inside or outside the terrain become more crucial than commitment to particular theories.

Experts in sophisticated fields can experience themselves as more "professional" even as their confidence in the content of their expertise declines. This is often visible in the arrival of ideas from other fields. Content boundaries are less important than boundaries marked by role or style: the more heterogeneous the material, the more sophisticated the expert. In sophisticated fields, arguments often end in something like a draw, settling on an outcome that in one way or another can be said to reflect a balance among competing considerations, taking everything into account, and expressing the general ideological temperament and associations of the field as a whole.[5] What seems to hold these otherwise indecisive modes of argument together is a shared sensibility about arguments that one cannot make and a practice of transforming opposed alternatives into tendencies to be balanced, generating an outcome.

Professional style is more than a complex performance with a limited repertoire of argumentative moves. Experts in sophisticated fields also develop a shared posture toward their own practice that sustains strong advocacy and congenial agreement. One needs to be able to take the materials seriously, but not too seriously, to inhabit them professionally but not religiously. Such a posture can also seem "sophisticated," although a better word might be "disenchanted" or "désabusé." International law is such a field. Professionals are aware that at one time jurists in their field cultivated devotion to various "theories" of international law: explanations of the relationship between international law and a world of sovereigns. They learn that "naturalism" slowly gave way to "positivism" in the nineteenth century, and that both theories were resurrected in various forms in the first half of the twentieth century. They also learn that no one is a "positivist" or a "naturalist" anymore. All such theories have risen up for disputation and become available to be harnessed in argument. An international law professional today ought to be an eclectic and savvy strategist, drawing on all these theories and their progeny. The question to which these theories respond—what makes law binding as law—remains central to expert practice, in the sense that one should have lots to say about it, but it is also important to realize that there is no clear answer and it would seem professionally naive to expect there to be.

The practical arguments with which these theories were associated have also proliferated within the boundaries of good practice. As a sovereign, I can say that without my consent I am not bound, but I am not able to say that my will entitles me to take what I can get. Consent is one thing, force and will something more extreme. Similarly, you can argue that what your opponent is doing is illegal because it "shocks the conscience of all mankind," violates the principles and standards of the international community or the duties implicit in sovereignty itself, but you cannot rest your argument on a command from God, ethics, or ideology. By eschewing these extremes, the profession ensures that every plausible position can be associated with both approaches to international law's legality. Positions that do not blend both are outside the frame.

The result is a distinctive argumentative form, in which expert discussion clusters within boundaries marked by a shared professional sense for the plausible. Although small differences along the horizontal axis may be presented as sharply different, the extremes invoked to distinguish them are themselves situated between positions understood by everyone to be beyond the pale: implausible positions for a professional to take.

International lawyers may argue robustly about the basis for claiming that an opponent should treat a normative proposition as binding, but the idea that the question could be cleanly resolved by a doctrine—the "sources of law," for example—seems naive and outdated. Instead, the field offers an array of

Figure 5.11 Asserting International Legal Entitlements: The Plausible Terrain

different reasons for asserting that a norm binds, ranging from the idea that the roots of law lie in the consent of sovereigns to the idea that international norms reflect a kind of natural law of the world, and a shared professional intuition that the "bindingness" of rules is, at the end of the day, not that important anyway. Sources of law doctrine provides a vocabulary for staking out positions on a continuum between two broad clusters of ideas, while the scholarly debate between "positivist" and "naturalist" theories of law that once crossed swords in the discipline ended in a draw.[6] Small doctrinal differences—how much practice is required to ground a rule of "customary" law, what must be shown for "changed circumstances" to vitiate prior consent—are debated by invoking the difference between a law grounded in sovereign consent and a legal regime rooted in community values. Every international lawyer needs to know how to make arguments across this field of possibilities. More important than this argumentative pattern is the sensibility with which it is used. But to take these arguments too seriously places you outside the terrain of a professional practice that moves easily among considerations of policy, ethics, and realpolitik strategy in arguing about what norms to follow when. Arguments that would have marked you as beyond the domain of law altogether a century ago are now necessary to prevent appearing as a narrow and old-fashioned "legalist."

Development professionals today have a similarly disenchanted and sophisticated relationship to the definition of development. To be a competent player, one needs to be able to argue across a range of positions that have emerged over the past half century while understanding that defining "development"

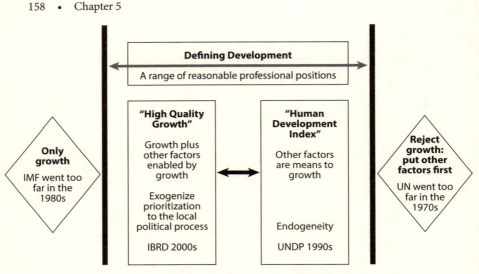

Figure 5.12 Defining Development: The Plausible Terrain

is a fool's errand, displaced by the more practical question of what to do in particular circumstances. In arguing about what to do, however, one must articulate a path between what one proposes and "development." Disagreement about where that path ought to lead is part of the bread-and-butter struggle among development professionals about what to do. One axis of disagreement, for example, concerns the relative importance of economic growth and other more "social" indicia of progress. Experts share a sense for the range of plausible professional positions that they often associate with the approaches taken by particular countries or institutions at a given time, as well as a sense for the institutions that "went too far" in one direction or another.

Within this frame, a very robust debate can be generated among positions that differ only marginally but invoke in the minds of their opponents extremes that lie outside the realm of the plausible. Any of the extant positions—"high quality growth" to "human development index"—evoke attention both to growth and to other factors. A painstaking process of argument that ends up anywhere on the continuum can be said to reflect a "balance." People who work in the development field often feel passionately about where their institution has set the balance relative to other institutions—they are more humane or hard-boiled than their colleagues across the street—while also realizing that debates about such things get in the way of the practical alliances and institutional positions that will be necessary to get a desired policy adopted.

When experts in such a situation turn from argument to decision, they often imagine themselves arriving at the position by carefully weighing and

Figure 5.13 Distilling Professional Wisdom from Policy Argument

balancing the alternatives and arriving at an acceptable outcome. If it is acceptable, any outcome will reflect a balance—and since it reflects a balance, in principle any outcome might be acceptable to reasonable experts. Sometimes the result is a congenial drift toward a position that allows all participants to affirm their positions of principle and reject everything extreme. In the development context, for example, there is a long-standing debate about the amount of change necessary to get development going. Is development something that happens once in the life of a nation, like the industrial revolution, or is it simply the outcome of steady policy oriented to efficiency or growth? For many development professionals, this is an issue best resolved by a balanced professional wisdom, as suggested in figure 5.13.

SOPHISTICATED RULE BY ARTICULATION

In sophisticated fields, self-evident performative assertion gives way to ever more diverse argument undertaken in a doubled style that can shift from earnestness to irony, from engaged to dispassionate, and from sophisticated to disenchanted. It remains difficult to explain why some arguments succeed or persuade while others fail when the vocabulary has become so plastic. It is hard not to conclude—or at least be suspicious—that "something else" is going on. Moreover, if expert vocabulary is this indecisive and open to argument, it is understandable that people might decry the significance of expertise in global political and economic life and wish for something different: perhaps something more directly "political."

The internal dynamics of professional communities is certainly one thing that is going on. Style and professional hierarchies as well as the prejudices, biases and blind spots of professional communities all matter more when the content of expertise is so malleable. The authority of argument can be less a function of the content of an argument than of professional values and virtues articulated indirectly: things like balance, modestly, elegance, virtuosity, workability. These attributes may make an argument persuasive, a professional virtuous, and a profession legitimate. Expert communities assess excellence differently and attribute virtues like "judgment," "objectivity," "discernment," "boldness," "rigor," or "originality" in different ways. A proclivity to modesty or bravado will resonate differently among policy makers or politicians speaking the same language. Individual experts in a field also bring the strengths and weaknesses of their psychological styles to their work: from extroversion and introversion or intuition to hysteria, paranoia, narcissism.

Fields of expertise are often proud of their biases, just as individuals may be proud of their personal styles: we are the humanitarian ones, the judicious ones, or those who understand the needs of business. Many expert communities work hard to promote the special insights they bring to problems. Sophisticated fields are often proud of their eclectic inclusiveness. Having taken everything into account, they have no bias. Everything that might be contested has been raised up from common sense and turned into a factor to be evaluated, weighed, and balanced.

The biases and blind spots of these expert communities lie in their remaining unexamined common sense and their shared unwillingness to reopen the outcomes of past struggle that they now experience as fact. These can be fleshed out by empathetic interpretation: what must they be thinking to argue in this way or to stop arguing at that point? Comparative analysis may also be useful as the alternative disciplinary maps I sketched in the past chapter suggest.[7] What do international lawyers see that military strategists do not, what problems do they find easy or difficult to confront, how do their styles of engagement conduce to authority in different settings? One can compare expert practice in different national settings or historical periods to shed light on the potential advantages and disadvantages of each. Were the authority of these experts increased, what problems would become easy to solve, what intractable? Who would get their attention, and who would be invisible?

In looking for blind spots and biases, however, it is easy to underestimate the flexibility of expertise, particularly in sophisticated fields. Professional deformations are not straightjackets. Opposing interests and ideas really have been domesticated into their argumentative material. Differences between fields have become differences within them. Within "free-market" ideas there lurks an exception for "market failures" that can be interpreted broadly or narrowly. A "free-market" policy could turn out, if properly structured, to be more friendly to "workers" than its "socialist" alternative. Military professionals may be too prone, or not prone enough, to use force. Economists do have a vocabulary for values other than efficiency, just as lawyers have a robust vocabulary for criticizing reliance on rules or litigation, for broadening exceptions, for promoting alternative dispute resolution, structuring administrative discretion, and appreciating the role of political life in constituting the rule of law. Political scientists do have a way of speaking about the influence of rules in international affairs even if they like to preface their accounts of multilevel games and predictive stability with denunciations of "idealistic" lawyers.

Nevertheless, many diplomats also do see the world from the foreshortened perspective offered from the UN headquarters building or flying among conferences and summits, commissions and expert working groups. The sites of prior international engagements loom large—Passchendaele, Somme, Munich, Bretton Woods, or, closer to our day, Vietnam, Cambodia, Bosnia, Rwanda, or Iraq. Each stands for a "lesson" that shapes reactions to new problems. Navigating on such a map can substitute for navigating in the world—for assessing the actual consequences of actual policies in contexts to come. High up there, it is easy to expect the Potemkin village of intergovernmental institutions to operate like the domestic institutions—courts, administrations, parliaments—on which they were loosely modeled. The expert's mental map discourages engagement with things below the line of sovereignty. International lawyers focus on what happens outside and between national jurisdictions: in Antarctica, in outer space, on the seabed. International policy makers imagine themselves in a space above sovereignty, a space in which sovereigns mingle, communicate, have "disputes." For something to get into this space—to be "taken up on the international plane"—it must be a grave matter, a serious breach, cause material damage, result in irrevocable harm, shock the conscience—or meet any of the numerous other substantive tests for reversing the presumption that things below the line of sovereignty are immune from international policy making.

Sovereigns can do as they like at home—for their actions to be respected on the international plane they must meet certain standards. These *deformations professionelles* can give international policy an odd shape. The international policy maker sees things like smoke or fish when they cross boundaries more clearly than when they stay close to home. The law of the sea classifies the world's fish species according to their migratory habits measured by their propensity to swim across international boundaries.

With clever and expansive interpretation, international policy makers in sophisticated fields may be able to stretch their materials to address these limitations, but they tend not to. International lawyers can make and unmake the boundary between war and peace, yet continue to imagine them as distinct. Although no one is a "neoliberal" and everyone knows all economic transactions might be subject to political control, in practice the default idea of limited government and global economic "flows" and "forces" limits the malleability of the expert material when it comes time to ratchet up regulatory power. Although everyone understands how to reconfigure contract into property and both into sovereign power, a default assumption about the distinctiveness of public and private, capital and labor, limits what might otherwise be a more flexible set of expert modes of engagement. Capital and private right travel "naturally," public policy and labor only exceptionally.

It is easy for international lawyers and policy makers, preoccupied with sovereignty, to underestimate the worlds of private and economic law or to overestimate the military's power to intervene successfully while remaining neutral or disengaged from local political and culture struggles. When experts identify international environmental law with the environmentally protective norms, they overlook the many legal arrangements that encourage or enable despoliation, although international law offers the environmental despoiler, like the war criminal or the human rights abuser, a great deal of comfort and protection. This would instantly become visible were such a person to become a client. When foreign policy experts overestimate the technocratic nature of economic concerns, they underestimate their ability to contest the distributional consequences of transnational economic forces.

Thinking of their work as "intervention," down from a great height, international experts are prone to think there was no international policy *before* intervention and easily become preoccupied with debate about *whether or not* to intervene. This obscures ongoing engagement with local conditions and the extent to which all regimes are today the product of transnational meddling and influence. The idea that one should not intervene without good reason and good authority erects a conceptual hurdle in front of every humanitarian initiative. What standing do we have? Innumerable worthy international policy initiatives have crashed on the rocks of hesitation to engage. Policy makers often imagine one might intervene in a place like Kosovo or East Timor neutrally, to "keep the peace" or "rebuild the society," *without* effecting the background distribution of power and wealth. This is a dream that there might be an international governance that does not govern.

Experts share maps of time as well as space. International policy makers situate themselves in a grand story of the slow and unsteady progress of law against power, policy against politics, reason against ideology, international against national, order against chaos in international affairs over three hundred fifty years. In this story, international governance is itself a mark of civilization's progress. Progress narratives of this sort can become policy programs, both by solidifying a professional consensus about what has worked and by defining what counts as progress for the international governance system as a whole. This can redirect policy makers from solving problems to completing the work of a mythological history. A strong myth of professional progress often hinders the pragmatic assessment of specific initiatives. The failures of particular initiatives may be interpreted as warnings to do more, to intensify the effort, along precisely the same lines. Internationalists too often see themselves as continuously *becoming*, polishing their tools, embroidering their technique, strengthening themselves, that they might one day tackle global problems. In the meantime, failures reflect the primitive state of the work, the strength of their enemies, the long road still to travel.

Where biases are unexamined matters of common sense, they may be able to be brought into debate. Doing so adds to the sophistication of the field. Where contesting a bias would place one outside the expert community altogether, the boundaries of the field may themselves be contested. It has been by repeatedly contesting assumptions and field boundaries that modes of contemporary expertise came to be sophisticated—and disenchanted—in the first place. The promise that this time everything may finally be taken into account is what keeps them going. This is also what gives the outcomes of expert struggle legitimacy: this was not about winners and losers, but about finally getting it right. In one sense, there will always turn out to be a bias, in the sense that struggles are, after all, won and lost. In the next round, everything will not be taken into account if this result becomes a fact or prediction that need not be contested. But if it is contested, the pursuit of finally getting it right can begin again as something else that had been assumed needs now to be taken into account. At each turn, the struggle fades beneath the victory of what will have been reason.

SOPHISTICATED EXPERTISE: THE SEARCH FOR ALTERNATIVES

If not an ever more sophisticated expertise, what? The most familiar alternative to expert rule is thought to be politics. Expertise should be subject to an external check by interests and ideological commitments that reside elsewhere. Rule by experts should be subject to the demands of other powers and viewpoints: those of citizens, stakeholders, or those represented by politicians. Shifting the locus of struggle may change the outcome. Replacing international lawyers or development economists with politicians may alter the outcomes of struggle, just as replacing lawyers with priests or economists with philosophers might. Different modes of expertise have different blind spots and the status of forces in different institutions where experts work may be different.

People in struggle move among vocabularies of interest or ideology and more technical modes of articulation to take advantage of the shifts in relative authority that may occur as a result. Politicians stop speaking of national interest and talk about law or science. To interpret an opponent's technical proposal as the expression of an ideology or interest is among the most basic activities of expert argument, alongside an explanation of the interests and ideological commitments that will be served by one's own proposal. A discussion of ideology or interest is not an alternative to expertise: it is an alternative within expertise. Nor are these vocabularies more decisive or less sophisticated. To figure out what is in the interests of capital or labor, of the first world or the third, is to enter the realm of policy making, attuned to perverse effects, unexpected costs and benefits. The outcomes and how to interpret them will be disputed. Arguments linking policies to divergent interests and divergent policies to the same interest will be common: if you really want to favor the unemployed, do the opposite. Alternatives that seem stark turn out to be more nuanced and to allow room for more than one political interpretation. It is hard not to conclude that the only real antidote to rule by experts is more expertise.

Within sophisticated policy fields, expertise is a complex dialog among technical and more "political" considerations by people who situate themselves and one another on different sides of the technical necessity/ideological imperative boundary at different moments. Arguments can become associated with political positions because they share a family resemblance, rather than as the result of careful analysis of their consequences. A vocabulary familiar from the defense of a particular interest in other contexts may be deployed here as if it would favor the same interest. In contemporary development expertise, to focus on the prevalence of market failures is to position yourself in the center-left; to focus on growth rather than efficiency and develop strategies aimed at alternative growth trajectories that might be equally efficient with different levels of inequality is to position yourself still further to the left. All without a clear sense for the outcomes of policies associated with arguments of either type in particular contexts. Expert argument is a kind of subdivision of broader ideological debate. If the market failure people are ascendant in development policy, that may strengthen center-leftists elsewhere and vice versa.

Matters of style and professional identity are also involved. To challenge the expert work of people in sophisticated fields by linking it to political interests and ideologies can make you sound shrill, lacking in nuance. It can violate the style rather than discredit the content of expert work and mark you as an outsider. When protesters in Davos, or Seattle, or Geneva denounce the WTO as a tool of global capital, it is hard not to think they should probably break things down a bit more, get more precise, maybe go to law school. But somehow we also know that if they did, they'd likely lose their edge, dampen their sense for the politics of global governance, precisely as they refined their skills to participate in it. Searching for the politics of expertise this way takes us right back to expertise.

An alternative way to think about the boundaries of expertise would focus *internally* on the relations among experts rather than seeking to associate expert performances with social forces and commitments "outside" expertise. Expert articulations become effective when someone acts or thinks differently than would otherwise have been the case. The uptake of expert work has something to do with how other experts—including lay audiences—grant access, authority, or credibility. We might reposition the evaluation of expertise within the horizontal terrain of struggle, asking "who yielded" rather than whose interest or ideology prevailed. Expertise would be effective when it induced the social experience of yielding: when someone who was taking one path takes another, releasing the gain she had aimed to secure and allowing you to prevail. Yielding may be a matter of "being persuaded." This must happen, however rarely, but it is difficult to separate yielding to argument from yielding to authority no matter how someone describes her own shift.

From afar, it is easy to overestimate other people's freedom of maneuver and their susceptibility to good arguments or pressure. If we think of the global AIDS crisis as a matter of drug prices and delivery systems, of intellectual property and health care finance, it is tempting to imagine that one enlightened industrialist could make the drugs available, one enlightened judge could carve out an exception to the rules of intellectual property, one enlightened bishop could remove the impediments to education about the causes and consequences of HIV infection. We just need to get to him with a good argument. When we contemplate a missile strike to shock and awe someone into respect for norms, it is easy to think of the foreign dictator able to decide as a rational actor: if we raise the price, he'll get the message. When people do not get the message or fail to respond to argument, it is tempting to see them as irrational, blinded by greed, religious dogma, or ideology. But the targets of such arguments are neither rational people waiting to be convinced nor irrational fanatics. They are experts. They come into their roles as dictators, investors, managers, patent holders, or bishops precisely by routinizing themselves into a professional vocabulary and practice that makes it difficult for them to experience freedom of maneuver for either rational persuasion or irrational preference. They have reasons embedded in their roles and situation for what they do.

Yet, they may also yield. When and how they do so is a matter of neither rational argument nor the application of overwhelming force: it is some alchemical thing in between. Whether the experience of yielding feels like "being persuaded," "knuckling under," or some combination, the expert may feel a loss of agency: the other person prevailed. There is a further element in yielding that is worth noting. When an expert abandons his position in the face of another, there is a moment of vertigo when the felt necessity of the earlier position fades. Suddenly, the technical argument, interest, or ideological commitment that seemed to compel and justify his position gives way. The expert, at that moment, is free of his expertise. What generally happens, of course, is that he scrambles to an alternative "reason," replacing what has become a false necessity with one that feels real. But not always and not right away. In the moment of pause between, the doorway opens for expert discretion. In that moment we may glimpse an alternative to rule by experts: rule by people deciding responsibly in a moment of unknowing.

There is a tradition of understanding politics not as an alternative universe of ideology and interest, but as an experience of deciding in the exception, in the freedom of not knowing, released from expertise but not from responsibility. To expand the possibility for a politics of expertise in this sense would mean expanding the experience of decisional freedom in the practice of those who participate in the background struggles of global governance. Experts often flee from this experience. Their flight, their denial of freedom and responsibility is part of their self-presentation as an expert.

My intuition is that this flight from decisional freedom and responsibility is among the drivers for ever more sophisticated modes of expertise.

Comprehensivity and disenchantment operate as a robust defense to the idea of an outside. You can come to the expertise hotel, but you may never leave. These experts have thought of everything, heard all the arguments, mastered all the theories, and seen it all before. Although an allegation of capture by interests or ideologies imagines an outside to their reason, it underestimates the plasticity and comprehensiveness of expertise and imagines one could figure out what interests or ideologies require without asking an expert. In their disenchantment, experts know better. Although the tools of their expertise are not determinative, by operating within these routines, you can experience yourself the avatar of good judgment and wisdom. You are not taking a position: all the positions have always already been taken. Nor are you deciding. You are articulating the direction of right reason.

Yielding is the experience that everything had not been taken into account. If politics is the experience of deciding, it is an experience people in the most sophisticated fields only feel when they yield and in a moment of uncertainty inhabit a kind of personal responsibility for unforeseeable consequences. The arguments that experts level at one another can have this effect when they press someone to experience conditions of ambivalent, contradictory, or vague guidance from their expert vocabularies. Illuminating the limits and self-image of sophisticated professional practice may help to expand this space and encourage a form of expertise that could experience politics as its vocation.

PART III

LAW

CHAPTER 6

LAW AND THE GLOBAL DYNAMICS OF DISTRIBUTION

The legalization of global political and economic life has made legal expertise a predominant language of engagement in transnational struggle. Law offers a language of disagreement and justification nestled in a body of shared common sense and accepted facts, a set of roles and institutional practices giving form to their use, and modes for relating legal assertions to the material world of coercion and the social world of status or legitimacy. Legal rules constitute actors on a terrain of struggle by arranging entitlements and authorizations defining what it means to be a "corporation" or "state" or "citizen," each armed with a backpack of legal powers and vulnerabilities. Legal expertise then rules by articulation. People exercise powers, allocate funds, engage institutions and fire guns by expressing claims of entitlement or authorization. They use legal language to assert power, justify submission or allocate gains. When their articulations are effective, their assertions are confirmed. When legal materials register those outcomes as entitlements, they provide a baseline for the next round of struggle. Law seems to have a kind of social power to legitimate the operation both as a whole and in its particulars. As a result, we can read in legal norms and institutional arrangements both sediment of past struggle and the tools available for new projects.

In this chapter and the next, I explore two remaining puzzles, before turning to the role of law in modern warfare to illustrate the workings of legal expertise in contemporary global political life. Although people in struggle rapidly grasp the significance of law for the allocation of gains and losses or the consolidation of relative powers, the role of law in distribution remains underappreciated by scholars. In this chapter, I focus on law's distributive significance and the importance of legal rules and arrangements as stakes in struggle to fill this gap. A second puzzle is the continuing skepticism in the scholarly community about the existence and "legality" of law at the global level given the dramatic spread of legal expertise as a vocabulary of global political and economic struggle over the past century. In the next chapter, I revisit the history of international law's reinvention by scholars and practitioners over the past century to suggest an answer: the legalization of global life accompanied a dramatic fragmentation and internal pluralization of legal expertise. As the legal field became more sophisticated, in the sense I have explored in the preceding chapters, it became more useful, if also less decisive or analytically compelling.

Although international legal scholars have rarely made the distributive significance of law the focal point of research, there is a long tradition of doing so elsewhere. In the United States, the tradition is often said to have begun with Oliver Wendell Holmes, who famously asserted that "the judges themselves have failed adequately to recognize their duty of weighing considerations of social advantage."[1] Among the American legal realists, many of whom took up Holmes's suggestion in one or another way, Wesley Hohfeld and Robert Hale were particularly influential on my own thinking. Hohfeld for disaggregating legal entitlements into pairs—right and duty, for example—that focused attention on their oppositional or distributional relationship; and Hale for his account of the role of reciprocal threats of coercion in the bargaining power of those who engage one another on the basis of legal entitlements.[2] The postwar embrace of sociology and economics by American legal scholars expanded the tools for understanding the process by which social conflicts become transposed into legal arrangements and vice versa.[3] More recent works by Duncan Kennedy and others in the "critical legal studies" movement are the direct source for the approach I develop here.[4]

THE POWER OF LAW: COERCION AND LEGITIMACY

In the first instance, people struggle over legal arrangements because law promises enforcement: it signals a promise by an authority to back up its statements with force. If you trespass on my property, I can call the police. If you enter my market without a license, the state will make you pay a fine. But this is not all there is to it. Not all official legal arrangements are enforced: much goes unpunished or is settled among people with the state only vaguely in the background. Some normative arrangements are not backed up by the state, but by customary authority. At the international level, there is no state standing above the situation to enforce. Enforcement, when it occurs, is horizontal, undertaken by other states, by economic pressure, by media pressure, consumer boycotts, or military engagement. Some analysts have said that *only* where there is enforcement ought we to speak about law at all on the international plane. That makes some sense—a realistic prediction of coercion is central to normative authority. But rather than shrinking the domain of law, this approach has tended to expand it. Lots of social, political, economic, and military pressures have the effect of "enforcing" normative expectations transnationally. Reading back from them, we find lots of law.

The fact that so many people involved in global struggle do so in legal terms, seek legal gains, reframe their ideologies and interests in technical legal arguments seems to go beyond the coercive power law brings in its shadow. Or at least, we would need to understand that coercive shadow in very broad social terms. People sometimes use the word "legitimacy" to denote law's additional social power beyond the naked promise of coercion. Legitimacy in two senses: when people accept that something is "legal," it seems legitimate; and law itself has legitimacy as a mode of engagement, a set of procedures for dispute, a vocabulary of arguments for advocacy and persuasion.

In the first sense, law's power rests in its ability to create what we might call a "legitimacy effect." If you can get someone to accept that something is legal, you will create in them the feeling that it "should" be accepted. This allows law to serve as a force multiplier in international economic and political discussion. If bombing the city was legal—if the dead civilians were legally permissible targets—you can expect that fewer people with the influence to oppose the military action will do so effectively. If you can convince people that occupying the territory is "illegal," by contrast, it will take more political energy and will to sustain the occupation because fewer people will be disposed to let it continue and many who oppose it will feel empowered. This kind of power also has a dark cousin: the power that comes with violation. People who behead journalists undertake a strategic legal (or, perhaps better, illegal) maneuver, seeking the authority that comes from a perception that they are outside norms of legitimacy. They may pay a price: their struggle may become more difficult if opposition hardens its resolve in light of their violation of legal or ethical mores. But they may also gain a great deal: visibility, even "legitimacy" from others on the outside of what pass for universal norms.

It is a puzzle how law—private law, national law, international law, industry standards, corporate codes of conduct—came to have this legitimating power. Law's legitimacy is itself the ongoing outcome of struggle, over both the authority to speak the law and the authority of legal speech. For the moment, the outcome internationally seems to be a broad dispersion of authority to speak in legal terms and a broad recognition of the prestige and authority of legal claims. Although this state of affairs may or may not turn out to be stable, it seems rooted in the background ideas elites have about how things work, alongside ideas about what an "economy" is, what a "state" is, or how politics and economics work.

At the same time, however, one unfortunate idea many people in the global elite share—with my own grandmother, as it turns out—is the sense that "international law" hardly exists. There are some treaties, there is the United Nations, and that's about it. One Christmas, when I told my grandmother how much I enjoyed studying international law, she calmly asked, "But David, do they even have that?" And yet, Grandma knew, as people everywhere instinctively do, that the suitcase she brought on board at home still belonged to her when the plane landed overseas. When she traveled, she expected to be able to reason with people when she arrived in familiar normative terms, just as confidently as she expected every country to have a flag, a national flower, and a typical souvenir. She might not know the local language, but she did know when the hotel had failed to meet its obligations or the local shopkeeper had pulled a fast one. She was not alone. People around the world have expectations about law's reach, significance, and availability as a common language for talking about who ought to do or get what that go far beyond the world of treaties and UN resolutions. This expectation has a lot to do with the ubiquity of legal rules and institutions themselves. So long as people struggling for advantage experience the power of legal arrangements, the persuasiveness of legal arguments, and the effect of legal authority, my grandmother will continue to be correct in her prediction that she will be able to rely on it in otherwise strange locations.

Although it is easy to think of international affairs as a rolling sea of politics over which we have managed to throw but a thin net of legal rules, in truth the situation today is more the reverse. There is law at every turn. Even war today is an affair of rules and regulations and legal principles. Nor is the global market a space of commercial freedom outside of law. Global trade—even informal and clandestine trade—takes place in a dense regulatory environment among entities whose capacities and bargaining power are structured by legal powers, obligations, and privileges. The dispersion and fragmentation of economic and political power brought about by their globalization have only accelerated their legalization. The result has been a tremendous proliferation of law and the vernacular of legal expertise. The multiplicity and ubiquity of rules contribute to their legitimacy and to the expectation that they will continue to be available and useful.

Yet global life is governed less by a functioning *system* of rules and institutions than by a hodgepodge of local, national, and international norms, made, interpreted, enforced, or ignored by all manner of public and private actors. We live in a world of conflicting and multiplying jurisdictions, in which people assert the validity or persuasiveness of all manner of rules to one another with no decider of last resort. The footprint—official and unofficial—of national rules and national adjudication extends far beyond their nominal territorial jurisdiction. Every sovereign territory is penetrated by the effects of rules made and enforced elsewhere. And then there are the many overlapping private arrangements, financial institutions, and payment systems, an alternate world of private ordering through contracts and corporate forms, standards bodies. It was, after all, a network of impenetrable private obligations that tied the global financial system in knots in 2008 and has yet to be unwound. Even global liquidity is as much a matter of private leverage and securitization as it is a function of central bank determinations about the money supply. Private entitlements hold public coffers hostage, whether to foreign bondholders or local pensioners. The informal sector is also global. Informal rules and customary normative expectations are significant for multinational businesspeople as well as small-scale traders and migrants. Remittances, barter, trade and exchange internal to families or firms, black markets, and corruption rackets all have rules and institutions—and enforcement mechanisms. Stigmatizing them, ignoring them—or utilizing them—is, for every public and private actor, a strategic choice. Law's capacity for both strong advocacy and reasoned compromise, and its plasticity to strategic novelty, seem rooted in the tremendous array of possible legal arguments, precedents, and procedures that emerge from this transnational normative hodgepodge.

All this law is relevant for the struggles through which global political life and economic life are carried out in three broad ways. First, legal claims are often an effective tool for defeating rivals and consolidating gains. Legal rules distribute value and foreshadow coercive enforcement where that distribution is not respected. Second, law provides a language for advocacy, negotiation, and conflict resolution. People struggling with one another argue about their entitlements and use legal arguments to discuss the meaning and applicability of broad principles and ideological commitments. My grandmother had no knowledge of the foreign law of public accommodation. The arguments she expected to be able to make with a foreign hotelier had their roots in law as a repository of hegemonic meanings, moral injunctions, social rankings, and commercial expectations.

Finally, law is relevant for people in struggle because legal ideas, rules, and institutional arrangements structure the balance of power among individuals or groups, shaping the terrain on which they come into conflict with one another. Large and small countries, local regulators and global companies, central banks and global investors all confront one another on a terrain shaped by their respective quiver of powers and vulnerabilities. Over time, as legal rules and the outcomes of legal disputes consolidate winnings and lock in small differences of power, large dynamics of inequality can arise. In this chapter, I look at each of these in turn. In the next chapter, I consider the century-long transformation of international law that rendered it a sophisticated, comprehensive, and malleable tool for global struggle.

LAW: A MODE OF DISTRIBUTION AND THEREFORE STRUGGLE

Law's distributive role is no surprise to people engaged in transnational economic or political struggle. They work hard to understand and exploit legal arrangements favorable to their interests and to shape the regulatory landscape. Law distributes when it gives people entitlements and legitimacy that strengthen their bargaining power, either individually or as member of a favored group. Legal rules distribute when they consolidate gains, marking the line where coercion will enforce an allocation of value to us rather than to our competitors. Regulations alter patterns of distribution by changing relative prices. Law permitting some weapons and prohibiting others will advantage some armies over others. The fact that migration is more tightly regulated than movements of goods or capital affects the relative bargaining power of investors, workers, and manufacturers. Access to capital depends on a specific intersection of local and global financial rules and practices.

Despoiling the rainforest is not only an economic decision—it is the exercise of a sovereign legal privilege at the center of international environmental law. Each sovereign is legally privileged to exploit the resources and despoil the environment within its territory. When smoke crosses the border or harms become egregious, arguments for restraint can be mounted. The privilege (and its exceptions) allocates powers and responsibilities in a way that markedly weakens the leverage of all who would preserve the trees. Were the exceptions to expand effectively and the privilege shrink, the status of forces between despoilers and preservers would shift. Because it distributes, law has value for people in struggle, and is often also at stake in conflict.

What is less obvious is how thoroughgoing this distributive function is in global political and economic life. The ubiquitous distributional significance of legal arrangements in world political economy can be illustrated by considering David Ricardo's famous analysis of the "gains from trade" in light of his analysis of "rent."[5] Ricardo demonstrated the potential for "gains from trade" with a simple model taught in every introductory college course on the economics of trade: two countries producing two products with different resource endowments or technologies. The theory is simple, if somewhat counterintuitive: even where one country needs more inputs than another to produce both products (is at an absolute disadvantage in the production of each), there will be gains from trade if that country exports the product in which it has a relative or comparative advantage.

In the classic demonstration, illustrated in figure 6.1, although country B takes more inputs to make both radios and televisions, if country B exports four televisions to country A, country A can release two units of input, apply them to the production of radios, and export six radios to country B, which can use them to release six units of input. Applying those six units to TV production allows for the production of six televisions, a gain of two televisions overall. Country B has a comparative advantage in television production. By exporting four televisions and importing radios, it can gain value equivalent to two televisions. The principle could, of course, be equally well demonstrated from the perspective of country A, which has a comparative advantage in radio production. In this case, as illustrated in figure 6.2, country A exports six radios, allowing country B to release six units of input, apply them to television production, and export six televisions. Country A, in turn, is able to release

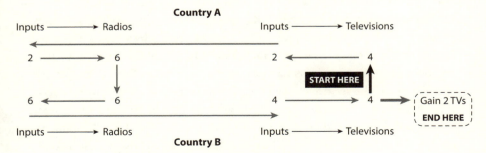

Figure 6.1 Ricardo: Gains from Trade to Country B

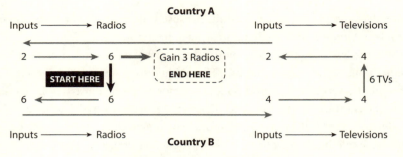

Figure 6.2 Ricardo: Gains from Trade to Country A

three units of input from television production, apply them to radios, and achieve a gain of three radios. This is all quite straightforward.

The struggle arises when the gains from trade are distributed. Will we end up with the equivalent of two more televisions in country B or three more radios in country A? This will depend upon an enormous number of variables which it is customary to treat as matters of "bargaining power" or as a kind of automatic consequence of things like the relative "productivity" of factors, "competitiveness" of economic actors, "price elasticity" of supply and demand in markets for these products. If lots of countries make similar radios at similar prices but country B is the only other place you can get televisions, for example, we would expect country B's bargaining power to be higher and a larger portion of the gains to end up there. What does the distributing is the market, setting prices for factors based on their productivity and for products based on supply and demand.

But what economists call "competitiveness" and "substitutability" depend in part on the legal and institutional arrangements that affect things like costs of production and barriers to entry in the two industries, the structure of these (and other) industries in both countries, the relative power of labor and capital invested in the two industries, the monopoly power of producers in each industry, the distribution of preferences and the process by which preferences are shaped in the two countries, and so on. Most obviously, if country B is the only place A's consumers can get televisions because B holds the patent for televisions, the relative competitiveness of the two products can be traced directly to a legal entitlement closing production to other nations who might otherwise bid down the price and shift gains from B toward A. Changing arrangements that have this kind of market-shaping effect could change a country's bargaining power, the competitiveness of its products, or the productivity of its factors and thereby affect the distribution of gains. As a result, they are worth struggling over.

Economic words like "competitiveness" and "productivity" have their parallels in political terms like "leverage" or "persuasiveness." They obscure the institutional arrangements that went into the bargaining power sausage. Each of these apparent facts ("he had more leverage, she was more persuasive") rests on legal entitlements, institutional arrangements, and vernaculars of persuasion that could be organized in different ways and are therefore themselves worth struggling over. Bargaining power depends on many things we associate with "power": relative size, prestige, wealth, or military might. Bringing relations of power to bear on the bargain occurs through institutions of one or another sort.

Consider colonialism. Regardless of who makes how many radios, if B is a colony of A, we would not be surprised to find the gains ending up with A. The colonial center, we would say, has the power to extract the gains. But how exactly? The "power" in a colonial relationship needs to be exercised through institutions, whether social, military, or legal. Did country A take the televisions by force? Did A preclude B from trading with other countries? Did it compel purchase of radios from A at above market prices? Perhaps there was a complex tax system—or set of currency controls and licenses—that ensured the prices paid in the two countries distributed the gains to consumers—or the tax office—in the imperial center. Or perhaps the institution doing the work is a social one: colonial elites so enamored with products branded in the mother country that they were willing to pay more. And things could be arranged the other way around: perhaps consumers in the mother country were compelled to purchase colonial products at higher prices as part of the overall colonial arrangement.

Ricardo recognized the significance of background social and legal institutions when he identified the centrality of "rents" to the distribution of gains from land. He was interested in how landlords holding highly productive land were able to charge more than the cost of production as demand increased and less productive land came into use. He wanted to explain how people deploying equal quantities of labor and capital in agriculture could nevertheless obtain different returns. Presuming the labor and capital were provided on parallel competitive terms in all locations, some land, he observed, was simply more productive. At any given time, the price of food would reflect the costs of labor and capital needed for its production on the least productive land in cultivation. Otherwise that land would not have been brought into cultivation.

If you put your labor and capital there, you would earn nothing. If you put it on the most productive land, you would earn the difference between your costs and those on the least productive land in cultivation. He called that difference "rent," which he attributed to "the original indestructible powers of the soil" over and above the labor and capital that had been applied equally in the most and least productive plots. The landlord had exclusive access to this "rent" because of property law: the landlord can call on the enforcement powers of the state to ensure that he alone receives the return above the cost of labor and capital necessary to produce the food on the most productive land.

Ricardo thought this was a bad arrangement. He thought landlords were less likely to make good use of those gains than other pluckier folks. They would consume it, waste it, sit on it, spend it abroad. One way to unravel landlord privilege as demand for food rose, he reasoned, would be to open Britain to grain produced elsewhere more cheaply. The price of food would no longer be set by the least productive plot in Britain, and the landlord would no longer have a free ride on his property in better land. In this sense, the landlord's rent was the product not only of property law, but also of the Corn Laws and all the other legal arrangements that kept the price of food high enough for him to reap this benefit. That is one reason he favored their repeal.

Ricardo's analysis had limits. As a theoretical matter, it is notoriously difficult to say what portion of the price of anything represents "rent" as opposed to the "cost" of production. It depends on what you attribute to "cost" and what you attribute to the "indestructible powers." If there is a market for land, the cost of acquiring the property right might as well be treated as part of the capital brought to the endeavor. Obtaining and securing a property right—an entitlement to rent—could be seen as another cost of production or the purchase of a needed service and the return a reflection of those costs.

But Ricardo was on to something. For one thing, there are situations in which there is no market for a landlord's entitlement. Suppose he and all the other landowners had inherited their land and they were not permitted to sell, by law or custom. Although it might seem reasonable to treat the cost of acquiring the property as a cost of capital if the landlord had paid for it or in retaining the land forwent equivalent investment opportunities, where law forbids that, we see more clearly the hand of power and it seems reasonable to call the gain an unearned rent, arising not from the soil but from the legal and social arrangements. Sovereignty is somewhat like this: there is no market for countries. What the elites of a "rentier state" have to play with are sovereign entitlements in a territory. They can license production, control the flow of labor, tax the proceeds, encourage or tolerate all manner of informal coercive demands for side payments, but they cannot sell out and buy another country. What they obtain reflects the indestructible powers of sovereignty.

There turn out to be lots of background legal rules that affect the landlord's ability to enjoy the full difference between the cost of production on his excellent land and on the least productive land. Perhaps agricultural workers are prohibited—or required—to unionize. Perhaps they are tied to the land as serfs. Perhaps some workers can move and others cannot. Perhaps banks are forbidden—or encouraged—to make loans in the agricultural sector. Just as the law of inheritance and property empowered the landlord to extract gains, workers (and bankers) will also be able to wield their entitlements (not to be enslaved, to exit for the next farm) to extract something. The gains arise not as a natural return on capital or reflection of the productivity of labor, but from the legal arrangements. Property, labor and sovereignty have no intrinsic value or indestructible powers. When those acting with the legal entitlements and vulnerabilities of property owners, laborers and state officials struggle with one another over value, the gain accruing to some at the expense of others reflects the relative strength of the legal powers they each brought along in their backpack.

In a sense, any economic gain could be understood to arise from the entitlement to exclusive use of the return from something. The soil, after all, has no economic power: it is just there. People have to add capital, labor and know-how to get food, the food has to be sold and the proceeds parceled out. Like the land, wealth, technology and labor are also just there: they have no inherent productivity or generative powers. A person has to have the entitlement, under some conditions, to use those things and retain the gain. Those conditions could be set in many ways: labor might be slaves, technology might be more or less exclusively owned, capital might be rationed, allocated or subsidized, and so on. And then the people who have these entitlements have to figure out among themselves how to divvy up the gains, bargaining in the shadow of their various powers and vulnerabilities vis-à-vis one another. Land, wealth, knowledge, and labor become economically productive only as legal institutions. The "indestructible power" in each case is the power of law.

To formulate this as a general proposition: legal arrangements distribute when they effectively exclude some people from participation in gains in the shadow of a promise of coercive enforcement. The landlord can have the trespasser imprisoned—or may have legal permission to shoot where his exclusive entitlement to the bounty of his land is threatened. A requirement that landlords bargain with a state-sponsored labor union or sell to a state market-ing board is equally coercive, forcing the landlord to accept less favorable terms than he could with individual peasants or buyers A prohibition on agricultural unions—or the law of serfdom—would coerce a bargain the other way. The law would not have to be official to do this work, nor would the coercion need to come from the state. In lots of situations, business practice and local custom are far more effective in conditioning access to gains from economic activity. In so doing, all such arrangements permit "rent" in the sense Ricardo identi-fied as the consequence of property rights to productive land. Globally, con-straint on participation in gain is ubiquitous, and differential access to returns is everywhere reinforced by entitlement.

When economists use the language of rent today, however, they have a more limited class of situations in mind: returns that arise when markets diverge from "optimal" or "competitive" prices and returns. Rent arises as a result of something "abnormal" or "distortive." In this picture, the image of a normal—or ideal—baseline of market transactions unimpeded by power is crucial. Without it, all returns would be as much a matter of Ricardian rent as a return on investment or recovery of cost.

In the legal field, for example, law and economics scholars Bebchuk, Fried, and Walker describe the potential impact of "managerial power" on execu-tive compensation this way: "Managers with power are able to extract 'rents'—value in excess of that which they would receive under optimal contracting—and managers with more power can extract more rents."[6] The word "optimal" does a great deal of work here. They have in mind a normal situation in which managers are the transparent agents of shareholders, disciplined by a competi-tive market in managers to work in the interests of shareholders and minimize agency costs associated with the need to hire managers in the first place. Rent, they explain, is the "excess of the pay obtained by him over what he would have received under a contract that maximizes shareholder value."[7] The au-thors then identify a series of social and legal arrangements that permit the exercise of manager power to divert to their own pocket part of what should be returned to shareholders, even in the face of shareholder supervision of pay by the board.

The idea that managers ought optimally to attend only to shareholder value is, of course, also a reflection of legal arrangements. It would be easy to structure corporations to ensure that managers were responsive to the state, to the com-munity, or to workers as well. Or we might think the arrangements of power that permit managerial capture of corporate profits are themselves normal: were shareholders to institute rules to force departure from them, they would be extracting rent from the poor managers. If we think of rent as the reflection of the power to exploit scarcity—here the power to divert corporate gains either toward or away from shareholders—then it would be rent all the way down. Economic returns always reflect a power to exclude, often a legal one conferred by contract or property or office or status or regulation of some kind.

The development economist Raphael Kaplinsky uses "rent" to analyze the distribution of gains in global supply chains, urging developing nations to improve their ability to extract rent by "upgrading."[8] His capacious conception of rent focuses on comparison rather than normality. For Kaplinsky, rent arises from any arrangement that permits firms to garner a larger share of the gains from production *than others* by excluding competitors from a source of value. He sees rents arising within firms when they invent or adopt new technologies, develop unique or improved skills, adopt new forms of organization, or institute changes in design and marketing that give them an edge over the competition. Some rents, he argues, are endogenous to the sector but are difficult for any one firm to obtain on its own: the ability to foster and operate networks, speed logistics, develop some kinds of quality, design, or human resource advantages. Clustering firms in an industry or relying on similar infrastructure can lead to competitive advantages for all firms in the cluster, Silicon Valley being perhaps the most well-known contemporary example. On a larger scale, Kaplinsky identifies rents that are exogenous to the industry as a whole: resource rents (the country has oil), policy rents (the government supports national champions at home and abroad), infrastructural rents (someone else paid for the harbor), and financial rents (institutions have been arranged to ensure credit is more readily available than it is elsewhere). His book is a plea for developing nations to adopt institutional arrangements that will permit their own firms to exclude others from gains generated across value chains. Firms, cities, regions, industries, and nations should all seek to upgrade their position in global value chains by increasing their privileged access to one or another moment in the production of value.

This approach is enormously useful because it denaturalizes the failure to capture gains. The gains from trade in radios and televisions are not distributed between country A and country B by the operation of economic forces. They are distributed among all kinds of players—the respective industries, their labor forces, their bankers, the consumers of each product—through struggle over the authority to exclude others from access to parts of the process through which value is generated. The issue is not your "competitiveness" or the inexorable laws of "supply and demand," but your inability to arrange things to exclude the other guy from the gains arising in a global value chain in which you participate. You have bargaining power if you can get the corner on one or another indispensable link in the chain, erect barriers to entry around the piece of global production you dominate, exercise relative monopoly power, and exclude competitors. The bargaining power of everyone involved—workers, investors, suppliers, distributors, suppliers of transport, retailers, consumers—depends on their ability to exclude others and coerce others to surrender gains. By definition, if you are not extracting rent, the others are.

Like many economists, Kaplinsky says little about the role of law in the battle for rent. He does acknowledge that rents endogenous to the firm "may be protected by unwritten process know-how or by formal entry barriers such as trademarks, copyrights and patents." Yet each form of rent he discusses depends on formal and informal legal or institutional arrangements. The bargaining power advantages he sees in the structure of firms, of finance, of labor relations, of consumer entitlement, and much more have their basis in legal arrangements. In some industries, intellectual property does provide the crucial lever. In others, it is the relative concentration of monopoly power at one place in the global chain—the large automotive manufacturer and credit institutions vis-à-vis both suppliers and retailers; or the major consumer product retailers through their dominance of access to large chains of retail stores and the contractual terms that structure relations with everyone else. Protection for innovation or access to an educated labor force may be crucial. So might privileged access to energy or transport, or privileged access to low-wage labor, or the privilege to despoil the environment. All kinds of technical standards relating to health or safety may affect who can secure the gains to be had from an exchange of televisions and radios.

"Rentier economies" are appropriately named: their development path is rooted in the access their elites have to value arising in their territory. But it is not the "indestructible power" of oil or natural gas that pours money into the sovereign wealth fund. It is the authority of legal arrangements. Were those arrangements to change—from sovereignty over natural resources to local formal and informal licensing, citizenship rules, taxation, and corruption schemes—there would be no reason to anticipate that a particular subset of the people who happened to live on top of an oil reserve would end up so rich. The division of gains among the Qatari government, Chevron, and the immigrant workers in Doha is the product of innumerable local and international, public and private legal arrangements.

The impact of legal rules on the allocation of rents between economic actors depends on the context—and on a network of other legal arrangements. Where compliance by suppliers with a new technical standard gives a large auto manufacturer a quality edge in their market, the resulting gain—and costs—will need to be distributed across the production chain. A large American or Japanese manufacturer may have effective monopsony power over their parts suppliers in Thailand or Mexico for any number of reasons: their size, know-how, prior investments, government support, location in a free trade zone, and so on. If so, they may have the "power" in negotiating contracts with suppliers to force acceptance of the new technical standard, imposing the cost on suppliers and capturing the full gain for themselves. But even here, the supplier may have cards to play. Perhaps they can "upgrade" to meet the standard at a lower cost, more quickly, more verifiably than their competitors, effectively excluding them from a new opportunity to contribute to gains generated when the manufacturer sells the cars. Perhaps they have a license for components necessary for quick compliance, receive subsidized credit to facilitate their upgrade, benefit from technology transfer and training programs enabling their labor force to make the change, or are simply the only firm permitted to sell to the manufacturer in the "free" trade zone. Contracting to comply with the new standard will represent an opportunity to upgrade and capture gains, rather than a new cost. The struggle over legal requirements—whether imposed privately or by regulation, adopted voluntarily or under pressure—occurs in the shadow of strategic assessments of this type. Will compliance offer a new opportunity to exclude and capture gain, or would it impose a cost and represent submission to the successful "upgrading" strategy of my competitors or business partners?

If you leave law out of the picture, it is easy to underestimate the potential to rearrange access to rent. Many economists speak about the strategic imperative for companies—and countries—to enter and hold "high-value" segments of the global production process. It is common to think of a ladder running naturally from natural resource exploitation through processing to assembly, manufacturing, design, branding, and invention. It seems a rule of thumb that high-wage "innovation" or "knowledge-based" activities will offer opportunities to retain a greater portion of the overall gain from economic activity in the value chain than low-skill manufacturing. Law is an important tool for encouraging people to move up the ladder.

But it is also important to understand how much this hierarchy of value itself depends on legal arrangements. A shift in intellectual property law and labor law, for example, might sharply diminish the exclusivity of innovation-based activities and reduce the availability of the privilege to access low-wage labor. At the margin, regulatory shifts in the many rules governing access to returns from different activities in global value chain can alter what is and is not a "high-value" activity. It is no wonder, therefore, that we also see intense struggle over those rules, undertaken in an extremely unruly and disparate fashion, among producers, consumer groups, investors, firms, cities, and nations.

By definition, not everyone can succeed—that's why it is a struggle. Upgrading is a relative accomplishment. A country might think that securing a low-wage niche through a special tariff arrangement would offer the opportunity to upgrade from agricultural to industrial labor only to find that others have easily secured the same advantage and compete viciously on price. A firm may think that locating the industrial capability to process logs into plywood close to the forest will secure it a privileged position, only to find those who finance the lumbering of the forest locked into a long-term contract with foreign plywood manufacturers. The local government may have gotten a cut for ensuring the exclusivity of their access to the trees. If there is a constitutional struggle in global economic governance, it is over the authority to allocate and secure privileges and other entitlements. At stake are not only economic gains, but the power to allocate in the next round.

The struggle over rent is not waged among nations alone, but through a complex set of struggles among domestic and foreign firms and governments. Although people speak about "Mexico" and "China" competing on price in low-wage manufacturing, the dynamics are more complex. Firms "within" each country and different offices "within" each government will have different interests—often aligned with other social groups or economic entities, whether inside or outside the nation. Nor will the impact of rule changes on "China" or "Mexico" be clear. Is a tariff reduction properly understood as a "concession" to foreign business or as an advantage for local consumers and the national economy? Short-term obstacles can often spur longer term advantages.

A few years ago, I visited a number of maquiladora firms in Mexico. They were creatures of development policy: situated in industrial parks constructed with government assistance and advice, purchasing inputs and exporting under licenses in free trade zones, individual owners receiving training from their government supported industrial association. All were concerned about Chinese competition: despite proximity to the US market, they simply could not compete on price. As we talked, it became clear that they had no clear strategy to compete with Chinese low-wage manufacturing other than to hope the government would come up with a different protected niche for them to occupy. Their strategic mentality was that of franchisers: astute managers of businesses whose design, cost structure, production method, and market had been provided by others. In China, meanwhile, development policy was aiming to upgrade: export-oriented firms should turn to the internal market and raise wages. The government's tools were regulatory, financial, and administrative adjustments. And they were pouring resources into universities, knowledge-based industries, and high tech. The market spaces opened up for others by these policies spurred economic activity in other countries. I had met assembly and textile factory owners in Thailand and Brazil who were far more nimble in their search for rents as the terrain shifted. In this sense, "Mexico" could not compete. But back in Mexico City, maquiladora manufacturing was last year's fad. I heard no sympathy for the plight of the owners I had been visiting. Mexican government policy was to upgrade: the energy was in high-tech, knowledge-based industry. At the same time, a nimble factory bread company was buying outdated cookie factories across the American South while a Mexican cement company embarked on a program of Asian and European expansion intended to circumvent quotas blocking access to the US market and ended up becoming a leading global player. A new division was opening between Mexican firms with access to global finance and those without.

Even the countries we call "rentier states" may or may not be able to capture the rent. Despite—or within the framework of—collective action through OPEC, oil-extracting countries compete with one another to offer a competitive rate of return to big oil. They have the normal tools of taxation, regulation and rules about foreign investment, alongside public spending powers of inducement at their disposal, and the informal mechanisms of coercion and corruption in which extractive industries are often embedded. Some may tax heavily while others may force the oil majors to invest in local firms or hire and train local labor. Some may promise to build infrastructure—or charge for infrastructure. Local militias and senior politicians may need to be paid off. The labor force will have some power to capture gains, depending on citizenship and migration law, family law, welfare law, labor law, and much more. Some may have the capacity to mobilize domestic savings or finance for exploration and development, others not.

Meanwhile, oil multinationals will have know-how, technology, expertise, access to capital, relationships with others in the chain of production, transport, refining, and distribution that will be protected by property, contract, corporate structure, and regulations of many sorts. From the perspective of big oil, it will come down to rate of return, a calculation of future gains and costs relative to other opportunities after factoring in the relevant risks. Their leverage will change over the course of an investment: at first, perhaps they compete with others for the license, later they will be the only game in town. Or the reverse: at the start, their power to withhold investment gives them leverage that will be foregone once the development is under way. They, the government, and all the local parties will seek to lock in their entitlement to rent—and will seek to renegotiate that entitlement whenever their leverage seems to strengthen.

In the end, the gains from trade will be distributed across these many claimants: inside the rentier state, inside big oil, among firms further along in the production process, suppliers, corporate home states, and consumers. In all these locations, the invulnerability to competition that comes with the ability to exclude allows someone to capture the gain. Whether that ability arises within the firm, within the sector, or within the nation, it will rest on entitlements, even where it looks like a quality or price advantage. It is in this sense that entitlements are the stakes in struggle.

LAW AS EXPRESSION: ADVOCACY AND RESOLUTION

Legal differences between and within countries at the most detailed level are contested by people who believe they unfairly exclude them from participation in economic gain. All countries now understand that you have to strategize your insertion into the global economy by arranging the institutions over which you have some control to enable economic actors you prefer to get and keep the gains. As a result, people have ample incentive to argue about the relative appropriateness of rules favoring themselves and other people and to develop a vocabulary for doing so. When legal reasons are effective in reallocating gains, law distributes by force of argument.

Legal materials offer people the opportunity to express particular gains in universal terms. Legal arguments sometimes pass smoothly into effective reception, articulation a decisive resolution of past struggle that others feel unable or unwilling to challenge. At other moments, they can be sharply contested by people preferring other outcomes. The vocabulary for struggle may be both narrowly technical and broadly principled and can often be associated with ideological alternatives and images of national interest common in general public discussion. As law has become an ever more global vocabulary of assertion and dispute, the lexicon of possible arguments has grown broader and more flexible.

Nevertheless, like other professional vocabularies of dispute, law reflects the shared experience that some kinds of arguments are inappropriate—and likely to be ineffective—on the international stage. It rarely seems appropriate in international affairs, even among determined adversaries, to argue that God intended us to win—or, for that matter, that our superior power means we can just take what we like. People may think that, may say it at home, but in transnational argument people shy away from asserting their interests this directly. They come up with "reasons": historical reasons, economic reasons, legal reasons, reasons rooted in common ideas about justice or utility. When representatives of the Islamic State of Iraq and the Levant spoke about their gains as confirmation of the will of God, it confirmed their outsider status almost as clearly as the beheadings that accompanied the video message.

It seems to be a quality of professional disputation to frame one's claims in an ostensibly general language. The result is often a somewhat—but not too—technical vocabulary of arguments: claims about what will work, how much things will cost, what the impact on health or growth or the environment will be. Many of the arguments people bring to bear have their roots in professional or academic fields like economics, development policy, political or social theory, or history. By the time they are brought to bear in policy discussions, rigorous analytics and careful research have often given way to a looser vulgate of "rules of thumb" and "best practice." When these arguments are effective, people experience them as analytically sound. When consensus weakens, they are more likely to be experienced as ideologically driven or the transparent expression of opposing interests. To function as a shared vocabulary of debate, law needs to be capacious enough for advocacy in both directions while creating the effect of decisive resolution frequently enough to seem both useful and legitimate.

I was first struck by this in the late 1980s when a young partner from a law firm I had worked for in Washington was asked to assist in the development of what became the Reagan and later Bush administration's Structural Impediments Initiative, a bold effort to get Japan to change aspects of its internal legal, institutional, and cultural landscape that were thought to disadvantage American companies seeking to do business in Japan. The job was to help frame the obstacles faced by these American companies so that they could be presented by the US trade representative in negotiations with the Japanese.

There was, of course, an element of bareknuckle demand for market access: we want more of the gains or we'll exclude you from our markets. But that left a great deal to be discussed. For one thing, how ought the USTR to distinguish between strong and weak claims by American industry for inclusion in the initiative? Everyone claimed that without government help, jobs would be lost in key congressional districts. Rather than simply assess their lobbying budget, it seemed useful to have a way of analyzing their claims in technical terms. The United States also needed a way of assessing the rule changes in Japan for which their arguments were strongest. This seemed to require some kind of common vocabulary for discussion with Japanese experts. It was not enough to say simply: we just want this more than you want that. Negotiation seemed to require principles, reasons, and some kind of distance between positions and interests. We needed a way to say that the rule changes we wanted would align things properly while their preferences would not.

The broad framework for thinking this through was provided by trade law. The existing trade agreements were too general to determine the outcome—and besides, the United States was hoping to extend those agreements, breaking new ground in its demands for changes by Japan. In a very general way, however, the trade system did offer a way of talking about legal and cultural arrangements. It begins by imagining that the governments of "Japan" and the "United States" aggregate political and economic interests of their respective societies and confront one another as representatives of those interests. At stake in the discussion are legal rules—tariffs and other regulations—that may be said to favor home country interests. To determine which rules can stay and which must go requires people to distinguish those rules that are part of the background necessary to support market activity and are presumptively legitimate from those that distort normal economic exchange and permit the extraction of rent and are presumptively dubious. Market-supporting rules should be enforced while market-distorting rules that functioned as "non-tariff barriers" to trade or otherwise rendered trade "unfair," ought not to be promulgated.

These terms did not have clear or settled meanings. There were a number of specific regulatory regimes constructed in the shadow of this idea, and people had a general sense about the distinction between market-supporting and market-distorting. There were clear cases on both sides: private law rules of contract and property, police protection, and stable financial arrangements, on the one side, subsidies for local business and regulations that explicitly excluded foreigners, on the other. From there, people could intuit a landscape of plausible and implausible arguments. They could imagine people pushing back and forth on the distinction: your rules distort, those favoring me support. There was a kind of loose background regime where these arguments could engage one another, located in a complex interaction among industrial lobbyists, academic experts, government officials (institutionally structured in different ways in Washington and Tokyo) participating in intergovernmental negotiations, all in the shadow of the General Agreement on Tariffs and Trade, other trade agreements, and the background consensus of the professional communities devoted to their interpretation.

And so the team went to work. Was the requirement that cars be outfitted to drive on the left in Japan a distortion permitting Japanese manufacturers already tooled up to produce them to capture gains that would otherwise flow to Detroit? What about the requirement that consumer products be labeled in Japanese? That technical manuals be written in Japanese? What about the regulations covering the teaching of English in Japanese primary schools? Each of these ideas was seriously discussed, along with hundreds of others, from Japanese land use arrangements, public infrastructure finance, and retailing practices to the American budget deficit and domestic savings rate. Since it is rules and rents all the way down, there is no principled or analytically precise way of figuring out what is background and what is distortion. It depends on what you think is normal.[9] Nevertheless, the Japanese were willing to undertake the discussion in these terms, and so were the Americans. The result was a satisfying and useful vernacular for struggling over the claims of American and Japanese industry for favorable rules. The seemingly unlimited potential to reinterpret elements of a nation's legal arrangements as "non-tariff barriers to trade" because of their differential impact on local and foreign actors was part of what made the legal vocabulary so appealing.

Many of rules that differed in Japan and the United States did not arise for discussion, either because everyone assumed they were part of a normal market-supporting rule system or simply because no one in industry thought to contest them. Lots of those rules allocated gains among different actors involved in economic activities linked to trade: between creditors and debtors, large and small enterprises, financiers and producers, and so forth. These battles had already been won and lost. After the Structural Impediments Initiative was concluded, it would have been possible to reassess the situation and search for regulatory tools that had escaped contestation but that could now be adjusted to strengthen the "bargaining power" or change the "competitiveness" of various actors: perhaps antitrust rules, labor law, environmental law, taxation, and so on. Looked at with new eyes, perhaps these also departed from the normal, permitted the extraction of unearned rent. And so the struggle would continue.

We might reimagine Ricardo's picture of trade to foreground the role of law in the distribution of gains, attending both to the uncontested arrangements

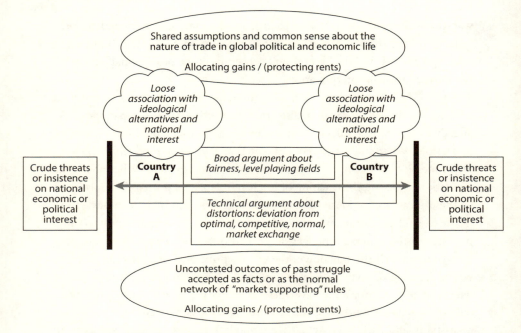

Figure 6.3 Professional Argument over Rules Distributing Gains from Trade

allocating gains and to the language for disagreement about whether those al-locations are normal rules supporting market competition and productivity or illegitimate intrusions of political power distorting competition to permit the extraction of "rent."

We can speculate about what makes the "rent" versus "cost" or the "market-supporting versus -distorting" vocabularies attractive for people struggling over the gains. One factor seems to be the analytic chiasma on which they rest. All gains could be said to reflect costs, if we include opportunity costs and the costs of acquiring, defending, and utilizing the entitlements to exclude others. In this sense, "rent" is simply a pejorative for profit or gain: other people's profits recast as unearned "rents" rather than reflections of their contributions. In another sense, it is rent all the way down: everyone's bargaining powers arise from the distribution of entitlements. There is no generally accepted and decisive analytic for drawing a line between background rules that support costs and those that generate rents. It depends on what seems ordinary and what seems the result of power. Similarly, all rules that affect relative prices might be seen either as "unfair barriers to trade" or as the normal regulatory infrastructure for market activity.

Another factor that made this vocabulary attractive was the subtle link between this apparently technical—if analytically not very robust—way of arguing and differing national and ideological visions of normal economic activity. It is clear that the opposing interests of Japanese and American business were at stake. People referred to what was going on as a "trade war." But neither party needed to say directly, "I'd like more of the gains, thank you." They could appeal to a purportedly neutral or shared analytic of "fairness": everyone should support and no one should distort the conditions for trade. The word "fairness" itself operates in at least two registers: as a technical synonym for trade based on market-supporting rules, and as a general normative expression of disapproval. Although this may seem an idiosyncratic case, the association of "war" with technical argument is routine. Even when presidents speak about "defeating" the enemy or, as Vice President Joe Biden put it, "follow[ing] ISIS to the gates of hell," a military campaign takes shape and acquires legitimacy in arguments to Congress, to allies, or to the press, in a technical vocabulary of appropriate and proportional force.

The trade vocabulary is also open-ended in a way that makes it easy to associate with larger ideological commitments. The market-supporting/-distorting distinction is loosely linked to ideological disagreement over the appropriate scope of government. To someone who favors disembedding the global economy from political life, lots of rules (particularly in other countries) will seem like distortive licenses to extract rents. For others, more regulatory arrangements (at least at home) will seem part of the normal background to market bargaining. A trade war fought in these terms will accommodate a vicious struggle over the allocation of gains—as well as over large-scale ideological positions—while also remaining sufficiently technical to permit a wide range of intermediate resolutions. After all, once the matter has been settled, the outcome will be normal: anything else would be an illegitimate distortion.

The outcome of arguments tethered, however loosely, to national interests and ideological positions also distributes power among those interests and positions. The persuasive power or legitimation effect of Japanese and American demands in future struggles was affected by their relative success in the Structural Impediments Initiative. While the initiative was under way, people were assessing—and reassessing—the relative "power" of American and Japan. Was Japan's spectacular success in penetrating American markets—and America's dismal record in reverse—a sign of American decline? Or had Japan been cheating, burdening its economy with government interference for short-term gains in ways that set the stage for a future decline or postponed an inevitable reckoning with American manufacturing prowess? The ideological stakes were also clear. The East Asian Tigers were being touted at the time as examples of the economic development success that comes with neoliberal policies of deregulation and trade liberalization. Japan was chastised for the reverse: unfairly structuring their internal market and supporting their export leaders for advantage. If it turned out that the Japanese legal and institutional arrangements targeted by the initiative were acceptable, the persuasive effect of arguments for market liberalization would be reduced and the legitimacy of strategic government intervention as a tool of economic development increased.

It remains a puzzle how experts experience their engagement in argument using a vocabulary with these characteristics. That it would be useful to have a vocabulary for advocacy and resolution that was linked, but not displaced, by interests and ideological commitments, and that was technical in feel but plastic enough to permit a range of positions and resolution, is clear. Using the vocabulary leaves a feeling that one both is and is not speaking about interests and ideologies, and that resolutions are analytically defensible but not analytically required. When I have discussed the "market-supporting/market-distorting" framework with trade professionals over the years, I have found a kind of looseness in their relationship to the rhetorical tools of their profession. The most sophisticated players in some way know—and don't know—that the distinction rests on a commonsense baseline understanding of the normal relationship of government to economic life about which there is no consensus. They know their apparently technical discussion is also—or ultimately—about ideology and interest in just the ways the technical distinction assumes away. But somehow all this conduces to a kind of sophisticated satisfaction. The point is not that it makes sense analytically, or that it avoids ideological and political commitments, but that it is useful, is shared, functions as a way to discuss and resolve differences—perhaps precisely because it straddles the technical and the political. Theirs is a sophisticated disenchantment.

Whatever the experience of using this kind of technical-strategic vocabulary in struggle, all kinds of people have learned to do so. It is not only—or even primarily—the US trade representative and his or her counterpart in Japan who debate these assessments. People everywhere in transnational economic life argue to change the rules so they can capture gains. They identify points in the production process where value is generated and try to position themselves to exclude others by deploying entitlements. They urge the government to take a stand against their adversaries and defend what they have extracted from governments at home and abroad. Some of their successes sink into the background while others come to be contested by their adversaries as "unfair" departures from normal market arrangements.

No authority stands in the background overseeing, adjudicating, and enforcing the outcomes of these battles over the distribution of gains. The World Trade Organization, often imagined as providing a governance framework for global trade, is simply one space among many for carrying on the struggle, where the uncertain line between market-supporting and market-distorting rules can be argued out. Nor is the WTO itself structured as a governing institution above member states. At best it provides a framework for horizontal bargaining among governments about tariffs and regulations that can be understood to function like tariffs, along with a dispute resolution mechanism whose enforcement depends on the relative willingness and ability of member governments to exact or bear costs vis-à-vis one another.[10]

The common framework for discussion is more vocabulary than institution. People contest rules favoring their adversaries by expanding an analytic frame loosely rooted in what they understand to be "trade law": part national statute, part precedent from other disputes and other regimes, and part simply what they imagine any law worth the name would stigmatize as "unfair." In this they are not unlike my grandmother confronting a foreign hotelier. The non-tariff barrier discussion is characteristic of many international struggles undertaken in legal language: at once technical and open to association with broader ideological positions and interests, sufficiently malleable to permit a range of possible (strong) arguments for various positions, and yet capable of defending outcomes in terms that sound at once principled and analytically sound.

LAW AND THE STATUS OF FORCES AMONG GROUPS

The countless individual struggles that drive global political and economic life leave patterns in their wake. The winners and losers are not only individuals or companies, but nations, regions, social groups, economic sectors, and ideological positions. The Structural Impediments Initiative was intended to adjust the relative power of industries, labor, commercial, and financial interests between Japan and the United States. It was widely understood as a test of the two nation's relative powers and of the persuasive authority of an ideological commitment to deregulation. It affected the relative positions of importers and exporters, Japanese and American manufacturers, consumers and producers as they looked ahead to future conflicts of interest.

Legal arrangements everywhere affect the balance of power between groups, changing the bargaining power of individuals and firms in ways they are not able to change or negotiate away on their own. The status of forces between debtors and creditors, investors and public authorities, consumers and producers, both across national boundaries and within them, rests on legal rules and institutions that may be the product of intense conflict or simply an unintended byproduct of arrangements made for other reasons. Airline regulations affect costs and relative powers of consumers and airline industry players, banking regulations those between debtors and creditors, laws of war those between well-equipped modern armies and insurgents. Large firms and financial institutions often find it easier to exercise and enforce their entitlements transnationally than small firms, consumers, and workers. On the other hand, patterns of extraterritorial antitrust and international administrative cooperation may strengthen some medium-sized companies at the expense of large monopolies.

Third parties and struggles are also affected. Things the United States failed to achieve in negotiations with Japan were harder for others to achieve in parallel negotiations elsewhere. How far it seemed possible to go in questioning the distortive impact of Japanese background rules abroad affected the appetite of trade negotiators and commercial interests in other places. Success in challenging a Japanese background rule as a non-tariff barrier emboldened people to try similar arguments elsewhere. And there was also a backlash—perhaps the United States had pushed things a bit far and a greater respect for regulatory differences should be encouraged.

At stake is not only the distribution of gains, but the large-scale direction of society. Economies configured differently will operate differently, just as different allocations of legal capacities and authority will generate divergent polities. By tracing the impact of legal forms on the economic and political actors and activities they constitute, people can identify choices among different political and economic trajectories. They can struggle to identify and build alternative, even equally efficient or democratic, modes of economic and political life with diverging patterns of inequality, alternate distributions of political power and economic benefit, more or less space for experimentation or contestation.

Although the significance of legal arrangements that shift power among groups is widely understood, the responsibility of those arrangements for economic and political outcomes is routinely overlooked. In September 2010, I traveled to Yaroslavl, Russia, for a meeting organized by then Russian President Medvedev's office to consider the efforts necessary to lay the foundation for a "knowledge-based" Russian economy to reduce dependence on extractive industries. In 2011, in Astana, Kazakhstan, I heard a great deal about the president's plans to develop a more diversified economy. In 2012, planners in Doha described their plans to lay the foundations for a "knowledge-based" economy by 2022 to reduce their reliance on natural gas. Mexico had this in mind as they moved from low-wage manufacturing to high tech. So did China. In all these cases, the tools were legal and administrative changes to reallocate opportunities to garner rent in the name of social transformation: adjusting rules on credit, education policy, immigration, intellectual property, local autonomy, export and import licensing: turning the levers of state power to allocate gains to those who would innovate as they had once been turned to those who would industrialize. By changing the rules, the privileged sectors—investors, innovators, entrepreneurs, national champions—would be strengthened.

Although people feel confident they can identify the levers necessary to change the allocation of power and wealth among social groups, economic sectors, or individual firms, this rarely translates into the feeling that something could be done about inequality, whether locally, nationally, or globally. People who readily understand allocations among firms, industries, or nations as the outcome of struggle nevertheless interpret patterns of inequality as in some way natural. People intended to move people from the country to the city, transform peasants into factory workers, remodel low-wage industries into innovation clusters, but no one intended inequality. People intended to liberate capital here, expand liquidity there, open these markets, restrict access to credit somewhere else, manage exchange rate fluctuation, and expand opportunities for securitized investment, but no one intended fiscal "imbalances."

One answer may be the tendency of past wins and losses to sink back into the "normal" or even the "constitutional." Large changes that emerge from struggles sometimes do seem "constitutional": they shift the institutional terrain, settle some debates while opening others, strengthen some political and economic actors while weakening or excluding others. The powers of a sovereign wealth fund that began as an instrument of policy can come to seem part of a nation's constitutional separation of powers. Within the European Union, a change in the institutional structure for managing bailouts—like the 2012 European Stability Mechanism—may consolidate a distributive settlement of risk among economic players and narrow the channel for political debate within and between member nations. The invention of new legal instruments—the "credit default swap"—may destabilize settled expectations and risk allocations. Over time, they may come to seem indistinguishable from property rights with longer historical pedigrees. Calling a result of struggle "constitutional" may also help to make it so. Constitutionalization—locking some things in, locking some actors out—is as much a strategy of engagement as a map or foundation for government.

The background common sense of expert vocabularies may constitutionalize inequality in this sense. International lawyers, for example, typically share an unstated presumption that the world of international politics is somehow prior to and more real than the artificial net of international rules they have created: the member states are somehow more real than the international institutions in which they are members. Real states like Israel are somehow automatically more legitimate and solid than legal "entities" like the Palestinian National Authority. On a larger scale, the idea that religion is part of the prehistory of international law helps consign religious ideas and institutions to the margins of international politics, just as international law's understanding that the commercial world of the market and the private world of the family lie outside its purview distributes power over families to states while disempowering states relative to the global economy. All these ideas generate narratives and institutions and expectations that shift the powers and statuses of people. When international law speaks in the language of universals, it acts as a cloak covering the distributive practices it authorizes and accepts.

The relative status of law itself may also be a factor in the distribution of power and the consolidation of inequality. In the field of development policy, for example, the relative authority of economics has outpaced that of law or other social sciences for more than fifty years. When development economics supported strong development states pursuing import substitution industrialization, there were sociolegal strands of thought in law that might have raised questions about the plausibility of a development program so dependent on an effective administrative state. In later decades, when development economics supported weak states, deregulation and open markets, legal expertise might again have raised questions about the plausibility of bringing market-ready institutions into being by calling for them in legislation. The relative hegemony of economic ideas—and the absence of robust legal objections—influenced the balance of forces among elites who favored and disfavored particular policies. The result encouraged the opening of markets without countervailing policies to blunt the potential for sudden changes to unravel local capabilities further or allow new kleptocrats to retain whatever gains were captured.

To say that international law is a "game of the middle powers" is to say that European nations more readily find themselves occupying the symbolic "center" of the global legal order than of the global military or even economic system. By contrast, when the United States speaks in the name of national security, it places an issue on a terrain where Americans are accustomed to deference from European allies. When the world's elites understand an issue like torture in legal terms, European positions may seem more compelling. If they can be reinterpreted in security terms, American positions may have more weight. As war becomes increasingly something to be debated in legal terms, the Europeans find themselves able to punch above their weight in global debates about the legitimacy of one or another campaign. The increasing hegemony of human rights and international adjudication as a framework for diplomacy seems to have deepened inequalities between African and European states.

When people feel their powers reflect a constitutional settlement, the status of forces wrought in the last battle is not only maintained, but also naturalized. This tendency to interpret relative power as a fact of the situation rather than the outcome of prior struggle takes us back to rents. Or, perhaps better, to the obverse of rents: all those arrangements through which gains are distributed that recede from view into the "normal" world of competitive costs and comparative productivity. But global poverty and inequality, like spectacular wealth and military prowess, are not just facts to overcome. They are byproducts of struggle underwritten by legal arrangements and defended in legal terms.

THE DYNAMICS OF DISTRIBUTION AND INEQUALITY: CENTERS AND PERIPHERIES

Global inequalities rest not only on the legal outcomes of individual and group struggles settling the status of forces among them but on arrangements that affect the dynamic interactions among those who lead and those who lag. Indeed, the link between inequality and the legal arrangements among groups is most visible when differences compound dynamically: when the rich get richer, the poor, poorer. People readily intuit that winners rig the game. Although the mechanisms differ, in every society winners find ways to change the rules to make future gains easier to garner. That is why they play for rules. That also happens globally. Large transnational investors and corporations, for example, have used their leverage with their home and host countries to promote treaties guaranteeing the enforcement of commercial arbitral awards, thereby disempowering host state national judiciaries, shifting authority to a professional community of well-paid international arbitrators, and empowering the commercial interests most well represented in the arbitration process.

But the legal foundations for dynamic gains are not only a matter of rigging the rules. Legal arrangements structure patterns of interaction between rich and poor in a variety of ways that encourage the compounding of gains. A conventional way to imagine this would be to shift the focus from people to a larger structure: winners don't rig the rules, the system is already rigged in their favor. This is a common and very useful way to conceptualize global political economy, not as an endless series of struggles among people and groups, but as a biased system or structure. Nevertheless, a midlevel focus on struggle to capture gains, such as I have proposed here, also has much to contribute to our understanding of law's implication in the dynamics of inequality.

For a long time, global inequality was interpreted against the background of a relatively stable relationship between a "first world" of developed nations and everyone else. The main players in the story were the developed nations of the North Atlantic, whose balance of power (or balance of terror) stabilized their domination of a world system before, during, and after colonialism. This arrangement was both naturalized and critiqued. Many global elites—even those most concerned about poverty—tended to imagine that differences between rich and poor reflected a historic fact: some nations "had developed" through an industrial revolution, while others had not yet done so. Once political equality was ensured through decolonization, it seemed appropriate to expect economic inequality to be addressed nationally, if with a bit of foreign aid and expert guidance. Global inequality was an unfortunate fact, rather than the product of ongoing institutional arrangements.

Many social scientists—sociologists, economists, historians—responded to this elite sensibility by developing interpretations of the linkages between wealth in the first world and poverty elsewhere. Historians and anthropologists reexamined the institutional, social, and economic structures associated with colonialism and found parallels in contemporary patterns of global trade, production, and diplomacy.[11] Development economists formulated a range of theories linking underdevelopment in the South to development in the North in a relationship of "dependency."[12] Immanuel Wallerstein drew on these strands, starting in the 1970s, to develop a mode of analysis rooted in the identification and description of "world systems."[13] The aim was to build an interpretation of the relationships among political, economic, and cultural changes on a global scale over long periods: power, knowledge, and capital are exchanged worldwide in structures that generate and reproduce inequality. The central image associated with world systems analysis is the relationship between a "center" and a "periphery." The analytic project is to identify the institutions and social arrangements through which unequal patterns of exchange are enabled and to trace changes in those arrangements over time.

Although the economic fault line between an "underdeveloped" third world and a "modern industrialized" first world no longer defines global economic relations, the intellectual tools generated by these critical traditions remain useful for understanding the process by which the outcomes of struggle generate patterns of inequality. Global political economy is characterized by social and economic dualisms between leading and lagging sectors, regions, economies, nations, and populations every bit as entrenched as the old line between an industrialized "center" and an underdeveloped "periphery." Dualism now crisscrosses national boundaries in a variety of directions, generating inequality within and among national economies along many different axes. The schism of leading and lagging rends the political economic life of nations, cities, and regions as much as it divides the world. And things remain remarkably unequal.

Political authority aggregates in leading cities, regional powers and global hegemons, each with a hinterland of subordinate powers. Economic gains also aggregate as firms or industries capable of extracting a disproportionate share of gains are able to invest, attract talent, raise wages, sustain financial institutions, raise property values and support government services while those with whom they interact at the periphery face competitive pressures that diminish their capacity on each of these dimensions as it becomes ever more unaffordable to break into the geography, institutional system, or mode of production characteristic of the center.

Conventionally, center-periphery analytics have been associated with social science traditions that emphasize the dynamics of a *system*. It has seemed necessary to identify the "center" and "periphery" *of something*: a field, a geography, a history, or world system within which something is the center and something else is the periphery. The system provides the coherence, holding the center and periphery in a relationship, raising the temptation to treat the system as the agent of inequality: the system permits the center to exploit and dominate the periphery. I propose to focus on dynamics of struggle without framing them in a constituted order or system. Imagine the global situation as a kind of dualism without system, generated by the continuous struggle through which gains are distributed. Which legal and institutional arrangements permit gains to aggregate, empower some and not others in future struggle, lock in differences in knowledge, bargaining power, or leverage? Detached from a "system," the asymmetric or hierarchical relationships may be spatial, temporal, or just a matter of mental emphasis. The crucial point is relational: inequality between them compounds as a result of legal and institutional relations affecting their interaction.

This kind of dynamic is easy to see in global value chains, which are often organized around a lead firm or firms able to capture and hold gains disproportionately.[14] Global distributors like Walmart and Carrefour, for example, might be understood to be at the "center" of a value chain running from clothing manufacturers in Bangladesh to consumers in Europe or America. Parts suppliers who must adjust production to meet standards demanded by global automakers may find themselves in the "periphery" of their supply chain. We would not be surprised to learn that lead firms are able to extract a disproportionate share of the gains from trade within the chain, just as first world consumers may have more rent-extracting power vis-à-vis global retailers than their suppliers in Bangladesh.

The dynamic question is whether these differences become self-reinforcing. Leaving aside, for the moment, the legal arrangements that make this possible, it is easy to imagine that lead firms will be able to invest in "upgrading" unavailable to firms at the periphery operating on thinner margins. Firms in the center may be able to use relative monopoly power to intensify competition among potential suppliers or extract know-how generated at the periphery for use elsewhere while protecting their own intellectual property in ways that intensify their bargaining advantage. Suppliers spread across the "periphery" of the global productive system may lack the knowledge, confidence, or experience to utilize the bargaining power they have. As gains fail to come their way, they may find themselves ever less able to figure out how to capture rents, competing in a race to export at the lowest cost, further eroding their share of the gains and their ability to upgrade. Scale often matters a great deal. Large firms with large transaction volume may have access to different financing terms or technical expertise, for example. Lead firms may have greater influence over the public hand across the value chain. Prestige may also play a role. Actors positioned at the "center" may come to be treated as having more bargaining power than their stock of entitlements and authorities would support were they put to the test. When gains at the center are self-reinforcing and firms at the periphery find themselves increasingly unable to extract rents, the global value chain has unleashed a dualist dynamic of downgrading at the periphery and upgrading at the center.

Gunnar Myrdal's loose analytic framework for thinking about economic and social dynamics is useful here.[15] He starts with economic inequality between regions within one country and aims to understand the tendency of differences to become more pronounced over time. In the normal course, he suggests, gains in one region are self-reinforcing.

> The system is by itself not moving toward any sort of balance between forces but is constantly on the move away from such a situation. In the normal case a change does not call forth countervailing changes but, instead, supporting changes, which move the system in the same direction as the first change but much further. Because of such circular causation a social process tends to become cumulative and often to gather speed at an accelerating rate.[16]

Movements of labor, capital, goods, and services are media through which the cumulative process evolves.[17] This is a tendency, not an iron law. In the relationship between the wealthy North and the poorer South, the inner city and the suburbs, the industrial and agricultural sectors, it is difficult to know how change will compound. Expansion in one locality may have "backwash effects" in other localities. The wealthier region may draw further investment, people, and energy from poorer regions toward it, making it ever more difficult for a poorer region to move ahead. Migrants with skills may leave the poorer area, further reducing its potential. But it is also possible for new wealth in one region to stimulate growth elsewhere. Accumulation in one region may generate "spread effects" elsewhere. Mrydal anticipates that the "whole region around a nodal center of expansion should gain from the increasing outlets of agricultural products and be stimulated to technical advance all along the line."[18] What might seem like a backwash effect—outward migration of the talented— may also have countervailing spread effects—the return of remittances or know-how. Centrifugal spread effects may affect localities farther away, where favorable conditions exist for producing raw materials for the growing industries in the centers; if a sufficient number of workers become employed in these other localities, even consumer goods industries will be given a spur. Spread effects may stir sufficient expansionary momentum to overcome backwash effects from the older centers allowing new centers of self-sustained economic expansion to emerge.[19]

Myrdal emphasizes that there is no reason to anticipate that these forces will cancel one another out, or that spread—or backwash—effects will dominate. It depends, he says, on all kinds of social, institutional, and other conditions. In the same way that Kaplinsky expanded the range of factors that might contribute to "rent," Myrdal opens the analysis to a wide range of "institutional" factors that might link what happens in leading and lagging areas. His method is less an analytic than a list: a checklist of salutary and perverse effects that can arise and an evocation of the vicious and virtuous cycles that can unfold. He orients the analysis to identification of linkages, potential positive and negative effects, vicious and virtuous cycles, relatively stable situations and tipping points at which good or bad things compound quickly. As a planner, one can only remain attentive to the emergence of positive or negative movements and adjust conditions as best one can.

Myrdal has relatively little to say about the specific role of law in the dualist dynamics between unequal regions.[20] He does consider the importance of the welfare state where "state policies have been initiated which are directed toward greater regional equality: the market forces which result in backwash effects have been offset, while those resulting in spread effects have been supported."[21] He contrasts this with developing nations where the absence of such policies has allowed differences between regions to accelerate or where a state functions as a force multiplier for the wealthy.

> The term "state" is used here to include all organized interferences with the market forces. . . . The traditional role of the "state" in this inclusive sense was mainly to serve as a means for supporting the cumulative process tending toward inequality. It was the economically advancing and wealthier regions and social groups which were the more active and effective in organizing their efforts, and they usually had the resources to stop organizational efforts by the others. And so the "state"—which stands here for organized society—usually became their tool in advancing their interests.[22]

At the global level, Myrdal notes that the absence of a world state to counteract backwash effects makes the global situation more like that within those developing nations where an ineffective state allows inequalities to grow. Although this is worrisome, he is at least reassured that the global situation is not akin to the historically more common situation of an "oppressor state" linked to the interests of the wealthy interfering so as to heighten and confirm inequality.

On that score, he may have been too optimistic. If we take his invitation to consider the "state" as the sum of "organized society," and consider legal arrangements across the world, there is a great deal of "state" in global political and economic life. Law is present whenever gains are distributed, facilitating their aggregation or ensuring their dispersion. Legal entitlements constitute actors, allocate opportunities for gain, and establish patterns of bargaining power in these midlevel relationships of differentiation and influence. By placing the Ricardian/Kaplinsky analytics of rent alongside Myrdal's analysis of the dynamic relationships among centers and peripheries, it is possible to trace the role of law not only in the distribution of gains, but in the process by which inequalities are reproduced or exacerbated.

At the simplest level, whenever law distributes gains or reinforces differences among social, economic, or political groups, it may initiate a center-periphery dynamic if the winners are able to use their rents to capture further gains out of reach to those who lost out in the first round. Those with monopoly power in the initial round have resources their competitors do not when it comes time to invest in all the things Kaplinsky identifies as rent enhancing: new organizational arrangements, new technology and skills, economies of scale, and so forth. Similarly, legal arrangements facilitating rent capture at the periphery will facilitate upgrading there in the second round. Beyond its initial distributive impact, law affects center-periphery dynamics in at least three other ways. Law can link or delink economic activities in the center and periphery. The most obvious example is tax and transfer from leading to lagging. Another would be legal rules that aim to integrate productive activity in leading areas with productivity elsewhere such as local content, employment, technology transfer, or investment requirements that link firms benefiting from privileged market access arrangements or free trade manufacturing zones to firms and people in the periphery. Of course, legal rules can also tilt the other way, as when lead firms are prohibited from discriminating in favor of local or lagging providers.

Legal arrangements may also speed or retard flows between a center and periphery. Most obvious would be citizenship and immigration rules that facilitate or impede migration, or banking and currency regulations that impede or expedite the flow of capital in one or the other direction. The impact of law on center/periphery flows may not be immediately visible. Anticorruption enforcement, for example, may stigmatize off-budget transfers that benefit the periphery, consolidating the center's lead in access to more formal financing. Family law, social security, and labor law may have as important an impact on migration as law explicitly regulating immigration.

Finally, law may affect the relative powers of centers and peripheries to play for rules that would affect their relations in these various ways. Firms at the center may be permitted to lobby and contribute to campaigns and gain preferential access to regulators. Firms at the center may themselves be the regulatory authority. Firms at the periphery may find their efforts stigmatized as corruption or may be too small and numerous to find leverage with rule makers. Or they may be national champions with powerful government allies. Constitutional arrangements may also enhance the powers of peripheral regions in the way states with small populations are privileged in the US Senate.

In analyzing the overall impact of legal arrangements on center-periphery dynamics, Myrdal's typology of "welfare states," "oppressor states," and the "absence" of a state is helpful. In the first instance, one can canvass each of the four kinds of legal arrangements—allocating gains to a center, linking/delinking centers and peripheries, speeding/impeding flows, allocating power over rules—to determine which function to strengthen the center's grip on resources ("oppressor state" analogs) or distribute capabilities and resources back to the periphery ("welfare state" analogs). Globally, as Myrdal recognized, the legal arrangements that influence economic activity in the "absence" of a state will often be more important.

Myrdal's "welfare state" has an analogy at the global level in the many rules that affect bargaining power or determine which economic activities will be relatively "high value," "productive," or "competitive" in the sense I explored in earlier chapters whenever these rules encourage the capture of rent at the periphery. Measures to link leading and lagging sectors or regions productively with one another are common in national legal regimes: local hiring or content requirements, corporate mandates that prioritize links with communities or unions alongside shareholders, lending requirements and incentives targeting credit to peripheral actors, zoning practices linking permits to an office tower downtown with the establishment of a shipping facility in the ghetto, and so on. Many could be translated to the transnational level. Corporations could be discouraged from offloading workers on the state for tax and transfer welfare and encouraged or required to find something these workers might productively do. Many international regimes—the WTO, the European Union, the United Nations—contain rules, administrative arrangements, and explicit policies that aim to strengthen the world's economic and political peripheries and disrupt the backwash effects of economic mobility. Specialized systems of trade preference entitle some poor countries to exclude others from their export markets, capturing more of the rent than would be possible in direct competition with other global producers.

It is also easy to imagine international legal arrangements designed to encourage global spread effects and counteract the tendency of gains to compound in centers. Many aspects of the 1970s project for a "New International Economic Order" aimed to link economic gains in the industrialized world with transfers to less developed regions, encourage the spread effects of technology transfer and local control, ensure access to credit at the periphery, and strengthen the participation of peripheral nations in the machinery of international rule-making.[23] Legal arrangements designed to stabilize commodity prices, whether through administered buffer stocks or liquid futures markets, could alleviate the disproportionate impact of price fluctuations in peripheral markets. Where capital flight is restrained or skilled labor is prevented from leaving peripheral regions, sectors, and nations, spread effects will be stronger than otherwise. They would be stronger still if unskilled labor could move freely across the world, if capital investment in developing regions was required or trade structured to compensate for bargaining power advantages accruing to industries in wealthier economies. Go-slow provisions preventing rapid in- and outflows of speculative capital in thin peripheral markets are intended to serve the same function. Investment rules designed to slow repatriation of profits and ensure local equity participation, labor training, and transfer of technology all aim to mitigate backwash effects.

At the same time, many aspects of the global legal order function as a Myrdalian "oppressor state." Global political and economic winners are given extraordinary powers: the UN Security Council veto for World War II victors is the most visible, but weighted voting arrangements across the international institutional system distribute rule-making power in ways that consolidate the capabilities of the center. The relative powers of creditor and debtor nations in international financial institutions is a striking example. Legal arrangements also affect the tendency of Myrdal's forces of "migration, capital movements and trade" to impoverish poorer regions. Capital mobility rules that permit rapid capital flows in and out of smaller economies, immigration laws that favor the movement of highly skilled workers to the center and prohibit unskilled labor migration, corporate and antitrust laws that encourage consolidation of large distribution chains and discourage the emergence of "national champions" in the periphery or that favor global investors and the "public-private partnerships" of the center but stigmatize the state-owned enterprises of the periphery, intellectual property rules that force global protection for the center's innovations while disfavoring trade in generics and innovations based on copying at the periphery may all generate backwash effects in poor countries. Intellectual property regimes protecting global pharmaceutical and entertainment industries from competition in the developing world and targeted immigration policies reinforcing brain drain are only the most well known.

Many have argued that the trade system compounds the advantages of the leading states who designed it by easing free movement of industrial products while exempting agricultural goods, by focusing on access to markets rather than access to capital, and by focusing on free movement of capital rather than stable public or private access to credit. These rules address challenges to the rent-capturing capacities of firms and nations in the center while leaving challenges at the periphery unaddressed. The WTO's most-favored-nation-based bargaining structure may advantage large economies with multiple trading partners who can force concessions from smaller markets they seek to enter while resisting pressure to open their own market by offering offsetting concessions. Over time, this may consolidate the emergence of market leaders in large economies and impede their emergence elsewhere. At the same time, interests of concern to big powers get on the agenda for global negotiation more easily and more powerful players are able to bargain for rules that support their existing strengths while shielding their weaknesses. The relative success of the global North in placing trade in services and intellectual protection on the world's trade agenda and the failure of the Doha Development Round of trade negotiations are illustrative. Nor is it surprising that as the leading economies negotiated ever lower tariffs among themselves on manufactured goods in the context of the General Agreement on Tariffs and Trade, trade in textiles continued to be covered by a different and more restrictive legal arrangement, the Multi-Fiber Arrangement.

A broad focus on liberalization and deregulation by global rule-making institutions may exacerbate dualist tendencies. Joseph Stiglitz and Andrew Charlton argue that the WTO's insistence on liberalization has a differential impact on poor countries with less capacity to adjust internally.[24] If factors cannot be readily shifted from radios to televisions in country B, opening the economy to the import of radios will not lead to expansion of exports in televisions. It will either demolish the domestic radio sector or place pressure on returns to inputs—here, predominantly wages. If international arrangements force an opening to imports while prohibiting internal arrangements to ease the shift toward television production—perhaps by stigmatizing them as "unfair" or "market-distorting"—country B may not only fail to participate in gains from trade, but may end up worse off. These conditions are pervasive in poor economies, they argue, and without reform, the WTO will continue to distribute gains disfavorably for poor nations and place them in ever more ruthless competition with one another for low-wage manufacturing. Again, where this compounds the relative difference in rent-capturing ability, there will be dualism.

To identify the precise mechanism by which the WTO "forces" countries to liberalize requires an assessment of the socioeconomic impact of rules. Stiglitz and Charlton argue that the pressure to open developing economies arises in part from the most-favored-nation requirement that bilateral concessions be granted to all members of the global scheme. This, they claim, discourages the more specialized arrangements that might shield poor econo-mies while they adjust internally to be able to take advantage of gains from trade. They suggest a corrective: a new global legal arrangement in which all nations would commit to provide "free market access in all goods to all developing countries poorer and smaller than themselves."[25] This seems plau-sible, although a great deal depends on how the most-favored-nation require-ment and the many exceptions to WTO requirements are interpreted and ap-plied over time, as well as how their alternative would fare once professionals began to argue about its meaning and scope of application. My own sense is that Stiglitz and Charlton underestimate the extent to which the existing texts of trade law leave room to defend internal policies.

They are not alone: a shared elite understanding that the WTO "requires" liberalization has tightened the effective meaning of the WTO's rules. Particu-larly in the heyday of neoliberalism, elites in the developed and developing world expected the rules to require deregulation—may even have favored it themselves—and forewent investment in the technical capabilities to assert otherwise.[26] Deregulation is also easy to negotiate: contravening rules, like tariffs, can be costed out and traded. It may also be easier for negotiators to identify distortive rules in the developing world where administrative ca-pacity is thin and industrial policy relies more directly on state ownership, tariffs, subsidies, and licensing schemes than in the more complex regulatory regimes of the industrialized North. In the WTO training sessions for third world bureaucrats that I observed during this period, I was struck by the focus on training participants from poor countries to translate internal poli-cies into the kind of non-tariff barriers to trade that could be negotiated away. Very little attention went into training for offense.

A focus on overtly "welfarist" or "oppressor" legal arrangements is a helpful starting point for identifying the role of rules in global inequality. The more common international situation, however, is the one Myrdal identifies: the ab-sence of a global state intending either to strengthen gains by leading sectors or mitigate backwash effects. All kinds of legal arrangements nevertheless dis-tribute gains, affect the links between leading and lagging regions, speeding or retarding flows of various sorts between them, or distribute authority to play for rules. The easiest way to imagine the impact of law in the absence of a global state is to think about the legal geography or terrain on which economic activities occur. As in any real estate market, it is clear location matters. And as in any city, what matters about location is a function of legal rules determining who can do what where in relation to whom.

Sometime in the 1990s, I heard a London finance maven advising a conference of the superrich on the significance of 1989. His theory was simple: from 1929 until 1989, the terrain on which one could securely and productively invest capital was small. Lots of places were behind the iron curtain, others lacked institutions capable of protecting investment or its productive use. In the terrain open to investment, capital was plentiful relative to labor, and therefore labor was dear while capital faced low returns. After 1989 and the development of liberal institutions across the world of "emerging markets," the terrain for productive investment expanded enormously. The result: capital shortage and labor surplus in the space relevant for productive investment. Time to get out of labor and into capital. It was a dubious story in many ways, but his basic instinct was correct: geography matters. And geography is a legal construct.

The legal geography of the world affects the distribution, flows, and linkages between centers and peripheries as well as returns to capital and labor. In a legal world in which banking, finance, Internet construction and management, and high-tech communication sectors were national monopolies regulated as public utilities in the national interest, the global clustering of these resources and capabilities in "global cities" and "silicon valleys" might be less pronounced. The absence of a global capacity to mitigate backwash and enhance spread effects is itself legally enforced. The legal privilege of every nation to dissent from global arrangements raises an insuperable hurdle in front of efforts to defeat national efforts to consolidate advantage at the periphery by appeals to global norms as well as international efforts to adopt welfarist legal reforms. The territorial separation of public law jurisdictions and the global enforceability of private law together ease the mobility of factors (other than labor) and reduce national capacity to adjust regulations to capture gains, making backwash mitigation more difficult and spread effects harder to encourage from the periphery.

Although many nations seek to give their local industries and national champions a bargaining and rent-capturing advantage, states differ radically in their ability to do so—or to resist efforts by other nations to prioritize competitors. Powerful economic actors often have greater capacity to press for rules both globally and transnationally, particularly where their interests align with powerful states. This is not only the result of disproportionate power in global rule making. A few powerful national regulators write rules in collaboration with leading industrial players that officially or unofficially regulate their industries worldwide.[27] The influence of American (and European) regulators on global airline, entertainment, pharmaceutical, software, and other high-technology industries is clear. Countries with political capacity, energy, and recognized expertise can often expect cooperation with and submission to the extraterritorial effect of their preferred regulation in a world where the extraterritorial effect of each nation's jurisdiction is legally a function of a willingness to assert jurisdiction and the ability to generate cooperation or acquiescence in its exercise.

Single jurisdictions that are home to dominant players in a global industry or sector often have an outside impact on rules governing that industry everywhere. Banking and tax havens that draw capital disproportionately to places like Switzerland, Bermuda, and Luxembourg are the classic examples: small states using their regulatory capability in a world of mobile capital and territorially restricted taxation and criminal prosecution to capture rents. As that happens, the voice of the banking industry in those capitals strengthens, the sophistication of the industry there rises, the reputation of the tax haven grows, and ever more capital flows in. Global cities and their national government have enhanced capacity to tax and redirect those revenues to amenities—including regulatory oversight—conducive to an ever stronger financial sector. Although more capital may flow to tax havens from wealthy centers, the impact on the periphery where capital is scarce may be larger, particularly if reinvestment occurs disproportionately at the center. What is a tax collection headache for large wealthy economies may drain gains wholesale from more peripheral economies. Nations able to rely on effective income or value-added tax administration are less vulnerable and able to consolidate the advantages that accrue to nations that can afford an effective public administration. Tax havens can also have a massive backwash effect when they encourage corruption and the leakage of gains from poor countries with weak public fiscal controls.

Against the background of a global regime of sovereign independence and free capital movement, it has proved incredibly difficult for far larger states, even in collaboration with one another, to reverse the incentive for capital flight. Public international law makes collective response difficult, requiring near unanimity to restrain the sovereign privilege not to enforce foreign tax obligations. Meanwhile, the ubiquity of private work-arounds made possible by permissive national corporate, property, and contract law regimes further encourages backwash effects in places whose only potential for public policy of upgrading depends on effective taxation of corporate entities or wealthy individuals. The passive sociological impact of national rules—heightened by a global legal regime that facilitates the free movement of goods, services, and capital while discouraging distortive national regulations—varies with scale.

The size of the Chinese economy makes whatever approach they take to environmental regulation or wages of tremendous significance for relative costs elsewhere. A Chinese decision to lower manufacturing wages or devalue its currency may set off a cycle of effects in European and American markets, consolidating outsourcing and hollowing out domestic manufacturing capability.

In principle, regional trade agreements may heighten or lessen these effects, just as states may, from Myrdal's perspective, be either oppressive or welfarist in orientation. Unfortunately, trade agreements are not written by a global sovereign hand in the public interest: they emerge from hard bargaining among states that are nominally equal and substantively anything but. The balance of benefits in such agreements will not be equal, although the impact on center-periphery dynamics can be unexpected. The impact of Mexican wage regulation on wages in the United States was heightened by NAFTA, along with the impact of US corn production on Mexican peasant farming. Just as the agreement stimulated peasant migration to the United States by lowering the price of corn in Mexico, it also shifted Mexican manufacturing capacity to export industries both within and beyond earlier free trade zones. These shifts affected the relative returns to agriculture and industry in the two nations, reshuffling what had been centers and peripheries within each national economy.

Uniform transnational legal regimes may affect rich and poor in ways that encourage backwash effects. A UN-sponsored commitment to promote the "rule of law" and criminalize bribery or corruption will have a different impact on states with different national administrative capabilities or economic patterns of formality and informality. Some states may enforce effectively, giving their industries a handicap in some markets and a bargaining advantage in others. In others, anticorruption enforcement may become an opportunity for leading families, social groups, or industries to instrumentalize the state against their foreign or domestic rivals. Informal arrangements and unofficial or off-budget transfers that may perform functions less expensively than the administrative apparatuses that are affordable in the center may be stigmatized. Their suppression may reduce productivity at the periphery while new administrative controls may require funds better spent on arrangements more likely to enhance the potential to capture rent and upgrade.[28]

It is difficult to assess the likely overall impact of the diverse rules and rule systems that constitute the legal geography for global economic activity. But it is possible to develop speculative interpretations that may open new possibilities for strategy. Duncan Kennedy has argued, for example, that the fragmentation of Africa into numerous independent "nations," each with its own elite, may have set in motion political and economic dynamics both within African states and in their relationships with the economic powers of the North that undermined development.[29] Capture of the local political machinery by economic elites was easier, he imagines, while bargaining power vis-à-vis global economic players, whether multinationals or trade negotiators from the United States and Europe, was correspondingly weaker. For heuristic purposes, he contrasts this with China's rise as a single political and economic unit, able to engage the global economy on quite different terms. The objective of such a thought experiment is less reform—fragment the EU and unite Africa—than an opportunity to highlight the significance of background legal and political arrangements in ways that might lead to a reassessment of the potential for well-worn reform strategies and open the way for more dramatic rethinking.

His argument echoes themes introduced by Cardoso and Faletto for Latin America in the early seventies.[30] They argued that internal and transnational structures and patterns of political influence matter for economic development and may systematically disadvantage entire regions. The assimilation of Latin American elites into a hub and spokes global economy encouraged what they termed "dependent" development. Rents were captured and shared (if unequally) between local elites and foreign capital. This locked in patterns of production and trade that relied on foreign capital, reinforcing the hub and spokes model of trade and diminishing the potential for the development of Latin America's own internal market. Inequalities at home increased as elites participating in gains from trade used state power to reinforce their dominance. As a result, Latin American economies grew less robustly than they otherwise might, while entrenching economic and political arrangements that reproduced this development pattern. Although Cardoso and Faletto say relatively little about the role of law in dependent development, the linkages they examine between local elites and global capital, the control local elites exert on national policy, and the background conditions for foreign investment, import substitution industrialization, and participation in trade were all established in legal terms. Had those arrangements been different, the opportunities for rent sharing to compound as dependency may have been less. This kind of continent-wide sociological speculation aims to identify elements of the background legal and institutional geography affecting the political and economic relations of centers and peripheries that might be reimagined or contested.

In any large-scale story, there will be elements of Myrdal's welfare and oppressor states alongside the less visible rules of background geography. The power of center-periphery dynamics within the EU, for example, is only beginning to be understood. Although experts long thought the EU—like free trade—was everywhere a contributor to spread effects, it is now recognized that powerful backwash effects were also unleashed between regions by everything from trade and labor policy to the structure of monetary union. I was practicing law in Brussels as the post-1989 negotiations to link the ex-Soviet societies of Central and Eastern Europe to the European Union got under way. In the first phase, the ex-Soviet economies were encouraged to experience the "shock" of global market prices and placed in the bracing winds of the global free trade order, while member states in the European Union continued to benefit from a variety of national and regional arrangements to encourage spread and discourage backwash effects. As the ex-Soviet states moved from association toward membership, the framework for discussion was an extreme version of the Structural Impediments Initiative. The Eastern/Central Europeans would need to dismantle their entire legal and institutional structure and replace it wholesale with the *acquis communitaire* of existing EU laws and regulations alongside "state of the art" and "best practice" laws imported from one or another EU member state for everything from corporate forms to banking, investment, labor, and consumer protection. It was surprising how little attention was paid to the potential that doing so would initiate backwash effects, hollowing out such industrial, institutional, and human capital as had been built up in the East.[31] Similar rules in different locations—often without countervailing buffers and social safety nets—were likely to have very different impact. The integration of the German Democratic Republic into the Federal Republic offered a similar lesson in Myrdalian dynamics, despite massive efforts to resist the forces of backwash by public investment and subsidization in the East.

Recent work suggests that backwash dynamics continue to be encouraged by apparently neutral principles of European Law as they are interpreted and applied. Damjan Kukovec, for example, argues that general legal principles— "free movement" or "social considerations"—at the core of the endeavor are applied in ways that heighten the inequality between the economies of the European center and periphery.[32] The devil here is in the details—in the precise ways that universal principles turn out to have diverse meanings and get applied in ways that contribute to dualism. For Kukovec, the "free movement" principle is applied so as to open economies in the East, unleashing classic backwash effects, while the "social considerations" principle meant to limit or balance free movement is interpreted to protect labor in the West from competition, weakening the spread effects of growth to the East. Ermal Frasheri has argued that the structural and cohesion funds intended to reduce inequality across Europe in fact effected a net transfer from the periphery to the center, while general policies adopted in the name of "democratization," "rule of law," or "economic development" had the effect, at the periphery, of undermining parliamentary democracy, encouraging deindustrialization, and strengthening the security state.[33] In this way, a universal program designed to equalize relations across the EU turned out to accentuate the political and economic distance between the European center and periphery. Analysis of the differential impact of austerity policies mandated by the European Central Bank after the global financial crisis on economies at the periphery of Europe for which they meant compulsory internal devaluation and wage suppression has brought center-periphery analytics into popular discussion.

In each case, inequalities were deepened as people pursued political and commercial interests in the shadow of entitlement structures that set up an asymmetric and disempowering dynamic, legitimated by a cloak of self-narration that what is going on is either a natural and inevitable adjustment driven by economic facts or a hopeful kind of win-win upgrading across the EU. In some sense, "Brussels" is to blame. But it would be more accurate to pin the blame on the routine ways in which these principles were interpreted and policies applied by professionals without attention to their dynamic impact on inequality.

The dualist dynamics of inequality in global political and economic life are not fundamentally different from center-periphery dynamics in other settings. Inequalities arise and are deepened by a complex combination of powers and ideas within a legal framework within countries between regions, sectors, and social groups. Although it may have seemed that Myrdal's categories of oppressive states and welfare states paralleled the distinction between the developed and underdeveloped worlds, the situation was always more complex. State power has everywhere been exercised through a mix of formal and informal arrangements that actively encourage, discourage, and simply ignore spread or backwash effects. Since Myrdal wrote, many peripheral nations have developed more complex state machinery, while the national welfarist commitment of advanced nations has attenuated. In one sense, all nations are postdevelopmental, sitting on top of a history of development policy failures and successes. All countries today have political characteristics and face economic challenges once thought characteristic of underdeveloped societies. Politics has become a diminished shadow of economics as political institutions have been instrumentalized by economic interests. All face strategic choices among modes of insertion in the global economy, find their economies riven with market failures and information and public goods problems for which they lack instruments to respond, and find themselves talking about new strategies for growth rather than the efficient management of a relatively stable business cycle. And all states are a mix of "welfarist" and "oppressor" elements atop a complex background legal geography. As a result, the challenges of inequality and structural dualism are as present within as among nations.

In the metropolitan Detroit region where I grew up, the slow—and then very rapid—dynamic of inequality between the city of Detroit and its many suburbs arose as people struggled in their own lives for economic advantage against a background of racism, social expectations about the racism of others, and a legal structure that fragmented authority among dozens of small communities, each with independent responsibility for schools, police, zoning, and taxation. With only very weak regional or statewide mechanisms to encourage spread effects, backwash effects predominated as one after another suburb found itself pushed up or pulled down by the intense residential segregation by income, race, and ethnicity that resulted from the struggles of individual families to advance and preserve their property values and mobility expectations for their children. Without the racism, the results may have been different. With different regional legal arrangements, they would certainly have been different.

As everyone realized, for example, with "cross-district bussing," the capacity of families to capture educational rents by purchasing property in a slightly more exclusive suburb would have been seriously diminished. It is an open question whether enough wealthy whites would have moved even further out to consolidate their control over the most productive schools. Lots of law would have shaped the outcome, from commuter charges, gasoline taxes, and the structure of towns and school districts in outlying counties to the network of highways. At the global level, the interaction of social arrangements, political interests, ideological commitments, and legal arrangements are more difficult to untangle. But the situation is parallel. As in Detroit, the global potential for backwash effects rests on a combination of legal arrangements and attitudes. The world's elites share ideas—including ideas about one another's ideas—just as Detroit residents had varying background notions about the relationship between race and privilege. The power we call political "leverage" or economic "bargaining power" is a condensation of moves made possible by a context of expectation and interpretation as well as entitlement.

Tracing the spread and backwash effects enabled by legal arrangements shifts our focus away from "who did it" to "how did it happen." If we are looking for agency in the reproduction of inequality, it may be most useful to say that it rests with the system of entitlements and expectations that link people in relationships of relative privilege and vulnerability, with the habits of society, with the ideas, aims, and identities of the participants themselves, and with the objectives and enforcement authority of the state. These are the "indestructible powers" that give rise to rents and facilitate spread or backwash effects. As people act in the shadow of these authorities and constraints, the complex reciprocal relations between centers and peripheries unfold.

Law is important for people engaged in struggle because it enables the capture of gains, distributes power and resources between groups, and structures relations between leading and lagging regions, firms, and nations. Nevertheless, the distributive impact of law has rarely been a focal point in mainstream international legal scholarship. Several generations of international legal scholars from the world's political and economic peripheries have engaged the mainstream to identify and remedy patterns of disadvantage. Feminist legal scholars have done likewise. Important and insightful as their contributions have been, they have so far not succeeded in placing distributive issues at the center of mainstream concern. Part of the explanation is the mainstream conviction that political economy issues lie outside international law's mandate. Economics is for economists and politics is what one hopes to beat into the plowshares of legal order. World political economy seems to require large-scale narratives of historical necessity—the nature of capitalism—or ethnographies and micro-sociological study of globalization's impact on very particular communities and transactions, neither of which lie within the skill set of most international legal professionals. And they have been more interested in other things: whether international law exists, how it binds sovereigns, and adds up to a workable and potentially universal legal order. As they have pursued these interests, however, they have reformed and reimagined international law in ways that have made it a sophisticated tool in distributive struggle. In the next chapter I explore this surprising turn. Worried about law's frailty and faithful to its universal and humanist promise, experts in the field have encouraged an increasingly sophisticated vocabulary for political and economic struggle.

CHAPTER 7

INTERNATIONAL LEGAL EXPERTISE: INNOVATION, AVOIDANCE, AND PROFESSIONAL FAITH

Across the twentieth century, as law expanded its reach into global political and economic life, legal professionals transformed their understanding of what law is and how law works. As legal expertise became sophisticated, plural and eclectic, law became an ever more powerful strategic tool for people struggling for advantage on the global stage. Today, a map of legal exposure, risk, and opportunity is part of the basic toolkit for political and economic actors operating transnationally. Yet when people reflect on the role of law in global affairs, they rarely focus on law as an instrument of distribution or cause of inequality. They may use legal argument and assertion ruthlessly for political or economic gain, but they think about international law more benignly as a sign of the potential for order and justice in global affairs. This chapter explores the relationship between these two sides of contemporary international legal expertise: an expanding practice of struggle wrapped in the promise of justice. It is a relationship sustained by a kind of professional faith or practice of fealty that strengthens law's authority while weakening the profession's sense of responsibility. The chapter ends with a suggestion for turning the internal diversity and pluralism of contemporary global legal activity toward a more responsible professional practice.

A possible explanation for the profession's aversion to exploring law's engagement with conflict, distribution and inequality might be a disconnect between the hard-boiled view of practitioners and the preoccupations of scholars arguing for international law's larger significance and potential. In the late nineteenth and early twentieth centuries, for example, as practitioners were expanding law's role in transnational commercial affairs and building new public institutions, many scholars were focused on clarifying and limiting the norms that would count as legally valid, shrinking the corpus of international legal rules just as practitioners were pushing the boundaries in all directions. Practitioners engaged in global struggle today are also more likely to think of law first as a strategic tool or frustrating limit than are academics focused on legal activity as constitutive of global legal order. Military professionals understand law as a tool for shaping the battlefield, businesspeople have become strategists of regulation, harnessing public and private standards to define their brand, defend their market, and distribute gains across global value chains, and lawyers promote their skills to anyone with an international project who might find it useful to assess the status of forces affecting its realization. Scholars do tend to see something else: a fragile and virtuous legal order of imperfect rules foreshadowing a future cosmopolitan order for a world of political conflict and economic competition.

But the relationship between practical savvy and scholarly vision is more complex. Scholars routinely adjust their ideas with an eye to their practical impact. They work hard to reinterpret what might be visionary as practical and what works as visionary. This double agenda is useful and reassuring for people who use legal assertion in struggle. Their legal assertions are also visionary, linked to order and justice. When you ask international lawyers, academic or practical, about their ongoing projects, proposals, and engagements, they readily describe the immediate terrain of their struggle with clarity. If you ask them to reflect on that experience—what it says about law and the world—they interpret their activity in a vocabulary that foregrounds a larger purpose for law as a contribution to order and justice rather than as a tool of distribution and instrument of struggle. To realize the promise of an ordered and just world, today's tentative shoots must be nurtured and honored. Increasingly, these perspectives have merged: people struggle technically for particular projects by making arguments about law's larger purpose, promise, and destiny and see its larger purpose prefigured in their ongoing technical projects.

Both activities are undertaken in the shadow of faith, a faith that precludes some kinds of self-reflection. Law's role in distribution, inequality, and conflict are leeched out: they belong to politics or to economic competition. Law is a nobler thing. Perhaps this explains the strange professional attachment to the idea that law remains a weak overlay on a political and economic world for which it has no responsibility. Both the profession's strategic pragmatism and its ethical self-confidence are on the line. To focus on law's role in conflict and injustice not only tarnishes law's usefulness in particular struggles but may compromise a noble promise for humanity. As a result, although the imagination and methodological inventiveness brought to legal work opened the door to understanding law's ubiquity as a mode of power, international lawyers—scholars and practitioners—have not stepped through.

The turn to faith emerged as scholars grappled with two intellectual puzzles that plagued their efforts to retheorize an ever more expansive, diverse, and plastic legal practice and corpus of legal materials: the problems of international law's "legality" or normative authority and of its enforcement or practical power. After a century of intellectual work in the shadow of a proliferating legal practice, these puzzles are no closer to resolution. The result is a kind of disenchantment with explanation and a merger of technical and intellectual work sustained by professional faith rather than confident theory or compelling sociology. The modern international legal profession is a case study of sophistication through disenchantment.

I tell the story here from an American perspective, although it took different forms in different places. Scholars have been divided among themselves about how best to light the path by which practical work might promote the legalization of international affairs. Their differences have defined schools of thought and national traditions, divided the profession within the United States, distinguished it from European thinking about the field, and affected the shape of national traditions everywhere.[1] Theoretical differences within the field have sometimes become linked with doctrinal or national positions and been articulated in political struggle. In the run-up to World War II, the Roosevelt administration proposed to think about international law more flexibly to abrogate or avoid what had seemed to be clear obligations of neutrality, and their Republican opponents fought back in the name of the international legal order as a whole.[2] The Manhattan and Yale schools of public international law disputed the wisdom and legality of the Vietnam War and other American Cold War interventions in methodological terms: was international law a matter of limiting rules or fundamental values?[3] Differences in legal theory divided supporters and opponents of the Iraq War both within the United States and internationally. The academic debate between European constitutionalism and the distinctly American blend of "policy pragmatism" and neoformal "rule of law" tracks closely the broader ideological debate between European social democracy and American neoliberalism. The association of theories with opposed political projects has diversified the field and given all theories a tendentious and overdrawn feel. These differences continue to offer a repertoire of moves for people in struggle. For the discipline, a shared sense that none of the theories emerged triumphant from a century of debate has become prevailing wisdom. To be a sophisticated international law scholar or practitioner anywhere today is to be an eclectic and jaded borrower, enlisting arguments from across the spectrum of ideas about international law's legality and power to sustain its promise.[4]

Not every international lawyer or legal tradition is comfortable with this new sensibility. Periodically, anxiety about the effectiveness or existence of so plastic a medium arises and new theories and empirical studies are brought forward to demonstrate that international law really does bind and is effective and that people do comply with it "as law." The fragmentation of international law has also raised anxieties about its integrity and coherence as a constituted legal order. When this happens, new constitutionalist visions and projects arise alongside new interpretations of law's coherence and new techniques for managing a fragmented corpus of materials and arguments. From the other side, neoformalists push back against international law's creative expansion, consigning ever more activity to the political or the economic. These bursts of renewal and attack are increasingly short-lived. A sophisticated and disenchanted professional sensibility no longer needs them: technique has embraced the plurality of theory as it harnessed the fragmentation, deformalization, and reformalization of norms. This is not the only destiny for legal pluralism, but it seems to be where we are. The chapter ends with a suggestion about what else might be imagined.

THREE INNOVATIONS: PRACTICAL INNOVATION AND SCHOLARLY REINTERPRETATION

The eclectic sophistication and disenchantment of the contemporary international legal profession were hard-won. They arose in part from a century of technical innovations wrought in struggle as people grappling with one another wrestled with the legal fabric, extending its reach and internalizing their differences within it.[5] The contemporary professional sensibility is also the product of scholarly reflection and theoretical innovation: the disenchantment that comes with a century of unsatisfactory answers to foundational questions. Although I focus on the theoretical side of the story to draw attention to the turn from unsatisfactory theory to practices of faith, it is worth recalling the drama of law's engagement with world historic struggles.

The expansion of law's reach in global affairs and the breadth of practical innovation since the late nineteenth century are difficult to overstate. The dispersion and globalization of economic life have made the legal arrangements that hold it together a focal point for struggle everywhere. Colonialism was a complex and diverse legal institution that became ever more institutionally and doctrinally nuanced as empires transitioned to mandate supervision and self-determination. Decolonization and the integration of imperial dominions into the global political and economic order have turned out to be more complex still. The spice trade, slave trade, and opium trade all generated legal innovations. Trade during and after industrialization sharply expanded the density and diversity of transnational legal forms. The global mobilization of commodities from sugar to oil, waves of expansion in the territory available for capital investment, and the integration of global labor markets into world production process each required new legal doctrines and institutional arrangements. New institutions and bargaining arrangements, a body of common principles and precedents to draw on, and a proliferation of new topics and new actors, both public and private, have made the contemporary law of trade more complex still. Consular and diplomatic life in the nineteenth century was the site of great innovation: special statuses, new remedies and modes of dispute resolution, specialized courts and tribunals. The institutional transformation of diplomacy in the aftermath of the world wars, decolonization, and the end of the Cold War produced an institutional terrain for global political conversation that crisscrosses governments, corporations, and civil society, all of which search for a common language of engagement. The story has been told many times: new kinds of law, new actors, new subjects, new institutions. And every year more of each.

This was not the result of a smooth global reform extending the role of law across new problems and territories. It was the result of struggle: of colonial expansion and resistance, of Cold War decolonization and nonalignment, of hot and cold conflicts between contending ideologies, commercial powers, and political blocks. Wars were fought and victories enforced in legal terms. There were, after all, Soviet and Nazi theories and practices of international law, just as there were Western liberal ones.[6] For elites in the world's semiperiphery, international law was a tool of self-invention and promotion just as it has been for Republicans and Democrats in the United States.[7] People promoting and opposing labor rights, environmental protections, or civil and political rights have done so in legal terms. The war on terror has harnessed the legal architecture of global finance to pressure outlier nations, individuals, and groups. Global financial institutions and wealthy investors have expanded their power over cities and nations alike. Industrial sectors have battled for dominance as corporations have struggled for exclusive access to resources and markets. In each of these struggles, people have pulled and pushed on the legal fabric, searching for ways to expand their quiver of powers and open chinks in their opponents armor.

At the same time, "internationalists" associated with global legal and institutional arrangements have also had projects: to secure the peace by collective security; to complete the state system through self-determination and the management of national minorities; to strengthen global regulatory and administrative authority; to advance the project of legalization by promoting the use of legal precedents, principles, and institutions by new actors in new fields of endeavor; and to promote things like free trade, human rights, or international criminal law and the institutions built to implement them in the name of universal values. It should not be surprising that people promoting legalization would find opportunity in the diversity of legal arrangements and arguments thrown up by ongoing struggle and seek to internalize them within an ever more comprehensive and sophisticated legal field. In one sense, of course, law reflects winners. The UN Security Council affirms that there were five great powers in 1945, although Germany and Japan had only recently almost been more powerful than all of them. The internal diversification of the legal fabric, however, reflects not only wins but games played. Whether global struggles are won or lost, each side had something to say that drew on, expanded or reframed law's vocabulary. The sophisticated eclecticism and internal diversity of the field reflect this history of arguments and assertions made.

The expansion of the international legal world was accompanied by a century of innovation in the field's vision of what international law is and how one should reason within it. From the mid-nineteenth century, as "law" came to be associated with national sovereignty, "international law" became an act of imagination and argument by analogy. A scholarly profession developed rapidly to undertake and promote that imaginative construction, developing theories—arguments, really—for the existence, scope, and content of international law in a world of national sovereigns. Over the next century, scholars urged an ever more realistic understanding of law diffused through the fabric of interaction and communication among all the actors on the global stage, reinterpreting the legal order in functional terms. This way of thinking about law further expanded international law's scope. Once law could be identified by its functions—as a technique of reciprocal enforcement, advocacy, dispute resolution, norm generation, consensus building, problem solving, or administration—wherever those functions are performed, there is law. International lawyers expanded their field's aperture to include national law and private law rules that affect transnational economic activity as well as informal or customary arrangements that function as law in global society. In a world where anything could be an avatar of law, much will depend on what people interpret law to be: law will become whatever people treat as if it were law. This sociological and interpretive expansion opened the way to grasping law's constitutive and distributive role in global political economy as well as its social power, legitimating and delegitimating as people denounce and defend global action in legal terms.

In the process, international law became a more dispersed and fragmented affair. The expansion of law's range was matched by an internal proliferation of legal principles, arguments, and doctrinal materials. The possibility to say ever more things in legal language increased the number of people who found it a useful vocabulary for self-assertion. As international materials multiplied, they became increasingly flexible. Rules were displaced by principles and differences in kind were reinterpreted as matters of degree. An ever more plural legal vocabulary embraced contradictory principles and purposes more readily. Nor were all legal rules of equal value or validity: some were more persuasive than others. Soon it became possible to use law both to make and to unmake familiar distinctions—war and peace, public and private, politics and economics, international and national—and to express a range of sharply different political viewpoints, enhancing law's potential as a tool of struggle. Law offered a way to do things with words: to denounce and defend, legitimate and delegitimate, define and redefine the battlefield or the market. Awareness of law's internal flexibility also increased the significance of professional interpretation. As international law came to embrace broad principles and require the balancing of conflicting interests, more would depend on the wise judgment of those who use legal tools.

Although these innovations might have made it easier to see the role of transnational legal arrangements in conflict and injustice, most averted their eyes. International lawyers and scholars did understand that disaggregating the legal order, merging it with social forces, loosening its claims to coherence and encouraging its strategic mobilization by people with all kinds of projects at various levels was a gamble: will legalization tame political and economic forces or be tamed by them? The answer, they could see, is as much a matter of interpretation as of fact, and ultimately, where one cannot know, one must choose to believe. The decision to embrace a disaggregated law as a functional cosmopolitan order is an affirmation of faith that now demands professional fealty.

It has the advantage of being a convenient faith, affirming the virtue of the professional project while strengthening individual claims made in its name. The idea that simply using international law contributes to a better world is an appealing thought for practitioners who frame their parochial claims as steps to a virtuous universal order. Scholars could imagine anyone using international legal institutions and arguments as a (perhaps unwitting) foot soldier promoting world peace through world law. Although many particular interests advanced in the name of international law might turn out to impede progress toward global order, international lawyers were hopeful. Practitioners might be transformed by using the tools of law and come to share the ambition for a better world. They might come to inhabit law as believers rather than use it as strategists, accepting law's limits for themselves as they urge them on others. Or it might turn out that as international law materials are used successfully, a legal order would sneak up on sovereigns, subordinating them to its limitations. Suddenly there would be institutional arrangements and argumentative paths it would be impossible to ignore. The profession was hopeful about a shared fiction: by interpreting the dispersed entanglements of law with everyday struggle *as if* they were or would become a global public order able to solve global problems, express shared values, and implement humanitarian aspirations, that day may be brought ever nearer.

This double project—making international law diffusely useful while lauding the results as ethical progress—requires careful interpretation and strategic skill by both practitioners and scholars. No longer the jurist waiting to be asked what is and is not legal, the international lawyer has become a strategic partner for businesspeople, civil society advocates, politicians, and military commanders, while *also* thinking strategically on behalf of international law. International lawyers play for gains and for rules—and also for a better world. Even the most focused advocate is rarely indifferent to international law's future. The tools work and the arguments persuade only when they can be linked to a future order that will civilize conflict and implement universal values. Whether you are prosecuting a war criminal or drafting a code of corporate responsibility, you are playing a long game for the legal order as much or more than you are struggling for victory in the case. Their eyes on a long game, international lawyers have a powerful motive not to investigate law's role in conflict, injustice, or inequality. These are better seen as stubborn facts to be addressed by a revitalized cosmopolitan law in the hands of inspired practitioners.

FAITH AGAINST DOUBT: THE ORIGIN OF A PROFESSIONAL RIDDLE

To believe in international law's future you need to accept its existence. To see the hand of *law* in so diverse a practice of global push and pull you need to believe that people would not have fought, won and lost in the same way without the normative pull of legal obligation. Unfortunately for international lawyers, just as their field was expanding dramatically, doubts on this point were at their peak. How can a legal order be built on the horizontal political interactions of sovereign states? In what sense can we say that international norms, institutions, arguments, and assertions are really "law"? Perhaps they are just power in a pretty dress, "compliance" nothing but lipstick on interest. A hundred-year rearguard action against such doubts turned out to be a blessing in disguise, however, propelling the emergence of the sophisticated and disenchanted professional sensibility we encounter in the profession today.

The classic formulation of the philosophical problem was by the English legal theorist John Austin in *The Province of Jurisprudence Determined.*[8] As the title suggests, his intellectual project was to understand the distinct nature of law by determining its boundaries and limits. Law, he maintained, is the command of the "sovereign," a power whose authority is backed by sanction, is routinely or habitually obeyed, and is itself not subject to the command of another. Sovereignty, for Austin, is outside of, above, or before law.

> Whether a given government be or be not supreme, is rather a question of fact than a question of international law. A government reduced to subjection is actually a subordinate government, although the state of subjection wherein it is actually held be repugnant to the positive morality which obtains between nations or sovereigns. Though, according to that morality, it *ought* to be sovereign or independent, it is subordinate or dependent in practice.[9]

As Austin saw it, the absence of a higher sovereign power meant that international law was not law "properly so-called" but a matter of morality called "law" only by analogy.

> The so called law of nations consists of opinions or sentiments current amongst nations generally. It therefore is not law properly so called.[10]

> The positive moral rules which are laws improperly so called, are laws set or imposed by general opinion: that is to say, by the general opinion of any class or any society of persons. Some are set or imposed by the general

opinion of persons who are members of a profession or calling; others, by that of persons who inhabit a town or province; others, by that of a larger society formed of various nations. . . . And laws or rules of this species, which are imposed upon nations or sovereigns by opinions current amongst nations, are usually styled the law of nations or international law. Now a law set or imposed by general opinion is a law improperly so called. It is styled a law or rule by an analogical extension of the term.[11]

Had international lawyers not started with Austin, they might have interpreted the nineteenth-century expansion of sovereign power differently: not as a threat to the existence of international law, but as a permissive shift in the content of the rule system from mutual restraint to an order more respectful of autonomy. To see the autonomy of sovereigns instead as a matter of political and historical *fact* excused international law from responsibility for what was permitted or possible in its absence. Even after international law's dramatic twentieth-century expansion, it remains common to associate it only with constraint, rather than to acknowledge its role in privileging what sovereigns do, whether despoiling the environment or making war.

Austin's conceptual challenge to the "legality" of international law has animated international law practice and thought ever since. Not because international lawyers *agreed* with Austin, nor even because they felt he was particularly significant. Some did, many did not. Rather because international lawyers and scholars were determined to reconcile their own acceptance of national political sovereignty with a passionate dream of a better and cosmopolitan international order achieved through law. Austin gave voice to an anxiety they felt. Modern international law was born in the paradoxical relationship between the dream of an international legal order and a sense that both the practical reality and conceptual significance of "sovereignty" stood in the way.[12] Resolving the tension between the "fact" of sovereignty and the promise of law gave international lawyers a common intellectual and practical project.

There was a lot of work to be done. By the end of the nineteenth century, international law had worked itself into a corner. An international law handbook for diplomats in 1800 would have contained a wide range of sensible strategic advice and information about what to expect when representing your country: part Machiavelli, part Robert's Rules, and part Emily Post.[13] The law of nations was as much a part of the accepted background for global political and economic life as the common law was for Americans at the same time. Lots of people asserted "rights" rooted in the law of nations: sovereigns, property holders, diplomats. Sovereign rights were exercised by aristocratic authorities, corporations, and private parties: privateers could exercise rights of war, the East India Tea Company could exercise sovereign powers, and the world was divided into all manner of overlapping political entities with varying degrees of autonomy. What we now distinguish as international public and private law were all mixed up. King Leopold of Belgium was said to "own" the Congo in what would later seem a strange fusion of property and sovereignty. Moreover, far from a uniform terrain of homologous states, the world itself was understood to be divided among civilizations and between those who were and were not "civilized." Legal powers and players were different within and between these domains.

By the end of the nineteenth century, the situation was altogether different. Within the legal field, distinctions had sharpened between law and politics, law and morality, national and international, and public and private international law. The domain for "international law" kept getting smaller and more conceptually distinct. Diverse arrangements of "sovereign rights" gave way to the idea of a single type of actor: the "sovereign" nation-state. This was a novel and not altogether persuasive proposition when most of the world remained part of various colonial and imperial dominions. Nevertheless, echoing Austin, the unique authority of "sovereigns" was understood to be more than the sum of their legal entitlements: it resided in history and expressed the priority of politics over law. As late as 1924, British legal scholar Percy Corbett gave expression to this idea in analyzing the League of Nations' authority over the Saar, where it exercised all the rights of sovereignty without qualification but did not possess what he called the *nuda proprietas* of sovereignty. That remained with Germany.[14] The absent *nuda* was not simply another legal interest—the right, say, of reversion—but a more elemental form of political power that an artificial creature of law like the league could not possess. The consolidation of "sovereignty" in the imagination as a singular and absolute kind of political figure placed international law under suspicion and opened rules long understood to be valid to suspicion and challenge. In response, international lawyers developed theories about—and arguments for—the "legality" of international law just as the global normative order was expanding.

The explosion of innovation that launched the renewal of international law and opened the door for its modernization took place in percussive bursts. Martti Koskenniemi focuses on the emergence of a cosmopolitan liberalism of a generation of international lawyers in the Europe of the 1870s.[15] World War

I sparked another remarkable period of intellectual and institutional innovation in Europe among political scientists and international lawyers.[16] The two dozen years after 1945 saw a further expansion of international legal materials, legal institutions, and professional communities fueled by decolonization, the United Nations, and American hegemony. The scholarly center then was the interdisciplinary discussion in the United States—in New Haven and New York—that interacted with the world of the United Nations and legal intellectuals from the postcolonial world. The proliferation of sites for international adjudication and advocacy that began in the 1970s and exploded after 1989 with the rise of the human rights movement gave another generation the opportunity to reimagine the field.[17]

As each generation faced a wave of technical innovation and expansion demanding interpretation, people found new ways to blend the reality of sovereign power and the promise of law's normative power. As people reimagined the field, they also extended its reach and added to the toolkit available for people in struggle. The projects that followed considered both the normative and the enforcement side of the legality problem: how could legal norms be distinguished from other norms, and how could legal enforcement be distinguished from the exercise of unrestrained political power? Any number of scholars might be chosen to exemplify the kinds of intellectual moves that reinvigorated the field in the shadow of Austinian doubt. For Koskenniemi, Hersch Lauterpacht's centrality to the technical practice and academic sensibility of midcentury international law makes him exemplary.[18] I have always associated this set of moves with Hans Kelsen, whose turn from sociological realism to faith is right on the surface.[19]

Kelsen begins by rejecting the notion, familiar from Austin, that law has behind it the absolute power of "sovereignty" or the "state."

> The assertion that back of the legal order is a power means only that the legal order is by and large efficacious, that its norms are actually observed. . . . The state as a power back of law, as sustainer, creator, or source of the law—all these expressions are only verbal doublings of the law as the object of cognition, those typical doublings toward which our thinking and our language incline, such as the animistic presentations according to which "souls" inhabit things; dryads, trees; nymphs, springs. . . .[20]

Reasoning about law on the basis of mental images and abstract concepts should be replaced by a more realistic assessment of law's actual effectiveness. The "state" we imagine is "only a picture."

The state is conceived of as having existence in space, and, accordingly, events are distinguished as happening within the state and without the state. We speak of internal and external affairs of the state. The object of national law is *within* the state; the object of international law is *without* the state . . . [however] the idea of the state as a body in space having an "inside" and "outside" is only a picture.[21]

The key to law's validity is the fact of coercion: "Law . . . is a coercive order not because the idea of the legal norm induces men to proper behavior, but because the legal norm provides a coercive measure as a sanction."[22] When a national legal order successfully harnesses sanctions to normative propositions, Kelsen imagines it resting on a *grundnorm* articulating the law that is "efficacious."

Turning to international law, Kelsen asks whether the same might be said. Here the importance of interpretive articulability is front and center: *can it be said* that international law is efficacious in the same sense?

International law is law in this sense if a coercive act on the part of the state, the forcible interference of the state in the sphere of interests of another, is permitted only as a reaction against a delict and the employment of force to any other end is forbidden—only if the coercive act undertaken as a reaction against a delict can be *interpreted* as a reaction of the international legal community. *If it is possible to describe the material which appears in the guise of international law* in such a way that the employment of force directed by one state against another can be *interpreted* only as either delict or sanction, then international law is law in the same sense as national law.[23]

What began as a turn from abstraction to the real world of coercion becomes a matter of interpretation.

Kelsen acknowledges, moreover, that interpretation is a matter of choice. War, he reflects, has been interpreted in two ways: as outside of law—"neither a delict nor a sanction"—and as "forbidden in principle" by international law and therefore either delict or sanction.[24] "It would be naïve," he says, "to ask which of these two opinions is the correct one, for each is sponsored by outstanding authorities and defended by weighty arguments."[25] The interpretive choice is a political and ethical one: do we choose law or a world unrestrained?

The situation is characterized by the possibility of a double interpretation. . . . It is not a scientific, but a political decision which gives preference to the *bellum justum* theory. This preference is justified by the fact that only this interpretation conceives of the international order as law. . . . From a strictly scientific point of view a diametrically opposite evolution of international relations is not absolutely excluded. That war is in principle a delict and is permitted only as a sanction is a possible interpretation of international relations, but not the only one. We choose this interpretation, hoping to have recognized the beginning of a development of the future and with the intention of strengthening as far as possible all the elements of present-day international law which tend to justify this interpretation and to promote the evolution we desire.[26]

The result is a professional project: to affirm and "promote" the significance of law in international affairs. If you—and others—chose to look at international law as an order, it would be one. Anything less would be to choose a world of unrestrained conflict.

A turn away from concepts to reality, a confrontation with the pluralism of that reality and the indeterminacy of interpretation, and a renewal of the will to interpret for order and to promote a future of ever more effective international law: across the twentieth century, generations of scholars and practitioners made these Kelsenian moves in one or another way. As they did, they came to see law everywhere, dispersed throughout global society and available for people with projects of all types and to reinterpret power as law made visible. In 1989, for example, the *Harvard Law Review* reexamined the relationship between jurisdiction and statehood to encourage courts to consider transnational solidarities and interests alongside national interests in assessing assertions—and refusals to assert—national jurisdiction outside a state's territory:

Rethinking jurisdiction . . . requires rethinking the state itself. It requires envisioning a state not as natural, bounded, and enclosed, but as constructed, boundless, and open, a constellation of authoritative behavior, or authoritative exercises of jurisdiction over individuals, events, and property. The "state," in this view, is the ever-changing snapshot emerging from these jurisdictional assertions, the very pattern of assertions of jurisdiction, *not* an entity that ponders whether to assert jurisdiction or not. It has no permanent inside and outside, no identifiable interests. In short, the state does not define the scope of its jurisdiction; rather, it is the jurisdictional decisions themselves that define the state.[27]

Nevertheless, the need to "promote the evolution we desire," in Kelsen's words, remained acute. The dream that legalization would enable a global humanitarian and cosmopolitan consensus, restrain self-interest in the name of global objectives, or offer effective tools to address global policy challenges remained on the horizon. Fealty to this dream would blunt recognition of what might otherwise be obvious: if people everywhere use law in struggle, it must be implicated in outcomes, just and unjust.

THE PROBLEM OF RULES: THE LIMITS OF CONSENT

For the international law profession, the scholarly road to agnostic eclecticism can be seen in changing answers to two central theoretical questions: how do we identify binding rules, and how are they made effective as law in the world? The late nineteenth-century solution to the first problem was consent. The distinction between law and policy or morality was sovereign intention of the sort expressed in treaties. Yet nineteenth-century international law contained many rules not established by treaty: it would be necessary to determine which could be said to rest securely on sovereign will. Even treaties would need to be assessed to ensure consent had not been vitiated by things like mistake, fraud, duress, or changed circumstances. The result was a new doctrinal tool—"sources of law"—for assessing the provenance of rules, codified in the 1924 Statute of the new Permanent Court of International Justice to guide the justices in their search for law. Unfortunately, the validity of norms was hard to prove and easy to challenge.

The 1900 US Supreme Court decision in *The Paquete Habana* illustrates the problem.[28] After a very lengthy and detailed historical investigation, the Court found that seizing "fishing smacks" as prize in war was contrary to customary international law. The recitation of sovereign practice was remarkable in its extent—page after page—and in the consistency of state practice. For many centuries, no sovereign seems to have seized a fishing smack. After affirming the rule, the Court applied it to the American Navy, striking a blow for the legality of international law more generally: "International law is part of our law, and must be ascertained and administered by the courts of justice of appropriate jurisdiction as often as questions of right depending upon it are duly presented for their determination."[29] *The Paquete Habana* is routinely cited as a textbook example of sources doctrine at work, illustrating the proper way to demonstrate the validity of a customary rule, and as the leading American authority on the binding power of international law itself. Prior to 1900, no authoritative ruling on this point was needed. It was simply obvious that international law, like the common law, was part of the nation's legal system. The need for articulation marked the beginning of the end for customary international law in American courts. More importantly, if every customary rule would now need historical proof as elaborate and uncontradicted as that in *Paquete Habana*, there would be very few norms of customary law. Much that had been legally regulated no longer would be.

International lawyers tried all kinds of things in the following decades to flesh out the normative catalog. Some launched private projects of "codification" to restate the norms in force with clarity and precision. They promoted codification by treaty, despite the limitations this placed on the norms that could be articulated. They worked to articulate a default rule to permit resolution of a dispute where no legal norm could meet the new pedigree requirements.

Perhaps a court could decide on the basis of equitable criteria, *ex aequo et bono* in the words of the Permanent Court Statute. Perhaps a solution could be deduced from the nature of sovereignty itself. In 1927, for example, the Permanent Court held in the *S.S. Lotus* case that the territorial bonds of sovereignty are superior to bonds of citizenship because sovereignty *was* by nature territorial, while admitting there was no rule of custom or treaty to this effect. Once it was possible to reason from the nature of sovereignty, the door was open to finding duties as well as rights, and looking to the nature of the international legal system as a whole to find principled means for settling disputes. In 1974, United Nations sought to clarify these background entitlements of sovereignty in the Charter of Economic Rights and Duties of States, whose multiple and conflicting terms further widened the scope for international legal argument and assertion.

Already in the Hague Conventions, a move from legal rules to broad principles was under way. It was difficult to come to agreement on rules of war beyond the prohibition of a few weapons and protocols for the treatment of medics and prisoners. Such narrow rules seemed to affirm that the rest of war was outside law all together. Perhaps the few rules we had could be seen to embody underlying principles of more general application. Or perhaps agreement could more easily be reached at the level of principle. A principle might also slide more easily into the reasoning processes of military professionals. The principle that military force must be "necessary" and "proportional" to its objective brings the entire battlefield into law while mirroring the military's own logic: concentrate your force, no wasted effort. It echoes the kind of moral distinction soldiers and citizens will want to make: no wanton destruction or unnecessary killing. Over the next decades, as hundreds of "codifying" treaties were adopted, the search for multilateral consensus generated ever more broadly framed provisions, often of uncertain normative status or meaning, which might be useful but require interpretation.

The turn to principles brought political and ideological differences into the legal fabric, softening the line between law and policy or morality. Rather than a threat to the legality of law, jurists saw confirmation of law's increasing strength and usefulness as a kind of principled gravitational field for sovereign interaction. It could serve as a general vocabulary of statecraft and toolkit for innovative solutions rather than simply a checklist of obligations, limits, and entitlements. Oscar Schachter put it this way in 1962, praising what he saw as UN Secretary-General Dag Hammarskjold's skillful use of international legal principles in diplomacy:

> Hammarskjold made no sharp distinction between law and policy. . . . He viewed the body of law not merely as a technical set of rules and procedures, but as the authoritative expression of principles that determine the goals and direction of collective action. . . . [He felt] the fundamental principles of the Charter and international law embodied the deeply-held values of the great majority of mankind and therefore constituted the moral, as well as the legal, imperatives of international law.[30]

The technique of fusing these opposing elements into workable solutions cannot be easily described; it is more art than engineering and blueprints are not likely to be available. Certainly, an essential feature lay in the nature of the general rules which guided him. They were, in the main, principles derived from Articles 1 and 2 of the Charter; in that basis they already commanded, in a psychological and political sense, high priority among the values formally accepted by the governments of the world. They were flexible in that they did not impose specific procedural patters or detailed machinery for action; they left room for adaptation to the particular needs and the resources available for a given undertaking. . . .

It is also of significance in evaluating Hammarskjold's flexibility that he characteristically expressed basic principles in terms of opposing tendencies (applying, one might say, the philosophic concept of polarity or dialectical opposition). He never lost sight of the fact that a principle, such as that of observance of human rights, was balanced by the concept of non-intervention, or that the notion of equality of states had to be considered in a context which included the special responsibilities of the Great Powers. The fact that such precepts had contradictory implications meant that they could not provide automatic answers to particular problems, but rather that they served as criteria which had to be weighed and balanced in order to achieve a rational solution of a particular problem.[31]

Schachter was correct: the abundance of principles—very often in tension with one another—greatly increased the usefulness of international law in diplomatic struggles. Parties on all sides of conflict were increasingly able to articulate their political positions in legal terms.

Whether this would lead to a "rational solution of a particular problem," however, was at best uncertain. The ability to express interests in legal terms may also strengthen everyone in the belief that their cause is just and compromise uncalled for. It may encourage weaker parties to overplay their hand—or stronger parties to press beyond what makes long-term sense. Schachter had confidence that the flexibility afforded by the "dialectical polarity" of law would be in good hands with Dag Hammarskjold because he shared faith in the promise and objectives of international law.

> He regarded himself as a man of law, in part because of his formal legal training, in part, it seemed, because of his intellectual delight in the subtleties of legal analysis. There was also perhaps an element of personal sentiment in his attitude, for he had a manifest pride in his family's legal background and especially in the contribution made by his father, Hjalmar Hammarskjold, and his brother, Ake [Ake Hammarskjold, registrar and later judge at the Permanent Court of International Justice]. Much more important, however, than these considerations was the conviction, which he increasingly expressed, that the processes of law, and, as he put it, the principles of justice were crucial to the effort to avert disaster and to achieve a secure and decent international order. That this conviction went far deeper than the conventional homage paid to the rule of law soon became evident to one who shared his professional interest. It was more than a belief in a distant goal; it inspired and influenced his actions from day to day, and it is not surprising that one of the first tributes paid him by an ambassador who knew him well was to describe him as "imbued with the spirit of law."[32]

In the hands of the faithful, a flexible legal fabric that embraces ethical and political differences opens the way for a forward-looking diplomacy that is "more art than engineering."

Meanwhile, a half century of reasoning and arguing had shifted the terrain for thinking about law and sovereignty. In 1949, Justice Alvarez of the

International Court of Justice had positioned himself at the cutting edge of the shift in his *Corfu Channel Case* opinion:

> By sovereignty, we understand the whole body of rights and attributes which a State possesses in its territory, to the exclusion of all other States, and also in its relations with other States. Sovereignty confers rights upon States and imposes obligations on them. . . . This notion has its foundation in national sentiment and in the psychology of the peoples, in fact it is very deeply rooted. . . . This notion has evolved and we must now adopt a conception of it which will be in harmony with the new conditions of social life. We can no longer regard sovereignty as an absolute and individual right of every State, as used to be done under the old law founded on the individualist regime, according to which States were only bound by the rules which they had accepted. Today, owing to social interdependence and to the predominance of the general interest, the States are bound by many rules which have not been ordered by their will. The sovereignty of States has now become an *institution*, an *international social function* of a psychological character, which has to be exercised in accordance with the new international law.[33]

If a sovereign was a social function constrained by rules beyond its consent, the "legality" of legal rules and principles had floated free of any Article 38 pedigree. The terms of Article 38 could still be used to *argue* for and against particular rules. Indeed, it would be an impermissible and unprofessional tactic to assert that the line between law and politics, rule and preference, did not matter or could not be drawn. It could be drawn in lots of ways. But there was no right place, no compelling theory, no ultimate juridical test of just where it should be drawn. As a tactic in struggle, everyone could insist that their preferred rule had a more solid pedigree and reject their opponent's position as a mere policy preference. This practice could now be undertaken more lightly, lawyers on all sides understanding that the line between legal rule and preference was fluid in their hands. Arguments about the status of rules could be effective, but less because they were persuasive than because they fit with professional habits and expectations. A sophisticated discipline had arrived.

In the years after the Second World War, argument in this spirit moved the goalposts for assessing the legality of international law; "legality" would now be a matter of social and political fact rather than an analytical conclusion. A determination by jurists that a norm is valid is, when you think about it, just another argument. The real question is whether the argument persuades, whether the norm functions to change behavior. This could be answered only in practice, not by analysis of Article 38. Take the definition of customary law as "evidence of a general practice accepted as law." Lots of questions arise: How much practice? What evidence shows a practice to be "accepted as law"? Is the practice of important states more significant? States directly affected by the custom? Dissertations could be written in response, but in practice, they would just be fuel for further argument. In diplomatic practice, however, lawyers readily intuit the evidence that will be *most* compelling: recent practice of the state you are trying to persuade, practice of similar or allied states, and so forth. As a lawyer evaluating evidence to put in the diplomat's speech, one does not think "valid/invalid" but "useful/less useful" or "more persuasive/less persuasive." The result will rarely be the absolute confirmation or repudiation of a possible rule, but something more nuanced, a matter of more or less. Some people would be persuaded, others not.

This approach sharply expanded the number of actors whose responses to legal claims would be significant and who could be understood to carry a brief for international law as a whole. If nongovernmental actors could argue successfully that major corporations violated an "emerging international principle" requiring a "precautionary" approach to environmental damage, they could be understood as part of the legislative and enforcement arms of the international community, contributing to the growth of the normative fabric. Through "naming and shaming," the human rights movement would simultaneously strengthen and enforce international norms. When using international law, moreover, it often makes strategic sense to bracket the question of what is in the normative catalog. Although General Assembly resolutions themselves are not "binding," they may be authoritative in a softer way, persuasive and useful reference points in disputes about what is and is not appropriate sovereign behavior. Oscar Schachter went so far as to catalog the legal and political significance of "nonbinding international agreements," finding parallels with binding arrangements and acknowledging their usefulness as diplomatic tools.[34] If enough people argue for a sensible principle and bring their collective power to bear, they might get a result, even if the norm they proposed could never make it through the sieve of the doctrine of sources. As actors embraced this possibility, the normative material proliferated and legal arguments were increasingly part of global political practice.

Environmental activists were among the first to seize the initiative, promoting new principles only loosely tethered to international documents, reports, and scholarly tomes. Philippe Sands noted the still "limited implementation and enforcement" of international environmental law, which he felt "suggests that international environmental law remains in its formative stages."[35] One thing it did have, however, was a catalog of principles. "Although no single international legal instrument establishes binding rules or principles of global application, several general principles and rules of international law have emerged, or are emerging in relation to environmental matters."[36] He notes that the principles "temper" one another, as in the case of the principles of "sovereignty over national resources" and "not to cause damage to the environment." Other principles that "emerged" in various international instruments and activities included "the preventive principle," "the precautionary principle," "the polluter pays principle," as well as the principles of "good neighborliness and international cooperation," "sustainable development," and "common but differentiated responsibility." Sands's principles rest on a smorgasbord of binding and nonbinding texts. To his mind, their emergence in the practices of advocacy and diplomacy are more relevant than their pedigree and might well be a matter of "more or less," depending on how far the principle had so far "emerged." To argue that norms culled from this material rose to the level of "general principles of law recognized by civilized nations" remained a heavy doctrinal lift. Nevertheless, arguments by analogy were often successful: a legal principle that worked over there might be a reasonable approach over here. Where these arguments are effective, law's march forward continues.

This shifted attention to the process by which the persuasiveness of norms could be *encouraged*. For Sands, that meant transforming them into workable and more specific "standards" and harnessing them to innovative "legal techniques" that might encourage their implementation. He had in mind reporting requirements, impact assessments, attaching liability to environmental harm in national legal systems, and "improved enforcement procedures and dispute settlement machinery."[37] The field had shifted from making norms to enforcing and implementing them. In that work, one could remain agnostic about whether they really were *legal* norms.

For the contemporary international lawyer, the problem of rules is not a problem. The legality of international law is not inherent in the norms but created in their use. As a result, everyone now speaks a loose jargon of principle and policy. The distinction between law and politics has blurred along with that between legal science and political science. Has international law devoured the political, or has politics turned international law into another language of interest? It is impossible to tell. To look at this situation with late nineteenth-century eyes is to lament the loss of law's special status. The contemporary international lawyer has simply outgrown such questions. As a sophisticate, she realizes rules have no pedigree and law has no special province to be determined. Acting as if law had normative power sometimes works and, if we believe, may yet bring us a better world.

THE PROBLEM OF POWER: LEGALIZATION WITHOUT LIMIT

The turn from validity to the persuasiveness or effectiveness of rules presented a different problem of legality: identifying the machinery of specifically *legal* enforcement. A century ago, it was obvious the machinery for enforcement was weak. Experts bemoaned the still primitive stage of international society and yearned for courts and other institutions to implement the normative catalog they were composing. Over the years, they imagined other enforcement possibilities. The horizontal interactions among sovereigns might be reinterpreted as acts not only of "auto-interpretation" but of reciprocal enforcement.[38] Together, they could be understood as a primitive functional equivalent for the vertical systems of interpretation and enforcement found in "mature" national systems. The enforcement pressures brought to bear would be not only military power or direct sanctions, but a wide range of social pressures that are part of "legitimacy." If we attribute these powers to law, we could conclude that the legality of international law resides in its social power to legitimate and delegitimate.

The picture that emerged is of a self-reinforcing legality blending normative creation and enforcement. People make assertions about what law requires. Their assertions go into the world armed with a backpack of social, political, and economic power. Where the assertions are met with acquiescence or agreement, the norms were legal. At the same time, assertions of power carry little backpacks of legal authority. When they are successful, they were legitimate. In both directions, the (successful and persuasive) use of law strengthens the legal fabric as a whole.

This is an elegant, if analytically somewhat circular approach to the problem of legality. It is hard to see how one could disentangle the social or military force brought to bear on behalf of a norm from the additional effect of law's legitimating power. If the power of law is merged with the powers that make law effective, it is hard to know whether the result is marvelously juris-generative or wild overreaching by international lawyers. If you approach international law with an attitude of suspicion, in the tradition of Austin, it would be easier to conclude that what is going on is simply the assertion and pursuit of sovereign self-interest. The legal language is nothing but a convenience to fool whoever may be taken in. But if you are a believer, someone who chooses, following Kelsen, to see the world in legal terms, you will witness the wonderful process by which civilization rises from the plain of brute force.

Once the legality of international law attaches to the power of social sanction, international law is an expression of power and an effect of coercion. It is difficult to see how this could avoid opening the door to a consideration of law's role in injustice or the violence and death of the wars it legitimates. But it has not. Rather than seeing the hand of power in the glove of law, mainstream international lawyers focus on the glove. They see *law* acting everywhere in the world and celebrate the ability of civil society organizations, individuals, or national judges to participate in global rule making. Where the outcomes are not desirable or when bad things happen in the name of law, they prefer to see the misrule of power dressing itself in legal justification.

One result of this professional posture is a kind of winner's logic. Whoever makes legal claims successfully has not only vindicated a parochial demand but contributed to the enforcement of a collective vision. Claims validated through enforcement must have had the wind of legitimation behind them. This idea has striking parallels in many seventeenth-century views of natural law. This also makes it very difficult to imagine law implicated in injustice or distribution: when legal claims succeed, everyone benefits. Those who "won" were successful agents of the whole. When George Bush challenged the United Nations to enforce international law against Saddam Hussein—or stand by passively while the United States took matters into its own hands—we can imagine a legitimation calculus whose outcome could be known only after the campaign was completed. Had the United States brought democracy to Iraq and beyond, the United Nations would have been delegitimated as the oracle of legality. If, as it happened, the campaign was widely perceived as a failure, the United States would be delegitimated in their claim to act on behalf of global order. One might untangle the legality from the success of the venture, but it would be hard to ignore their impact on one another. At the extreme, this can lead to the kinds of claims one heard when NATO attacked Serbia in defense of Kosovo: the action was legitimate, even if not, strictly speaking, legal. One would expect the law to catch up.

In 2003, Anne-Marie Slaughter analyzed the Bush administration's legal and political position in these terms in the *New York Times*:

> With the news that the United States was abandoning its efforts to get United Nations approval for a possible invasion of Iraq, yesterday looked to be a very bad day for staunch multilateralists. . . . That view is understandable,

but incomplete. . . . By giving up on the Security Council, the Bush administration has started on a course that could be called "illegal but legitimate," a course that could end up, paradoxically, winning United Nations approval for a military campaign in Iraq—though only after an invasion. . . . In 1999, the United States, expecting a Russian veto of military intervention to stop Serbian attacks on ethnic Albanians in Kosovo, sidestepped the United Nations completely and sought authorization for the use of force within NATO itself. The airwaves and newspaper opinion pages were filled with dire predictions that this move would fatally damage the United Nations as the arbitrator of the use of force. But in the end, the Independent International Commission on Kosovo found that although formally illegal—the United Nations Charter demands that the use of force in any cause other than self-defense be authorized by the Security Council—the intervention was nonetheless legitimate in the eyes of the international community. So, how can United Nations approval come about? Soldiers would go into Iraq. They would find irrefutable evidence that Saddam Hussein's regime possesses weapons of mass destruction. Even without such evidence, the United States and its allies can justify their intervention if the Iraqi people welcome their coming and if they turn immediately back to the United Nations to help rebuild the country.

The United States will now claim authorization under Resolution 1441. Most international lawyers will probably reject this claim and find the use of force illegal under the terms of the Charter. But even for international lawyers, insisting on formal legality in this case may be counterproductive. . . . The United Nations imposes constraints on both the global decision-making process and the outcomes of that process, constraints that all countries recognize to be in their long-term interest and the interest of the world. But it cannot be a straitjacket, preventing nations from defending themselves or pursuing what they perceive to be their vital national security interests. . . . That is the lesson that the United Nations and all of us should draw from this crisis. Overall, everyone involved is still playing by the rules. But depending on what we find in Iraq, the rules may have to evolve, so that what is legitimate is also legal.[39]

DISCIPLINARY RENEWAL AND PROFESSIONAL FAITH: THREE EXAMPLES

Hans Kelsen responded to the undecidability of theory with a plea for faith. Modern international lawyers who inherit a century of work on the problems of normative legality and enforcement remain in Kelsen's predicament. There is no analytically decisive answer to the riddle of international law's legality. As Kelsen observed, to see the operations of a legal order is a choice. International lawyers make all sorts of arguments about the specificity of normative pedigree, the special persuasiveness of legal norms, the singularity of legal enforcement, or the special powers of law to legitimate. Ultimately, however, an international legal argument is just an argument; an enforcement action just an exercise of power. International legal theory is just a collection of arguments you can try in discussion with a skeptic, none of them watertight. What makes international law a sophisticated and disenchanted profession is the shared realization that this is the case and a determination to forge ahead.

As a result, international law is best understood not as a philosophical mystery to be solved, but as a profession: the work of people who animate the practices, norms, and ideas that have been gathered in its name. What holds the field together is a professional identity that is part shared faith in international law's usefulness and long-term potential, part practice of fealty and strategic engagement on behalf of that faith, and part shared sensibility or posture aligning these ethical commitments and pragmatic strategies. To illustrate the importance of belief in the contemporary professional style, I revisit the arguments of three American postwar international law innovators: Myres McDougal, Harold Koh, and Louis Henkin. The choice is idiosyncratic: the selection would look quite different in other national traditions. They exemplify three subtly different American modes of professional faith associated with different professional practices and engagements with statecraft. Like Kelsen, each asks those in the profession to choose faith, responding to the failure of theory with professional responsibility.

Of the three, McDougal may be the most well known through his work with the Yale Project on World Public Order. He and his colleagues imagined the world as an open-ended "policy process" through which law is created, interpreted, and affirmed through a constant give-and-take. In 1955, McDougal described norm creation "as a process of continuous interaction, of continuous demand and response, in which the decision-makers of particular nation-states unilaterally put forward claims of the most diverse and conflicting character . . . and in which other decision-makers, external to the demanding state . . . weigh and appraise these competing claims . . . and ultimately accept or reject them."[40] It is possible to speak confidently about what the law "is" only after one has observed the outcome of the give-and-take.

At the same time, power is not an absolute prerogative backed by force: it is a more interactive and institutional effect that is often generated by people using legal terms and legal institutions. McDougal criticizes those who fail to understand law's role in power as aggressively as those who deny power's role in law.

> The process of decision-making is indeed, as every lawyer knows, one of the continual redefinition of doctrine in its application to ever changing facts and claims. A conception of law which focuses upon doctrine to the exclusion of the pattern of practices by which it is given meaning and made effective, is, therefore, not the most conducive to understanding. . . . Formal authority without effective control is illusion: effective control without formal authority may be naked force. A realistic conception of law must, accordingly, conjoin formal authority and effective control. . . .[41]

> Law offers, as we have seen, a continuous formulation and reformulation of policies and constitutes an integral part of the world power process.[42]

Would a law so closely allied with power still be law? If so, would it still be a good thing—the cosmopolitan law of the discipline's dreams? Many of McDougal's contemporaries thought he had both abandoned and undermined international law, confusing it with policy and great power prerogative. But McDougal disagreed. The key was to appreciate the significance of ethics in power itself, and to place confidence in the powers of free people to generate a law—and a world—worthy of their aspirations. In his view, to stand with virtuous power was a personal and professional choice, and to find law there the best path to law's own triumph.

> The moral goals of people—demands for values justified by standards of right and wrong—are not mere "abstractions" without antecedents or consequences. Such goals are rather the most constructive dynamisms of conscience and character and, when shared with others, are not "sources of weakness and failure" but rather the most dependable bases of power and successful co-operation. The moral perspectives of people, no less than naked force, are commonly regarded as among the effective sanctions of law. . . . To reject these growing common demands and identifications of the peoples of the world for a "profound and neglected truth" from Hobbes that "the state creates morality as well as law" and hence, to conclude that it is moral perversion for a nation-state to clarify its interests in terms of a wider morality, is as fantastic as it is potentially tragic. Certainly it neither accurately reflects the aspirations of the free peoples of the world nor effectively promotes the clear interest of the United States in a more efficient organization of these

peoples to suggest that the issue between the free world and the totalitarian is simply one of "relative power" and that distinctions between aggressor and non-aggressor nations are mere moral illusions serving to protect vested interests. . . .

It is urgently to be hoped that attacks upon law and morality which so profoundly misconceive law, morality and power . . . will not cause many of us to mistake the real choice that confronts us. People whose moral perspectives preclude the deliberate resort to violence except for self-defense or organized community sanction, have in the contemporary world only the alternative of some form of law. The choice we must make is not between law and no law or between law and power, but between ineffective and effective law. . . . A choice in sum between . . . illusory doctrines of "old fashioned" diplomacy, and spasmodic resorts to unauthorized violence, and, on the other hand, clear moral and legal commitments to freedom, peace, and abundance which are sustained by organized community coercion and which invoke, at both national and international levels, all the contemporary instruments of power, ideological and economic as well as diplomatic and military.[43]

International law was a terribly serious business, neither irrational politics nor rational law, but an ongoing project through which the world's people have the opportunity to choose a world public order of freedom and justice. McDougal did not offer a resolution to the problem of the legality of rules and their enforcement. He modeled a posture forward from its nonresolution: to choose law as an expression of values and a mobilization of "all the contemporary instruments of power" to their realization. It is difficult to separate so bravura a profession of faith from the context of high politics in which McDougal imagined international law being made relevant. His was a voice of the postwar American political ascendency as it contemplated another global struggle against the ideologies of tyranny. The significance of international law could be seen in its relation to what he saw as the most significant political challenge of the day for which all the instruments of power would indeed be necessary. The values he had in mind were not enumerated in legal process or a catalog of rights. They were larger than that: the aspirations of the free peoples of the world. Law should be subordinated to so great a cause. It was fortunate that to choose law was also to align with that future.

A second American response to the inadequacy of theories of legality focused on the legal process across a period in which American ascendency and world order seemed more stable and the work of law a matter of steady and often routine adjustments in commercial and government practice. The lineage for this approach runs to Philip Jessup's midcentury articulation of a transnational law and is best represented today by work on adjudicative and administrative networks. Harold Koh, past US State Department legal advisor and former dean of the Yale Law School, exemplifies the "transnational legal process" approach, although one might as easily focus on the rising tide of scholarship about "global administrative law."[44] Like McDougal, their focus is the sociopolitical process through which law is invoked, tested, and affirmed, but they have in mind the adjudicative and bureaucratic practices of commercial affairs and government. Philip Allott had famously asserted that the *travaux preparatoire* for legal agreements had no boundaries of space or time.[45] Koh identified law with its professional expression in the legal institutions of adjudication and administration within and between states.

It took intellectual work to interpret judicial and administrative bodies across the world as a kind of "network" that could be constitutive of a global legal order. Where McDougal placed his faith in the moral choices people would make—and the powers they would exercise—in the name of freedom, Koh relied on more routine patterns of interaction that would "create patterns of behavior and generate norms of external conduct which they in turn internalize."[46] For Koh, the judicial function has a direction: the transnational legal process is *normative*, generative of its own legality.

> Thus, the concept [of a transnational legal process] embraces not just the descriptive workings of a process, but the *normativity* of that process. It focuses not simply upon how international interaction among transnational actors shapes law, but also on how law shapes and guides future interactions: in short, how law influences why nations obey.[47]
>
> To summarize, the critical idea is the normativity of transnational legal process. To survive in an interdependent world, even the most isolated states—North Korea, Libya, Iraq, Cuba—must eventually interact with other nations. Even rogue states cannot insulate themselves forever from complying with international law if they wish to participate in a transnational economic or political process. Once nations begin to interact, a complex process occurs, whereby international legal norms seep into, are internalized, and become embedded in domestic legal and political processes.[48]

To use international law is to strengthen it and to find oneself transformed. The long arc of international relations can be bent toward law if people accept the responsibility to help it along. Wherever they may work, professionals can be agents of the international legal process, and Koh urges international lawyers to accept the professional responsibility that goes with this possibility.

> [The theory of transnational legal process] predicts that nations will come into compliance with international norms *if transnational legal processes are aggressively triggered by other transnational actors* in a way that forces interaction in forums capable of generating norms, followed by norm-internalization. This process of interaction and internalization in turn leads a national government to engage in new modes of interest-recognition and identity-formation in a way that eventually leads the nation-state back into compliance.[49]

> It is sometimes said that someone who, by acquiring medical training, comes to understand the human body acquires as well a moral duty not just to observe disease, but to try to cure it. In the same way, I would argue, a lawyer who acquires knowledge of the body *politic* acquires a duty not simply to observe transnational legal process, but to try to influence it.[50]

The legality of international law has no theoretical guarantor. The legalization of global political and economic life will be a victory to be won by professional commitment and personal acts of responsibility to put law to use. Legal professionals, in whatever setting they find themselves, should nudge government toward the use of legal procedures and vocabularies.[51] Although this might be done through external agitation—Koh cites the work of the international human rights clinic at Yale as one example—international lawyers in government or private practice ought also to think of themselves as a kind of fifth column within the establishment, loyal to the larger future of law alongside the interests of clients or governments, pushing clients toward law and encouraging them to push others toward law.[52]

Working for law requires a suspension of disbelief in law's dark potential. Were the legal fabric systematically implicated in violence and injustice, the orientation Koh advocates would make little sense. Koh's exemplary outliers—North Korea, Libya, Iraq, Cuba—were doubtless chosen to emphasize that even for such states, the transnational legal process was now normative. His choice also sends the message that international law is aligned with the broad interests of the established order whose center is underwritten by American power. Work for the law and work for the client align.

The Kingsbury, Krisch, and Stewart manifesto for "global administrative law" arrives at a similar moment of affirmation.[53] They encourage us to imagine a "global administrative space" stretching across all the diverse institutions that implement norms transnationally and to work to make that space more effective, responsible, and transparent by bringing the techniques of national administrative law to bear in one or another way on its procedures. In democratic national government, administrative law aims to link the bureaucracy to the democratic decisions of parliament under the legal control of the judiciary. Internationally, there is no democratic legislature and no controlling judiciary: global administrative law will be in some sense unmoored. Might it then become an instrument of tyranny, rendering undemocratic actors more effective?

> Our espousal of the notion of a global administrative space is the product of observation, but it inevitably has potential political and other normative implications. On the one hand, casting global governance in administrative terms might lead to its stabilization and legitimation in ways that privilege current powerholders and reinforce the dominance of Northern and Western concepts of law and sound governance. On the other hand, it might also create a platform for critique. As the extent of global administrative government becomes obvious (and framing global regulation in traditional terms of administration and regulation exposes its character and extent more clearly than the use of vague terms such as governance), the more resistance and reform may find points of focus. . . . Confronting these issues in administrative terms may highlight the need to devise strategies for remedying unfairness associated with such inequalities.[54]

That is the last we read about administrative law's dark potential. Kingsbury, Krisch, and Stewart affirm their confidence in its potential to improve the machinery of law making and application, and for the self-correcting operations of open global debate, a posture more plausible for people with long-term faith in the overall justice of the established order, whatever its current failings, than for outsiders beyond the circle of faith.

A third approach to professional faith in law's virtuous destiny focuses less on process than the remaking of consciousness among the world's elites. If people came to share an idea about the limits and direction for power, neither legal process nor all the enforcement powers of the free peoples would be required to compel it. Law could be taken out of the equation, replaced by a shared ideology of power. Although legal norms and institutions may point the way, a better world would require an awakening of spirit.

I first encountered this idea in a 1954 article by Wilhelm Roepke, a German ordo-liberal economist, reflecting nostalgically on the nineteenth-century world order.[55] He was an opponent of efforts to construct anything like a government at the European or global level: the very idea raised the specter of collectivism. But he marveled at the way he imagined the world to have operated in the nineteenth century.

> We realize that the problem of international trade is to find for it a legal-institutional framework which is at least approximate to that which intra-national trade can take for granted within the national borders. . . . But how has this been done in spite of the fact that there never was a world state? That is the capital question which we must answer.
>
> The solution which the Liberal Age had found for the problem of international order was of a peculiar and complex kind, and we may characterize its main features if we call it the universalist-liberal solution. . . . The functions of the non-existent but seemingly indispensable world state have been replaced by something else for which we may find the only parallel in the Res Publica Christiana of the Middle Ages. . . . We may call this substitute of the world state the international "open society" of the Liberal Age. It was a sort of *ordre public international* . . . .
>
> The international "open society" of the nineteenth century may be regarded, in a very large sense, as a creation of the "liberal" spirit. . . . We come here to a point of extraordinary importance without which we cannot understand fully the mystery of the international order of the recent past. What we mean is the genuinely *liberal principle of the widest possible separation of the two spheres of government and economy, of sovereignty and economic exploitation, of Imperium and Dominium, or of "political power" and "economic power"* (MacIver). This means the largest possible "depolitisation" of the economic sphere and everything that goes with it.[56]

Free trade was not the disciplining creed of international financial institutions and first world governments—it was the spirit of an age, enforcing itself in the minds of elites wherever they worked, in city governments, corporate boardrooms, local central banks, and dozens of national civil services. The shared commitment to the liberal principle—plus the gold standard—functioned as an "As-If-World-Government." If institutions were to be constructed at the European or global level, they should be designed to encourage that spirit rather than to legislate or enforce it.

After 1989, legal intellectuals developed a similar picture of human rights. In this view, the peoples of the world are united in a common civilization whose normative consensus operates as a foundational limit on political life expressed in the canon of international human rights norms. In 2001, a leading American international law text introduced the chapter on human rights by reference to Louis Henkin's 1990 argument that we had entered an "age of rights."

> The second half of the 20th century has been described as the "Age of Rights." That characterization reflects the view that, with the end of the Second World War, the idea of human rights became a universal political ideology and a central aspect of an ideology of constitutionalism. The ideology of human rights, of course, is a municipal ideology, to be realized by states within their national societies through national constitutional law and implemented by national institutions. But beginning with the promises made during the Second World War in the plans for a new world order, human rights became a matter of international concern and progressively a subject of international law. . . . What was once unthinkable had become normal by the end of the 20th century.[57]

This vision linked law's operations in the world directly to the common faith of the professional elites who govern in its name. The most significant law is not the law that is valid or persuasive or effectively enforced, but the law that is taken for granted: the law that needs no enforcement and raises no suspicion about its validity. The legality of this law is always already vouchsafed by it hegemonic position in the governing "ideology" of the global establishment. In Henkin's view, the "age of rights" has much in common with the world before Austin raised anxieties about legality in the first place. Following Henkin, we might say that when Ben Franklin packed himself off to Paris with Vattel in his satchel, international law was part of his "ideology" of what it meant to be a diplomat.

As I have argued in this book, elites do share many ideas about what governments are, what an economy is, what the appropriate objectives and tools of policy are, what problems demand attention, and which can safely be left unattended. They share ideas about law as well: what it is, what it requires, how it operates, where its limits are to be found. Their ideas are not all laudatory: a consensus that damaging the environment is a natural prerogative of sovereign power, that rules distorting economic activity ought to be withdrawn, or simply that the suffering and death caused in legitimate war is, well, legitimate. International lawyers have tended not to explore these possibilities, perhaps because it would complicate their veneration and jeopardize their effort to promote law as an ideology of governance.

The robust global machinery of advocacy and activism that has grown up around the promotion of human rights would not be necessary had they truly become axiomatic for people in power. In one sense, however, Henkin was correct. One rarely hears arguments *against* human rights. Governments routinely accuse one another of violating human rights and defend their own exercise of power on the global stage as a defense of human rights. As a vocabulary for the assertion of power, they have become hegemonic. People making assertions in their name customarily do so in a forceful style, as if the norms they represent were part of a settled global consensus that ought not to need to be asserted at all. The word "faith" is probably not the best description for the mental backdrop to these practices. Henkin does not ask his readers to "believe" in human rights or to choose law as the best interpretation of a global power process. He recounts the triumph of human rights as a historical fact: a new global political ideology has come.

The question is how to act in their name. Here, Henkin urges a complex professional posture on his followers. Where McDougal imagined international law professionals in Cold War statecraft while Koh imagined them in bureaucratic practice, Henkin imagines them as advocates bearing witness to a new truth. To act with zeal and fealty is certainly part of it. The human rights community fosters a habit of fidelity among the faithful, a shared commitment not to doubt or betray the human rights revolution before the unbelievers. But to play for ideological hegemony is also to play a long game that requires strategic and practical wisdom. One must take care: if you go to war in the name of human rights, you could both lose the war and disenchant the human rights vocabulary.

In his short 1990 book, *The Age of Rights*, Henkin offers a kind of epistle to the faithful. The book contains affirmations of faith alongside advice and possible arguments one might use when witnessing: what to say about competing "ideologies" like religion, socialism, or "development"; how to square so many violations with the existence of rights; how to handle the diversity of human rights practices in different nations; how to think about the false piety of the hypocrite; how to square the demands of an unreformed world with the fact of human rights triumph. These recall the concerns that moved Paul in his many letters to struggling communities of faith.

> Ours is the age of rights. Human rights is the idea of our time, the only political-moral idea that has received universal acceptance. . . .
> Despite this universal consensus, as all know, the condition of human rights differs widely among countries, and leaves more-or-less to be desired

everywhere. This may suggest that the consensus I have described is at best formal, nominal, perhaps even hypocritical, cynical. If it be so, it is nonetheless significant that it is *this* idea that has commanded universal nominal acceptance, not (as in the past) the divine right of kings or the omnipotence state, not the inferiority of races or women, not even socialism. Even if it be hypocrisy, it is significant—since hypocrisy, we know, is the homage that vice pays to virtue—homage, that governments today do not feel free to preach what they may persist in practicing. It is significant that all states and societies have been prepared to accept human rights as the norm, rendering deviations abnormal, and requiring governments to conceal and deny, to show cause, lest they stand condemned. Even if half or more of the world lives in a state of emergency with rights suspended, that situation is conceded, indeed proclaimed, to be abnormal, and the suspension of rights is the touchstone and measure of abnormality.[58]

The result for human rights advocates is a subtle and shifting combination of strong assertion and strategic calculation. In my experience, it would be wrong to say that human rights advocates "believe" they represent a settled ideology. They are committed to the practice of human rights advocacy as a path to justice. They have confidence in the power of advocacy *sans peur et sans reproches*. They are careful pragmatists about when and where to engage, and how to preserve the authority of speaking in the name of norms whose legality is not open to challenge. What holds them back from exploring the costs and benefits or unanticipated consequences of their advocacy, their role in the legitimation of conflict or the reproduction of inequality is less belief or faith than a shared practice that arises for each professional as a personal identity—*here I stand*—combined with strategic cunning. It is difficult not to be reminded of a similar injunction to the believer:

> Behold, I send you forth as sheep in the midst of wolves. Be ye therefore as wise as serpents and as innocent as doves.[59]

To associate human rights with injustice or bad outcomes both betrays the community of the faithful—"I knew him not"—and is bad strategy. If you bear witness, people will come to believe and act in the name of human rights. To affirm the downsides can only delegitimate law and retard progress toward a better world. The problem of legality—like the problem of faith—can be resolved only in the practice of a community of believers who balance pragmatic awareness and strategic calculation with a calm ethical self-confidence in their materials and their common work.

In the wake of twentieth-century efforts to renew and expand the field, the expertise of international lawyers is a combination of shared ideas and points of reference, shared projects and commitments, and a common sensibility. It is not ideas or doctrines that hold the field together—these are diverse and only rarely compelling. The faith required to inhabit and use them is part fealty, in the sense of a commitment never to deny or betray the field, the legality of international law, or the promise of its future. It is faith affirmed in community, through the shared experience of routine professional work as the faithful recognize one another and celebrate what sets them apart. This faith as practice is a habit of acting as if what is believed were true, a practical project in a fallen world: the common work of promoting, expressing—or holding one's tongue—as strategically necessary in a world that will only later be able to live fully the dream of cosmopolitan legality.

RESPONDING TO LEGAL PLURALISM

The modern sophistication of the international legal profession reflects an awareness of the diverse and contradictory quality of the available ethical commitments, legal norms, institutions and legal theories.[60] The practice of professional faith—an orientation toward the virtuous future of law—makes this pluralism tolerable. As in any community of faith, however, people also struggle with belief. Doubts and anxieties arise. In periodic response, the discipline generates new theories about how it all fits together. These function as a kind of belt and suspenders on professional faith. We would expect these to come in at least two voices: the impatient idolatry of premature solution and the reassuring balm of prefiguration in a still fallen world. We should understand contemporary international legal theory in this way: a ministry to a doubting church.

If there could be a dispositive account of systemic coherence, we would not need so difficult a practice: what we believed might come could already be seen. For all the nuanced sophistication of practice in their shadow, images of a policy process, legal process, or universal ideology are meant to be reassuring in just this way. Diverse action, action taken in doubt, also somehow adds up. The whole is more than the sum of parochial interests struggling with one another. Debates about the "fragmentation" of international law or the "proliferation" of international courts and tribunals across the turn of the past century arose in moments of anxiety and doubt when worry about the integrity of the legal "order" as a whole weighed on the profession. The work of scholarship was not to address the doubts they expressed: a dispersed and fragmented law cannot be put back together; a constitution for the world cannot be but a wish. When Austinian anxieties arise in these terms—Are we constituted? Is law whole?—all we can do is talk about it reassuringly, developing practical responses in particular situations, plowing the debate back into professional argumentative practice. Then we can again pick up the baton and return to the work of faith.

People theorizing coherence into a plural legal universe are sometimes tempted by the metaphor of constitutionalism. In public international law, scholars have encouraged the idea that the UN Charter provides a kind of "constitution," particularly when it comes to the use of force. Others have seen a "constitutional moment" in the emergence of human rights as a global vernacular for the legitimacy of power. Some have proposed the World Trade Organization as a constitutional order, perhaps in combination with the human rights canon. Specialists in comparative constitutional law sometimes find the key in relations among national constitutions. All testify to the wish that things were constituted—as well as the realization that there is as of yet no workable account of how the world's legal order coheres. In a sophisticated profession, coherence theories rarely stand the test of time. There are too many of them, they are too easily instrumentalized by people with parochial projects and the pressure of practical struggle continually reopens awareness of pluralism and returns the professional from the reassurance of theory to the practice of his faith.

Gunther Teubner's proposal for a transnational "project of constitutional sociology" is a particularly sophisticated constitutional theory.[61] Rather than privileging one doctrinal or institutional regime, he proposes to deepen the sociology of transnational regulation, adjudication, and administration to illuminate principles, rules, professional practices, and institutional arrangements, whether "public" or "private," which affect the "division of powers" among actors, sectors, and values in transnational society. The goal is to unearth the constitutional underpinnings of everyday interactions across and within semi-autonomous systems, each loosely associated with industries or domains of social practice or belief, each with its own rules and procedures, each pursuing its own particular logic: a health system, a sports system, a media system, a trade system, a pharmaceutical system, a scientific system, and so on. Governments—or diplomacy—form but one system among many. The identification of "systems" is not just description. It requires interpretation. Is there a global pharmaceutical system and an entertainment system? Or is there an international intellectual property system? Does the sports system stand on its own, or is it part of the diplomatic system or the entertainment system? Interpretations are strategic tools: this is a system, this is its logic. And now we have returned to professional practice, atop another sediment of theoretical sophistication. It would require a break with professional faith to harness the same analytic to make visible the coercive distributive struggles in which one or another professional practice is implicated.

In the United States, we are accustomed to thinking about the rules governing relations among the federal legislature, courts, and executive as "constitutional" because they are mentioned in the official Constitution and debated as such. If we think in more sociological terms, we may want to add other things: the distinction between public and private activity, the relationship between corporate and labor power, the relative prestige of coastal and midwestern or northern and southern culture, the distribution of power between cities and suburbs. Perhaps the enduring allocation of power between white and black citizens, between men and women or between rich and poor is "constitutional." The distributional consequences of treating one as constitutional and the other as a matter of history is hard to unravel, but it is likely to affect who feels empowered to contest or preserve which arrangements. The practice of constitutionalism—or systems analysis—is itself a space of distributive struggle.

In this book, I have advanced two responses to the experience of pluralism other than redoubling the practice of a doubting professional faith or embracing the idolatry of new coherentist theory. First is to lay down the burdens of faith and see law's role in the ubiquitous struggles of global political and economic life and the injustice that results. Martti Koskenniemi expresses this shift in perspective:

> Much of mainstream Anglo-American jurisprudence . . . approaches law in this way, as a hermeneutics of interpretation that aims to ensure the coherence of the legal order—and thereby the acceptability of the system of distribution of material and spiritual values that goes with it. There is much that is right in this jurisprudence. Law is an interpretive craft. But it underestimates the open-endedness of the interpretations and mistakes "coherence" as the point of legal activity. A better view is to take one step backwards, accept the irreducible indeterminacy of interpretation and the contradictoriness of legal argument (which, in any case, most lawyers accept), and build on the way legal argument brings out into the open the contradictions of

the society in which it operates and the competition of opposite interests that are the flesh and blood of the legal everyday.

Law is an argumentative practice that operates in institutional contexts characterized by adversity. . . . From this perspective, law is not a supporter of social consensus but a participant in its conflicts, giving form to social adversity in order to support some values against others, to affirm or contest prevailing distributionary structures.[62]

A second and allied alternative is embrace of the experience that things don't add up, that coherence fails, that incommensurability must be acknowledged. This road opens whenever there is a personal encounter with incommensurate difference and a loss of confidence in the availability of resolution within the canons of acceptable professional discussion. Lawyers may experience it whenever there are conflicts, gaps, or ambiguities in the law and it seems, if only for a moment, that they cannot be reconciled or bridged. In chapter 5, I associated this with the professional experience of "yielding" to the argument or assertion of another. The personal experience of legal pluralism that comes with "yielding" unmoors professionals from the confident sense that their expertise grounds their action. Suddenly, there is a choice: a moment of vertigo and professional freedom.

People recoil from this experience of pluralism. Experts turn back to faith or reach rapidly for the reassurance of theory and prior practice. But there is also a long tradition praising such moments in religious and political thought: the moment when "unknowing" and "deciding" cross paths, when freedom and moral responsibility join hands. It is what Carl Schmitt had in mind by "deciding in the exception"[63] or what Max Weber spoke of as having a "vocation for politics."[64] It is what Kierkegaard described as the "man of faith,"[65] or Sartre as the exercise of responsible human freedom.[66] This is what Jacques Derrida meant by "deconstruction."[67] The sudden experience of unknowing, with time marching forward to determination, action, decision—the moment when the deciding self feels itself thrust forward, unmoored, into the experience. In that moment of vertigo, the world's irrationality makes plain the constructed nature of theories about how it all fits together and the tendentiousness of practices in their name. Professional practice suddenly has no progressive telos, and international law opens as a terrain for politics, rather than a recipe or escape from political choice. It is in such a moment that the world could look again like 1648: open to being remade.

CHAPTER 8
LEGAL EXPERTISE IN WAR

The professional practices of legal experts inside and outside the military illustrate the work of expertise in contemporary world making and management. Warfare has been a central preoccupation and presented a kind of ultimate test for international law. It is hard to think of international law governing the relations among states without having something to say about war—when war is and is not an appropriate exercise of sovereign authority, how war can and cannot be conducted, which of war's outcomes will and will not become components of a postwar status quo, and so on. It is conventional to imagine that international law restrains war by making distinctions: this is war, and this is not; this is sovereignty, and this is not; this is legal warfare, and this is not. The terms with which these legal distinctions are drawn change over time. The vernacular may be more or less sodden with ethical considerations, more or less rooted in the specific treaty arrangements entered into by states. The distinctions may be drawn more or less sharply, may be matters of kind or degree. What goes on one or the other side of these distinctions may change, but the idea that law is about distinguishing war from peace, sovereign right from sovereign whim, legal from illegal conduct, on the battlefield and off, endures.

Discussions about international law and war usually unfold as if the participants were imagining an international law that would be able to substitute itself for sovereign power in a top-down fashion, first to distinguish legal from illegal violence and then, perhaps not today but eventually, or perhaps not directly but indirectly, to bring that distinction to bear in the life of sovereigns, extinguishing sovereign authority for war at the point it crosses a legal limit. The idea is that the articulation of right will discipline, limit, and restrain sovereign power when it turns to violence. International law proposes to bring this about through a series of doctrines, definitions, and arguments that *say* where war begins and ends, and then through an apparatus of institutions and relationships that are linked in one or another way to these doctrines and that are the locus for or the effect of these sayings.

Much work has been put into codifying the doctrines through which international law will be able to say what is and is not legal and to develop a canon of thought about how these doctrines are to be interpreted when making a distinction. On the institutional side, at the national level there is the apparatus of military justice, courts-martial, and penalties, the institutions of political and strategic command, of media commentary and popular engagement, of international approval and condemnation, and so forth. At the international level, lawyers have sought to empower the UN Security Council as the arbiter of war and to build an International Criminal Court both to adjudicate past wars and, more importantly, to signal and deter future sovereign departures from what the Court determines is legal. Recognizing the limits of such institutions, international lawyers concerned about war have adapted the twentieth-century reconceptualization of the international political process as an interactive process through which norms are made real in a horizontal society of states— through the enforcement authority of hegemonic states acting in the name of law, by disaggregated citizen action delegitimating sovereign activity, or simply by the increased military and political costs imposed on those who make war when or in ways which are understood by others to be illegal.

This conventional framework has serious limitations. It overstates the distinctiveness of war and peace as well as the extent to which international law can be said to be on the "side" of peace. It would be more accurate to say that the international law about war operates in two directions simultaneously. On the one hand, it offers a doctrinal and institutional terrain for a kind of combat over the effectiveness and limits of war that depends upon a professional practice of distinction and a series of institutional practices and sites for rendering these distinctions real in the operations of sovereign power. On the other hand, it offers a parallel doctrinal and institutional framework for transforming sovereign power and violence into right, continuing the projects of war by other means. By following these circuits between law and war in the operations of modern war, we may come to replace our image of a law outside war (and a sovereign power normally "at peace") with an image of sovereign power and legal determination themselves bound up with war, having their origin in war, and contributing through their routine practices in "wartime" and "peacetime" to the ongoing, if often silent, wars that are embedded in the structure of international life.

The doctrinal and institutional components of the international legal regime are in operation not only when they assert themselves against the exercise of military force or when they cabin violence within walls drawn by these doctrines. International law is equally—indeed, perhaps more routinely—the space within which war is conceived and validated and through which force is disciplined and rendered effective. It can be difficult to remember that the articulation and institutional enforcement of legal boundaries also expresses and continues projects of war. Yet sovereigns do routinely discipline and legitimate their military campaigns by pronouncing on the legality of bombing here or killing there. When this happens successfully, international law confirms the violent expression of sovereign power as right.

It is easy to understand the virtues of a powerful legal vocabulary, shared by elites around the world, which appears to distinguish legal from illegal war and wartime violence. It is exciting to see law become the mark of legitimacy as legitimacy has become the currency of power. It is more difficult to see the opportunities this opens for the military professional to harness law as a weapon, or for sovereigns to continue the exercise of power as right. Yet the humanist vocabulary of international law *is* routinely mobilized by as a strategic asset in war, just as the vernacular of legal right is inseparable from the enforcement of sovereign power. When humanitarian international lawyers say that compliance with international law "legitimates," they mean that killing, maiming, humiliating, wounding people are legally privileged, authorized, permitted, and justified. The military has taken the hint.

The American military have coined a word for this: "lawfare"—law as a weapon, law as a tactical ally, law as a strategic asset, an instrument of war. They observe that law can often accomplish what might once have been done with bombs and missiles: seize and secure territory, send messages about resolve and political seriousness, even break the will of a political opponent. When the military buys up commercial satellite capacity to deny it to an adversary—contract is their weapon. They could presumably have denied their adversary access to those pictures in many ways. When the United States uses the Security Council to certify lists of terrorists and force seizure of their assets abroad, they have weaponized the law. Those assets might also have been immobilized in other ways. It is not only the use of force that can do these things. Threats can sometimes work. And law often marks the line between what counts as the routine exercise of one's prerogative and a threat to cross that line and exact a penalty.

There is a kind of political continuity between international legal projects that seem to concern war and peace. When special courts are established by victors to adjudicate the criminality of opponents, it can be dressed up as the "return" of law and peace—but it is hard to avoid thinking that law is also the continuation of war by other means. Something similar is at work when the Security Council of the United Nations, itself established to institutionalize the outcome of the Second World War as a system of "collective security," is given the authority to determine the legality of wars today—when, for example, the "legality" of the Iraq War hung solely upon how France decided to vote. The legalization of the last war's outcome presses itself on the legitimacy of future combat. The situation is similar when a hegemonic "international community" sets up a court of general instance to try those who have, in their eyes, lost their "legitimacy" as sovereigns. Whether or not anyone is prosecuted, a war has, in some sense, been lost. We might say that, through law, not all wars need to be fought to be lost decisively. These engagements of the international law about war with the ongoing relations of sovereign power enforced by war are emblematic of a more general relationship between modern war and modern law.

On the one hand, modern war has engaged the bureaucratic, commercial, and cultural institutions normally associated with peace. On the other, what I term "modern law" has proliferated the doctrinal materials and interpretive methods that can be brought to bear in discussing the distinctiveness and legality of state violence. Lines are now harder to draw, both because the world of war has become more mixed up and because ambiguities, gaps, and contradictions in the materials used to draw the lines have become more pronounced. At the same time, however, there is a lot more line drawing going on. There has been a vast dispersion of sites and institutions and procedures through which legal distinctions about war are made. This proliferation of legally framed activity has made war and sovereign power into legal institutions even as the experience of legal pluralism and fluidity has unhinged the idea of a law which, out there, somehow distinguishes. It would be more accurate today to speak about an international law that places legal distinction in strategic play as a part of war itself, further proliferating and fragmenting the sites of its doctrinal and institutional operation.

Moreover, in the retail operations of law about war, the experience of irresolvable debate, or of debate that can be resolved only by reference outside law to the political or ethical, is ever more common. As is the experience, for soldiers and citizens alike, of vertigo amid the shifting perspectives from which killing is evaluated. It is difficult to say just how this will come out. New doctrinal tools may arise, old tools may regain their plausibility, institutional and doctrinal activity within the field may become less dispersed and more hegemonic. It may again become plausible to imagine an international law "outside" and "over" sovereign power, declaring and determining the limits of violence. In the meantime, however, international law about war offers a window onto the political and ethical consequences of the fluid and strategic relations among sovereign power, force, and law that characterize the experience of modern law in modern war—the experience of people who work with law and declare in its name.

DISPERSION: MODERN WAR AS A LEGAL INSTITUTION

In warfare today, the practice of distinction—central to both law and war— has been dispersed. The sites and technologies through which legal assertions about violence are translated back and forth into the vernacular of violence have proliferated. In this sense, law has infiltrated the war machine. Law now shapes the institutional, logistical and physical landscape of war and the battlespace has become as legally saturated as the rest of modern life. Law has become—for parties on all sides of even the most asymmetric confrontations—a vocabulary for marking legitimate power and justifiable death. It is not too much to say that war has become a legal institution—the continuation of law by other means. Not everyone follows the rules or even agrees on what the rules are and how they should be interpreted. Quite the contrary—people disagree about these matters all the time. Precisely as a result, the opportunities for law to make itself felt in the experience of those participating in modern war have multiplied.

The law that structures the macro and micro operations of warfare is broader than the "law of force," the "law of armed conflict" or "international humanitarian law." Law is certainly most visibly part of military life when it privileges the killing and destruction of battle. If you kill *this way*, and not that, *here* and not there, *these people* and not those—what you do is privileged. If not, it is criminal. And the war must itself be legal. Operating across dozens of jurisdictions, today's military must also comply with innumerable local, national, and international rules regulating the use of territory, the mobilization of men, the financing of arms and logistics and the deployment of force. War is waged across a terrain shaped by constitutional law, administrative law, private law, and more. As warfare has evolved, law about the environment, social security, land use, religious expression, finance and payments systems, government budgeting, privacy, as well as human rights, law of the sea, law of space, conflict of laws, law of nationality, jurisdiction are all implicated in the shape of warfare.

Background doctrines of property and contract, of privacy and financial accountability, channel the legal mobilization of violence, as do informal and customary laws of business practice, informal markets, and the clandestine flows of finance, information, goods, and people.

Wars now occur at the peripheries of the world system, among foes with wildly different institutional, economic, and military capacities. Enemies are dispersed and decisive engagement is rare. Battle is at once intensely local and global in new ways. Soldiers train for tasks far from conventional combat: local diplomacy, intelligence gathering, humanitarian reconstruction, urban policing, or managing the routine tasks of local government. Violence follows patterns more familiar from epidemiology or cultural fashion than military strategy. Networks of fellow travelers exploit the infrastructures of the global economy to bring force to bear here and there. Satellite systems guide precision munitions from deep in Missouri to the outskirts of Kabul. The glare of the modern media is everywhere, even as the politics continued by warfare has itself been legalized. Today's sovereign stands atop a complex bureaucracy, exercising powers delegated by a constitution, and shared with myriad agencies, bureaucracies, and private actors, knit together in complex networks that spread across borders. Political leaders act in the shadow of a knowledgeable, demanding, engaged, and institutionally entrenched local, national, and global elite, which also has institutional forms and professional habits. Discourses of right have become the common vernacular of this dispersed elite, even as they argue about just what the law permits and forbids.

War is also a professional practice. Militaries are linked to their nation's commercial life, integrated with civilian and peacetime governmental institutions, and covered by the same national and international media. Mobilizing "the military" means setting thousands of units forth in a coordinated way. Officers discipline their force and organize their operations with rules. Public and private actors must be enlisted in projects of death and destruction, which they must in turn explain to their families, their pastors, their comrades. Coalition partners must be brought on board. Delicate political arrangements and sensibilities must be translated into practical limits—and authorizations—for using force. Nor is the legal professionalization of warfare an exclusively first world practice. Indeed, it turns out the Taliban issues training materials outlining the rules of engagement designed to maximize the effect and legitimacy of their force in their own cultural time and place.

As a result, the sites at which official rules for war are given meaning and have institutional, political, or personal purchase have become many. Ideas about what war is and is not, what uses of force are and are not legal, which wars are and are not legally legitimate run through the political, institutional, and social fabric of societies. In each of the spaces in which war is made, the determination of what is and is not legal plays a role in constituting the entities who will act. Negotiations over participation in warfare are conducted in debates about the "rules of engagement"—who could do what, when, to whom? For politicians who will take the heat, it is important to know just how trigger-happy—or "forward-leaning"—the soldiers at the tip of the spear will be. Soldiers—and citizens—must be made in the image of these rules. At each of these sites, there are opportunities for adjusting, refining, and making the distinction between legal and illegal—and it will often be these distinctions through which the political debates are resolved, the families are able to feel proud, the allies establish a common front.

MODERN LAW: RHETORICAL STRATEGY

As the sites over which the regime of distinction has dispersed itself have proliferated, the doctrinal and conceptual materials used to distinguish war and peace or legal and illegal state violence have become even more fluid. No longer an affair of clear rules and sharp distinctions, international law rarely speaks clearly or with a single voice. That does not mean the making of distinctions is any less important. Whenever people call what they are doing *war*, they stress its discontinuity from the normal routines of peacetime and sharpen a collective identity against a common enemy. To shoot a man—or a woman—on the battlefield is not murder. Distinction establishes the legal privilege to kill. But just when does the privilege to kill replace the prohibition on murder? Where does war begin and end? What counts as "perfidy," "terror," or "torture"? Which civilians *are* innocent? As law has become an ever more important yardstick for legitimacy, the legal categories used to make those distinctions have become far too spongy to permit clear resolution—or became spongy enough to undergird the experience of self-confident outrage by parties on all sides of a conflict.

The law of armed conflict has become a confusing mix of principles and counterprinciples, of firm rules and loose exceptions. In legal terms, "war" itself has become a smorgasbord of finely differentiated activities: "self-defense," "hostilities," "the use of force," "resort to arms," "police action," "peace enforcement," "peace making," "peacekeeping." It becomes ever harder to keep it all straight. Meanwhile, warfare has come to comprise an ever wider range of divergent activities. Troops in the same city are fighting and policing and building schools. Restoring water is part of winning the war. Private actors are everywhere—from insurgents who melt into the mosque to armed soldiers who turn out to work for private contractors, not to mention all the civilians providing moral and physical support to those who bomb and shoot, or who run the complex technology and logistical chains "behind" modern warfare. In the confusion, military and humanitarian voices will often have a motive to insist on a bright line. For the military, defining the battlefield defines the privilege to kill. But aid agencies also want the guys digging the wells to be seen as humanitarians, not postconflict combatants—privileged not to be killed. Defining the not-battlefield opens a "space" for humanitarian action. Others will be moved to soften the distinctions, perhaps to permit military funds to be used for a police action, or to insist that human rights norms be applicable in combat. In a dispersed regime for articulating the legality of sovereign force, we can expect a constant push and pull, making and unmaking formal distinctions, in ways that reflect the calculations of actors pursuing very local strategies.

As it became a more plastic medium, international law offered an ever wider range of instruments for making and unmaking distinctions between war and peace, allowing the boundaries of war to be managed strategically. Take this difficult question—when does war end? The answer is to be found not in law or fact—but in strategy. *Declaring* the end of hostilities might be a matter of election theater or military assessment, just like announcing that there remains "a long way to go," or that the "insurgency is in its final throes." We should understand these statements as *arguments*. As messages—but also as weapons. Law—legal categorization—is a communication tool. And communicating the war is fighting the war. This is a war, this is an occupation, this is a police action, this is a security zone. These are insurgents, those are criminals, these are illegal combatants, and so on. All these are claims with audiences, made for a reason. Increasingly, defining the battlefield is not only a matter of deployed force—it is also a rhetorical and legal claim.

When people use the law strategically, moreover, they change it. The Red Cross changes it. Al Jazeera changes it. CNN changes it. The US administration changes it. Humanitarians who seize on vivid images of civilian casualties to raise expectations about the accuracy of targeting are changing the legal fabric. When an Italian prosecutor decides to charge CIA operatives for their alleged participation in a black operation of kidnapping and rendition, the law of the battlefield has shifted. As American military forces in the Middle East have changed their military objectives and strategy over the past years, they have also adjusted their rules of engagement with respect to civilian death. In broad terms, what had seemed legally acceptable collateral damage in an invasion came to seem a threat to the success of an occupation—and what seemed acceptable to enforce an occupation came to seem counterproductive in "counterinsurgency operations." The rules were tightened and civilian death was meted out more parsimoniously. At the same time, however, observers (and civilian populations) altered their expectations about the civilian deaths that would occur and that had to be tolerated. They pushed back, tightening the reins on the American forces yet further until *any* dead civilian seemed a rebuke to the legitimacy and proof of the failure of the mission.

As a result, there is now more than one law of armed conflict. Legal pluralism has arrived. Different nations have signed onto different treaties. The same standards look different if you anticipate battle against a technologically superior foe or live in a Palestinian refugee camp in Gaza and the legal materials are elastic enough to enable opposing interpretations. Amnesty International called Israeli attacks on Hezbollah "war crimes that give rise to individual criminal responsibility." Israel rejected the charge that it "acted outside international norms or international legality" and insisted that "you are legally entitled to target infrastructure that your enemy is exploiting for its military campaign." There is only the imaginary Court of World Public Opinion on the international stage to adjudicate such claims. The process by which diverse claims take institutional, political, and professional form varies, and a lawyer advising on the law of war must assess the institutional, political, social, and human context before making a prediction about how people with the power to influence the client's interest will interpret and enact claims about the distinctiveness of what the client contemplates doing.

A HISTORY OF MODERNIZATION

The fluidity of the modern law about warfare results from the long professional struggle I described in the last chapter. At least twice over the past two hundred years, international law concerning war has dramatically transformed itself in an effort to provide a satisfying vernacular of distinction. Across the nineteenth century, the broad considerations of ethics and policy that had preoccupied the international law about war for centuries—when is war just, when is war wise, how ought the sovereign to treat his enemy, his ally, his subjects, and so forth——were gradually leeched out. They were replaced by a series of sharp distinctions and clear rules that were either agreed between sovereigns (these weapons and not those) or deduced from the nature of war and sovereignty themselves (war and peace, civilians and combatants, belligerents and neutrals, law about going to war and law about conducting war). By the early twentieth century, the doctrinal materials had narrowed to focus on clear formal distinctions defined and agreed by sovereigns. War and peace were legally distinct, separated by a formal "declaration of war." A sharp distinction between public and private law made it seem reasonable to insist that private rights survived the violence of warfare, which public powers did not. It was at this moment that the "law of war" and the "law in war" came to seem sharply distinct—separate ways of judging the legality of making war and then, irrespective of the legality of the war, of judging the legality of weaponry and tactics.

At the same time, the idea of law's own disciplinary function in relationship to war changed. At the start of the nineteenth century, international law offered a kind of handbook of advice and good sense to guide the action of statesmen. It focused on considerations affecting the right to make war and the sensible limits of warfare. It imagined the jurist and the statesmen or military commander not as part of sharply distinct disciplines, but as part of a shared community of leaders struggling to make sense of natural law and national interest. By the end of the century, a more formal doctrinal law tracing its rules to state practice and consent—or simply to the nature of sovereign authority itself—offered itself as an external, autonomous, and in some sense scientific judge of the legality of sovereign action in warfare. It treated the distinctions between legal and illegal war, weaponry or tactics as best able to be drawn by independent jurists ruminating on the nature of sovereignty and the meaning of agreed texts.

Over the course of the twentieth century, international law shifted again. From the First World War forward, many international lawyers thought the effort to restrain war by rules unrealistic. Some turned instead to diplomatic promises and institutional arrangements to provide for the "collective security" and manage a process of "peaceful change," primarily through the League of Nations. For those who continued to pursue the doctrinal route, considerations of justice and policy that had been exogenized found their way back in. Distinctions came to be drawn less sharply, often as matters of degree rather than kind.

Agreed rules about weaponry were joined by broad principles—such as proportionality or military necessity—that expressed the limits of warfare in terms that seemed more pragmatic and could more readily be associated with reflections on justice. By the end of the Second World War, these doctrinal approaches were harnessed to the institutional framework of the United Nations, whose charter shifted the focus from the rhetoric of legal declarations of war and distinctions between neutrals and belligerents to the institutional management of threats to the peace and the use of force. Over the years, as distinctions softened, it seemed reasonable to consider applying elements of what had been the law of peace—particularly the law of human rights—on the battlefield, and blurring the boundaries between the legality of a war and the legality of weapons used and tactics chosen.

This transformation was supported by both military specialists and humanitarians. Both came to doubt the viability and usefulness of sharp distinctions. For the military professionals, bright lines can be helpful in the blur of combat, communicating a firewall between levels of combat to their own force, to allies and enemies alike. But they can also constrain in unpredictable ways. It will often be more useful to work with loose standards expressing broad principles, to weigh and balance the consequences of military action in light of its objectives. At the same time, ethical absolutes, let loose on matters of war and peace, can be dangerous, heightening enthusiasm for military campaigns beyond a sovereign's actual political capacity to follow through. They can focus attention in the wrong place, and it may not be clear, in advance, which tactic or weapon will, in fact, cause the least harm. The rule against use of chemical weapons on the battlefield seems to preclude the use of tear gases routinely used in domestic policing—a line that led to the widespread use of flamethrowers to clear caves during combat in Afghanistan. Moreover, narrowly drawn rules permit a great deal—and legitimate what is permitted. From a humanitarian point of view, it seems wiser to assess things comparatively, contextually, in more pragmatic terms.

These shifts did not happen everywhere at the same time or to the same extent, nor did they happen in a vacuum. They were part of a widespread enthusiasm and then loss of faith in the formal distinctions of nineteenth-century legal thought—in the wisdom, as well as the plausibility, of separating law sharply from politics, or private right sharply from public power. Within that framework, much depended on the details of national legal cultures and upon the political strategies of leading jurists and others in particular locations. More importantly, these shifts were not decisive. Remnants of each discarded sensibility remain. As a result, people now speak about the legal distinctions of warfare in three different dialects, each reminiscent of a historical phase in the discipline's development.

At the start of the twenty-first century, international law, taken as a whole, speaks about warfare as a matter of justice and wise policy, recollecting the early nineteenth century, as an object for juristic assessment through rumination on first principles and elaboration of valid rules, in a way that recalls late nineteenth-century thinking, and as a very twentieth-century question of legitimacy determined by the persuasiveness of justification to international elites, whose granting or withholding of legitimation in turn validates or invalidates the distinctions and judgments that are made. Moreover, these dialects have been changed by their encounters with one another. They have become methodological options, rather than simply what law is all about. Focusing on questions of justice and policy, for example, may be picked up in a spirit of eclectic pragmatism, alongside the languages of juridical forms and sociological legitimacy, or as a matter of methodological—even ethical and political—commitment, responsive to what seem the limitations of both nineteenth and twentieth century ideas. Those who today give voice to legal distinctions—legal professionals, statesmen, media experts, and law people—sometimes do so with passion about the mode of argument being made and sometimes with a kind of eclectic indifference to issues of method.

The transformation of historical modes of thought into styles of argument has arranged them in relation to one another as methodological positions on an imaginary continuum between political realism and ethical judgment. Each analytic style offers a somewhat different way to declare what is and is not legal without sounding as if you are simply saying what you believe or desire. In each style, legal pronouncements are "rooted" in sovereign consent, just as they are compatible with widely shared principles of justice. They have also pulled away from these roots, through a series of rituals and transformations which blend the two ambitions together. Those who speak about "just war" in legal terms, for example, may feel confident that they are expressing more than an ethical preference because they have derived their definition of "just war" by reference to the practice of sovereigns or the nature of an intersovereign society. Those who speak about the power of legitimacy feel they are doing more than restating political outcomes in legal terms because they have traced the attribution of legitimacy to rule following, perhaps because, in social terms, rules exert a kind of pull toward compliance or because the psychology of statesmen can plausibly be reconstructed to suggest rules were followed even when states didn't think doing so was in their best interest. As a result, in each of these three modes of distinction, law can be intertwined with sovereignty and with the violence of sovereign power while also being professionally practiced and articulated as if it were something altogether different.

Speaking in these ways, international law can echo with virtue and stand firmly on the side of peace while pursuing a proliferating institutional and

professional engagement with the practice of war. Defending this doubled professional sensibility has itself become an important disciplinary project. The
various rhetorical styles offer languages for tarring alternative modes of argument with the professional sins of either ethical or political subjectivism. In this
sense, defense of an autonomous legal doctrinal and institutional determiner
has been replaced by a professional practice of disciplining the boundaries of
legal argument itself to exclude political whim and ethical preference. In such
a profession, it is easy to mistake our ability to articulate law's autonomy—for
which we have numerous discursive tools ready at hand—for an actual capability to restrain the power and violence of war.

At the same time, however, the proliferation of styles has allowed for the
emergence of powerful antidotes to arguments that this or that death was legally compelled or justified. These antidotes—embedded in counterstyles of
professional argument—often unravel the confidence with which people have
asserted that this or that act of violence was legal or illegal. Indeed, it turns out
that none of these vernaculars of distinction holds up very well to thoughtful
criticism, which may help explain why there are three to begin with. An international law rooted in natural justice or wise policy seems unlikely to provide much of a solid foundation in a plural world. People will disagree about
what justice means and which policy is wise—indeed, they may go to war
over their disagreements—and it is hard to see how lawyers have any comparative advantage over sovereigns as auguries of justice or practical wisdom or,
on the basis of their vision of wisdom and justice, any independent platform,
expertise, or mandate for distinguishing the legitimate from the illegitimate.
That is partly why late nineteenth- and early twentieth-century international
lawyers thought a narrower catalog of rules rooted in sovereign power might
offer a stronger perspective from which to judge state behavior. It turned out,
however, that an autonomous regime of valid rules was insufficiently robust
to distinguish legal from illegal warfare with certainty. Agreed rules were too
narrow, principles were ambiguous and ran in too many contradictory directions, and it seemed difficult for rumination on sovereignty to crowd out the
actual exercise of sovereignty. That was partly why international jurists turned
to more social and interactive conceptions of the relationship between international law and warfare. But here there were also difficulties. The notion that
law is what it does makes it terribly difficult to distinguish law from whatever
happens in a convincing fashion. States did things for lots of reasons—just
when had law been the dominant cause? The idea that statesmen are persuaded
by law or that states act in the shadow of an international society that metes

out legitimacy ultimately rests on a hypothesis about the existence of the community international law is intended to express and to construct.

In the end, there are good reasons to be skeptical of claims made in any of these modes that this act of war *is* legal and this is not, that this *is* war and this is peace, or that this *is* legitimate and this is not. That doesn't mean such claims are unimportant or that they never persuade. Speaking this way can be quite satisfying, and not only because it can be pleasurable to speak confidently about violence that is and is not legal. These performances also routinely take institutional form, disciplining and excusing soldiers, making or ruining careers, identifying targets, emboldening or disheartening allies, comforting or demoralizing those who have killed or whose loved ones have died. This is knowledge that routinely becomes power, conjuring and shaping violence.

PEOPLE PURSUING PROJECTS BY ARTICULATION

International law is a set of arguments and counterarguments, rhetorical performances and counterperformances, deployed by people pursuing projects of various kinds. To focus on the expert practice of articulating legal distinctions, it is useful to suspend the effort to determine who is right. To understand what happens to ethics, to politics, and to professions themselves as they keep noses to the grindstone of legal argument in the face of all the killing that people do in war requires leaving to one side the question of whether this or that war is legal, whether this or that doctrine is valid or persuasive or made legitimate through enforcement—or which mode of assertion offers the most robust, effective, or appropriate style for legal work. Worrying about these things, arguing about them, giving opinions about them are all routine professional practices for international lawyers that one will surely want to master if one wants to work in the field.

Articulation becomes effective as force as people make legal arguments about war and all sorts of people have gotten into the act: military officers, human rights lawyers, Red Cross lawyers, demonstrators, ambassadors, presidents and prime ministers, media commentators, and, of course, law professors. People from many countries and cultures have done so: Americans and Iranians, Europeans and Australians, members of Hamas, Israeli public officials and judges and citizens, UN officials and East Timorese citizens. The sum of their statements is what international law has become. One way to imagine the dynamic that unfolds as this material is used is to picture its deployment in opposing projects.

There are those who speak the language of law and war for the purpose of strengthening their military hand—by disciplining and directing their forces, legitimating their actions and justifying their means—and those who do so for the purpose of restraining or weakening a military force by undisciplining and reorienting its forces or by delegitimating its violence. Leave to one side, for a moment, those who speak it for another purpose—say to strengthen the language of law itself by embroidering it into an effort to justify or restrain a military action, whatever the consequences. In this simple picture, there are those who claim to strengthen and those who claim to weaken the hand of force. We might think of these rhetorical positions as those of friend and enemy, or, perhaps more conventionally, of the national military and the international humanitarian. In every engagement, the one performs power as truth, the other speaks truth to power.

We can now begin to think about the model more dynamically. Where and how will modern law be brought to bear in modern war to further one or the other of these projects? Given the fluidity of modern law and the plasticity and dispersion of modern war, it will often be unclear precisely how a given statement might operate to strengthen or weaken the hand of force. Narrowing the rules of engagement, for example, may concentrate and discipline, or it may derail the effort, harnessing force to other objectives or demoralizing and delegitimating those who fight. A great deal will depend upon the larger regime through which statements are made, which offers an unending range of institutional maneuvers from denouncing to commending, from sensationalizing to routinizing. Even here, much is in doubt. Prosecuting a soldier may be a way of locating responsibility or avoiding it, focusing or distracting attention, strengthening or weakening a campaign.

We might, following Clausewitz, postulate that if all this claiming has any effect at all in war, whatever strengthens one side weakens the other. As a starting point, we might say that it will be in the interests of one party to advance whenever it is the interests of the other to rest or withdraw. Following his lead, we might begin with the hypothesis that whenever a claim for the legality of this war or this tactic would strengthen offense by allowing power to be exercised as right, we ought to expect the defense to think hard, not only about how to fight back so as to assert its own power as right, but also about how a claim of right might itself slow down the offense. The defense begins, then, by determining, if it can, that the attack is illegal, and speaking that truth to sovereign power. Of course, to be effective, this statement will need to pass through the institutions and regimes of law and politics and become a power which can, in fact, arrest the offense. In an opposite fashion, the offense must also make good its claim of right, through conquest, certainly, or more routinely through the capillaries of the world political regime through which such assertions succeed in strengthening one's hand in battle. Over time, where those who use the language have different—opposing—interests, it would be reasonable to expect that quite different performances will emerge that interpret rules or practices differently, stress different principles or precedents, shift among different dialects or frames of analysis, and resonate with different audiences.

As on the terrain of battle itself, of course, this may not happen. Someone may win and the struggle may end. Either may acquiesce in the legal determination of their adversary. Perhaps they were not able to think of a legal way to claim what would be in their interest. Perhaps they carry on insincerely, if emphatically. Perhaps they become convinced that what *seemed* to be in their interest should be sacrificed to the argument of the other side—they may, in effect, switch sides. For Clausewitz, the tendency to pause in war—for neither side to attack or withdraw—could be explained only by bringing other factors and other players onto the stage—the friction of physical, technical, and communication failures or the political calculations that emerge from mutual bargaining with third parties. Something parallel seems to be happening on the terrain of rhetorical engagement. Either or both parties may play for the attention of third parties, in ways that temper their claims, although this will often simply intensify their opposing assertions. There may be friction of one or another sort, the technologies and sites for making their assertions may not be found, and so forth. They may simply lack the intellectual or communicative resources to develop the argumentative antidote and make it stick.

As we observe the struggle unfolding, we can explore the effect of participation on those involved at a quite micro level of professional practice as well as the macro level of national strategy and the deployment of political capital. We can be on the lookout for professional deformations and structural biases that enter the struggle through the making and unmaking of assertions. As a general matter, we could say that in this rhetorical war of maneuver among argumentative styles, the terrain is not symmetrical between those who assert their power as truth and those who claim to speak truth to power. When you believe you exercise power as right, it will be tempting to treat those who speak to you in the voice of a truth as enemies or traitors—or to dismiss them as dreamers who have not understood how effectively you have already restrained, disciplined, and legitimated what you now perform. Of course, often those who aim to speak truth to your power will actually be your enemy or, if successful, will aid your enemy. As a result, it is easy to understand how important it will be for peacemakers to persuade those making war that knuckling under to the higher power of law will ultimately make them stronger, that those who speak truth to their power also share their realism, their pragmatism, their political savvy, and their commitment to the larger cause. They may be right in this—the party of war may have mistaken its interests, threatened to win the battle but lose the war, and so forth. But the effort to frame things in this way pulls those who seek to restrain the use of force by speaking truth into a strategic alliance with those whose power becomes truth.

At the same time, we must imagine that claims to make war in the name of right will rarely sound sincere or seem persuasive to those who believe the truth lies elsewhere—who oppose the war, are disgusted by the tactic, or simply expect themselves to be maimed or killed. They will be motivated to interpret those who would make legal assertions that discipline and strengthen the sword as perverse misuses of the rhetoric of peace to foul ends, conflating law with their own sovereign interest and ethics, uprooting it from a more general ethics, unraveling the careful process by which a more general and historical sovereignty had been codified as law. It will therefore be important for those who do seek to strengthen the military hand through law to make their assertions of right in a way that repositions them in alliance with the larger principles of law and peace. Their assertions may be correct—the party of peace may have mistaken its interests, sheathing precisely the sword that could have arrested a broader destruction.

Taking these two tendencies together, we should not be surprised, however, that those who exercise power as truth will be pulled toward ever more hyperbolic invocations of justice and law. The imbalance, then, lies in this: those who speak truth to power find themselves drawn into the collaborative exercise of violence, while those who exercise power as truth will tend to heighten the distance between what they do and what they say. Over time, justice will come to be articulated most robustly by those who make war, while war may well be made most effectively by those who began as masters of truth. This rather simple model suggests a hypothesis for exploration—that the back-and-forth of legal discourse about war tends toward a sharp differentiation of positions in which each is constantly motivated to align itself with or pose as the other. It is not surprising, in this light, that in law, enemies will sound like friends, and friends, enemies. Or that those who make war will speak as peacemakers, those who would restrain violence as strategic realists. We can expect a kind of endless dialog, proliferating itself alongside warfare—very different from the image of law as the voice and hand of the universal come to civilize swords into plowshares. The action is less vertical—law to power, power to law—than horizontal, between claimants, among selves and positions. Rather than truth mud-wrestling with power, we find a far more human interaction of tit for tat, in which death and destruction unfold alongside a dialog that seems to be terribly pertinent, but is nevertheless somehow about something else.

Pursuing the operations of law in war—and war in law—along these lines, we might see the practice of warfare and legal distinction, taken together, as part of a history of struggle, by humanitarians and military professionals, by friends and enemies, in times of "peace" and "war," over the relationship between international power and right. These struggles are normally not won and lost on the terrain of either rights or powers. They are not adjudicated by argument or force of arms—but through the variety of relatively small-scale technologies where assertion and action are blended together and their outcomes routinized into practices of governance and modes of global political or economic life. Over time, this practice may simultaneously become both power and right. In this sense, the law about war is not only an effective machinery for managing the military, for disciplining and legitimating recourse to arms, but also a part of the larger technology through which international power and right are made and known.

MODERN LAW AND MODERN WAR IN ACTION

Returning to the world in which modern law and war take place, it is not surprising how routinely political leaders now justify warfare in the language of human rights and international law just as military commanders frame strategic calculations in the language of law. They understand that violence one can articulate, disclose, and proudly stand behind will be more effective, sustainable, and legitimate. From a strategic point of view, we might imagine deploying a legal standard like "military necessity" or "proportionality" by calculating a kind of CNN effect, in which the additional opprobrium resulting from civilian deaths, discounted by the probability of it becoming known to relevant audiences, multiplied by the ability of that audience to hinder the continued prosecution of the war, will need to be added to the probable costs of the strike in calculating its proportionality and necessity—as well as its tactical value and strategic consequences. Claims about the legal distinctiveness of what one undertakes have become the currency in which checks can be written against one's legitimacy balance, their persuasive power determining the price to be paid.

But calculations in that currency are terribly difficult to make and sustain, while the conflation of right and power at both the micro and macro levels can lead people to lose critical distance on the violence of war. It is easy, for example, to substitute argument about the UN Charter for judgment about the ethical or political consequences of war. Yet it is difficult to think of a use of force that could not be legitimated in the language of the Charter. It is a rare statesman who launches a war simply to be aggressive. There is almost always something else to be said—the province is actually ours, our rights have been violated, our enemy is not, in fact, a state, we were invited to help, they were about to attack us, we are promoting the purposes and principles of the United Nations. Something.

Neither humanitarian idealism nor military necessity provides a standpoint outside the ebbs and flows of political and strategic debate about how to achieve objectives on the battlefield. Conversing before the court of world public opinion, statesmen not only assert their prerogatives—they also test and establish those prerogatives through action. Political assertions come armed with little packets of legal legitimacy—just as legal assertions carry a small backpack of political corroboration. As lawyers must harness enforcement to their norms, states must defend their prerogatives to keep them—must back up their assertions with action to maintain their credibility. A great many military campaigns have been undertaken for just this kind of credibility—missiles become missives. In this environment, the experience can be one of self-confident assertion and pride in the strategic shrewdness of one's assertions—but also of uncertainty and unease when one remembers the experience of being defeased from certainty by the assertions and powers of others in a plural legal environment.

In war, moreover, the assertions of opposing forces on questions of legitimacy and legality will echo across a chasm of difference in perspective. The legal and pragmatic assessment of wartime violence can heighten each side's confidence while stigmatizing their foe. For all sides, limiting civilian death has become a pragmatic commitment—no unnecessary damage, not one more civilian than necessary. The difficulty is determining what is necessary, necessary for what and for whom, and then making a claim to kill in a way that resonates. In today's asymmetric conflicts, it is all too easy to view tactics unavailable to one's own forces as perfidious, whether that means the shock and awe of bombing from a great height or hiding among civilians and placing one's weapons among the religious.

American Major General James Mattis, poised to invade Fallujah in Iraq, concluded his demand that the insurgents stand down with these words: "We will always be humanitarian in all our efforts. We will fight the enemy on our terms. May God help them when we're done with them." His juxtaposition of humanitarian claims and blunt threats was as chilling as his self-confidence. In war, it is terribly hard to remember how this will sound to other ears, particularly when the law of armed conflict has so often been a vocabulary used by the rich to judge the poor. No one, after all, experiences the death of her husband or sister as humanitarian and proportional. And everyone who believes in the legitimacy of their struggle will applaud its pursuit—the more so if it seems to be pursued by the least violent means available against a perfidious foe. It was equally chilling to hear the Iraqi insurgents in Fallujah respond to Mattis by threatening to decapitate civilian hostages if coalition forces did not withdraw. What could be more perfidious? Like Mattis, the insurgents were threatening innocent civilian death—less of it actually. Many will hear such a threat as a legitimate humanitarian effort to achieve a military objective with the least damage to civilian life, and that is how they will record it in their calculus of legitimate power.

When things go well, modern international law can provide a framework for talking across cultures about the justice and efficacy of wartime violence. More often, the modern partnership of war and law leaves all parties feeling their cause is just and no one feeling responsible for the deaths and suffering of war. Good legal arguments can make people lose their moral compass and sense of responsibility for the violence of war while politics and ethics have successfully been held at bay. It is in this atmosphere that discipline has broken down in every asymmetric struggle, when neither clear rules nor broad standards of judgment seem adequate to moor one's ethical sense of responsibility and empowerment. All sides assess their adversaries by the strictest standards and prefer permissive rules of engagement. Everyone has a CNN camera on their shoulder—but who is watching—the enemy, the civilians, your family at home, your commanding officer, your buddies? In this context, soldiers, civilians, media commentators, and politicians all begin to lose their ethical moorings.

There is no avoiding decisions about whom to kill in warfare. The difficulty arises when humanitarian law transforms *decisions* about whom to kill into *judgments*, when it encourages people to think death results not from an exercise of human freedom, for which a moral being is responsible, but rather from the abstract operation of professional principles. What does it mean to pretend the decision to kill is a principled judgment? It can mean a loss of the experience of responsibility—command responsibility, ethical responsibility, political responsibility. The greatest threat posed by the merger of law and war is loss of the human experience of moral jeopardy in the face of death, mutilation, and all the other horrors of warfare.

Modern war and modern law are conjoined in this new situation. It is a distinctively modern triumph to have transformed war into a legal institution while rendering law a flexible strategic instrument for military and humanitarian professionals alike. Professionals modernized the law of war to hold those who use violence politically responsible and applaud the law they have made as a global vernacular of "legitimacy." Unfortunately, however, the experience of political responsibility for war has proved elusive. Law may do more to constitute and legitimate than restrain violence, impressing itself upon its subjects in myriad dispersed sites of discipline and aspiration. It may accelerate the vertigo of combat and contribute to the loss of ethical moorings for people on all sides of a conflict. Pressing beyond modern law and modern war would mean feeling the weight of the decision to kill or let live. Most professionals—and citizens—flee from this experience. We all yearn for the reassurance of an external judgment—by political leaders, clergy, lawyers and others—that what we have gotten up to is, in fact, an ethically responsible politics. In the end, however, Clausewitz was right. War is the continuation of political intercourse in another language. For modern war, modern law has become that language.

War and law have teamed up to divorce politics from ethical choice and responsibility while structuring and defending a global political or economic order of ongoing and unequal struggle. Power has become a mixed matter of identity, strategy, assertion and discipline, authority and violence. Law and war have become oddly reciprocal, communicating and killing along the boundaries of the world system, at once drenched in the certainty of ethics and detached from the responsibility of politics. Working in partnership, modern law and modern war have enforced and pacified the boundaries of today's global architecture, while erasing their complicity and partnership with power and evading both ethical and political responsibility.

EPILOGUE
LET IT BE SO

As a law professor, I train experts. Many embrace the possibility that their generation could transform the world, and I hope they will. But I am cautious. Well-meaning experts routinely go terribly wrong, from the "best and brightest" in Vietnam through the planning and execution of the recent wars in Afghanistan and Iraq. Human rights activists, development planners, and international lawyers all have blind spots and biases, overestimate their insight, enchant the tools they have learned to use, and place faith in their discipline's potential above careful assessment of its accomplishments. They have learned to see order and system in the world rather than struggle, and too often experience their expertise as clear and persuasive, underestimating the plasticity, ambivalence, and conflicted nature of what they know.

Yet in another way, they also know all this. Sophisticated and accomplished experts wear their ambivalence and disenchantment lightly. And they press on. I have long found this the most puzzling aspect of expertise in the modern world. As I have explored it, I have come to believe that expertise is misunderstood. We think of expertise as specialized knowledge, when the background work of experts is continuous with the ways of knowing and doing of laypeople and princes alike. Expert knowledge is human knowledge: a blend of conscious, semiconscious, and wholly unconscious ideas, full of tensions and contradictions, inhabited by people who have projects and who think, speak, and act strategically. Style and role count as much as content. Although the work of experts has effects and is often undertaken with words, expertise is not made real though "persuasion" in a bell jar of ideas. Knowledge effects are all mixed up with power effects, as they are whenever humans engage one another. Even long-rejected and much-contested ideas continue to make themselves felt.

Perhaps most importantly, we excuse experts—as experts excuse themselves—from responsibility for the outcomes of their work. Sometimes this happens because we not noticing the outcomes, as international lawyers have long over-looked the distributive effects of legal rules, institutions, and arguments. More often it happens because we place responsibility elsewhere: in their knowledge or in the power of those who listened to their advice. Experts, we imagine, are being spoken by their expertise. It is not he who speaks, but the law—or economics—speaking through him. But knowledge is far more ambivalent than this. It must be inhabited to become effective and is always inhabited strategically.

Alternatively, we excuse the expert by imagining that others—the prince or people—decide. But power and decision are not like this either: princes and people must also think things through, act through assertion and argument, become effective through interpretation. I have tried here to imagine and de-scribe the habits of people who stand between knowledge and power in the hopes that if we see ourselves there we will understand ourselves as responsible deciders. That we will inhabit our expertise as fighting faith and experience politics as our vocation in just the sense Max Weber imagined: with passion, with proportion, and with responsibility in an irrational world that cannot be known or predicted.

The sensibility I have in mind requires a sense for the urgency and drama of the times: a sense that this is, indeed, 1648. A time when things are being remade in ways it is difficult to understand at first. Or a time like 1918, when people just know things have to be profoundly remade and both politics and economics are open for deep revision. These were not "end times" but mo-ments of rebirth. Apocalyptic language more often urges people back to their policy routines. The sensibility I hope to encourage requires an inclination to remain calm. Precisely because the situation is urgent, we ought not to rush to embrace the available levers or default in crisis to the most familiar.

I'm describing an impulse, an intellectual appetite, a critical suspicion. Where does it come from? In my experience, that is a very personal question. How did *you* come to feel things weren't right, that the solutions on offer were inadequate, and that taking the time to think hard about it might help? I suspect that as each of us reflects on the source of our intellectual vocation, the animus that fuels our scholarly work, we will find it in a different place. In our position in our family, our position in our nation, our society, our culture. In the position and practices of our country in the world. Perhaps in the teachings of our faith. Or in the disenchantments of our professional experience. But if you have this impulse, you are not alone. And you don't need to start from scratch. There is a long tradition of intellectual work lying alongside the mainstream routines of your professional or academic discipline on which you can rely. And there is community. Others, scattered around the world, share a similar impulse for innovative intellectual reflection, if probably for quite different reasons. Together, you can change the world. The spirit of 1648 is to begin.

NOTES

INTRODUCTION: COULD THIS BE 1648?

1. The Global Redesign Initiative resulted in a report published as Richard Samans, Klaus Schwab, and Mark Malloch-Brown, eds., *Everybody's Business: Strengthening International Cooperation in a More Interdependent World* (World Economic Forum, 2010).

2. Earlier studies of experts involved in global policy making—international lawyers, human rights activists, military professionals, economic development experts—include the following: For human rights: David Kennedy, *The Dark Sides of Virtue: Reassessing International Humanitarianism* (Princeton University Press, 2004); Kennedy, "The International Human Rights Regime: Still Part of the Problem?," in *Examining Critical Perspectives on Human Rights*, edited by Ole Windahl Pedersen (Cambridge University Press, 2013). For law and economic development: Kennedy, "Law and Development Economics: Towards a New Alliance," in *Law and Economics with Chinese Characteristics: Institutions for Promoting Development in the Twenty-First Century*, edited by David Kennedy and Joseph Stiglitz (Oxford University Press, 2013); Kennedy, "Some Caution about Property Rights as a Recipe for Economic Development," 1 *Accounting, Economics and Law* 1–62 (2011), and Kennedy, "The 'Rule of Law,' Political Choices and Development Common Sense," in *The New Law and Economic Development: A Critical Appraisal*, edited by David Trubek and Alvaro Santos (Cambridge University Press, 2006), 95–173. For international lawyers: Kennedy, "Lawfare and Warfare," in *Cambridge Companion to International Law*, edited by James Crawford and Martti Koskenniemi (Cambridge University Press, 2012); Kennedy, "International Humanitarianism: The Dark Sides," 6 *International Journal of Not-for-Profit-Law* 3 (June 2004); Kennedy, "Tom Franck and the Manhattan School," 35 *New York University Journal of International Law and Policy* 2, 397–435 (Winter 2003); Kennedy, "The Methods and Politics of Comparative Law," in *The Common Core of European Private Law: Essays on the Project*, edited by Mauro Bussani and Ugo Mattei (Kluwer, 2003), 131–207; Kennedy, "The Twentieth Century Discipline of International Law in the United States," in *Looking Back at Law's Century*, edited by Austin Sarat et al. (Cornell University Press, 2002), 386; Kennedy, "When Renewal Repeats: Thinking Against the Box," 32 *New York Journal of International Law and Politics* 2, 335 (Winter 2000); and Kennedy, "The Disciplines of International Law and Policy," 12 *Leiden Journal of International Law* 9 (1999).

3. For a strong recent polemic, see Patrick Wood, *Technocracy Rising: The Trojan Horse of Global Transformation* (Coherent Publishing, 2014), arguing that the outcome of globalization will be a form of scientific dictatorship.

4. Michel Foucault's work on modes of "governmentality" and "biopower" have spawned a large range of studies in this vein. See, in particular, Michel Foucault, *Discipline and Punish: The Birth of the Prison* (Alan Sheridan, trans.; Pantheon, 1978); Foucault, *Security, Territory, Population: Lectures at the College de France 1977–1978* (Michel Senellart, ed.; Graham Burchell, trans.; Picador, 2007); Foucault, *The Birth of Biopolitics: Lectures at the College de France 1978–1979* (Michel Senellart, ed.; Graham Burchell, trans.; Picador, 2008). For a comparative study of modes of "public reason," see Sheila Jasanoff, *Designs on Nature: Science and Democracy in Europe and the United States* (Princeton University Press, 2005).

5. Something of a divide separates those who focus on the importance of individual practice and achievement from those who focus on social conditioning in a "community of practice." A leading figure in the psychological study of expertise, Anders Ericsson, for example, has studied the professional development of skilled memory and other special cognitive aspects in skilled domains of performance, from business to music, sports, and the arts. See, e.g., K. A. Ericsson, ed., *The Road to Excellence: The Acquisition of Expert Performance in the Arts and Sciences, Sports, and Games* (Erlbaum, 1996). See also K. Anders Ericsson, Neil Charness, and Paul Feltovich, *The Cambridge Handbook of Expertise and Expert Performance* (Cambridge University Press, 2006). I find it difficult to understand the work of experts in global affairs without some sense for the interactions of individual psychological disposition and the complex institutional contexts and communities within which expert work unfolds. To understand expert work as "struggle," as I do here, requires a sense for the strategies of people pursuing projects on a constituted terrain. As a result, work exploring the cognitive process by which individuals become excellent is less relevant to my concerns. Consequently, the "communities of practice" approach has more in common with my own. The roots of this approach may be traced to the sociology of groups and religious communities, from Max Weber forward, to the American philosophical pragmatism of Pierce and Dewey with their focus on communities of inquiry and learning through participation in an occupation, or to the study of continuity and change in scientific knowledge communities, starting perhaps with Thomas Kuhn. One influential formalization of a theory of expert, professional, or craft knowledge is Etienne Wenger. See, e.g., Wenger, *Communities of Practice* (Cambridge University Press, 1998). See also Karin Knorr Cetina, *Epistemic Cultures: How the Sciences Make Knowledge* (Harvard University Press, 1999). Max Weber's notion of a "vocation" may be closest to what I have in mind: a complex constellation of individual desires, attitudes, and actions in a relationship to a context. Max Weber, "The Vocation of Science" and "The Vocation of Politics," in *The Essential Weber: A Reader*, edited by Sam Whimster (Routledge, 2004), 257–87.

6. See, for example, Donald MacKenzie, Fabian Muntesa, and Lucia Siu, eds., *Do Economists Make Markets?* (Princeton University Press, 2007); Michel Callon, *Laws of the Markets* (Wiley-Blackwell, 1998). Sheila Jasanoff adds elements important for my own approach: the significance of power differences in the reciprocal "co-production" of technical practice and social experience, and the ongoing work of boundary making and unmaking through which power is exercised within the worlds produced by technocracy and social practice. See, e.g., Sheila Jasanoff, *States of Knowledge: The Co-production of Science and the Social Order* (Routledge, 2006). This strand of expertise studies often traces its roots to the "actor-network theory" developed by Bruno Latour and Michel Callon. Latour famously proposed that laboratories transformed the world outside the laboratory to resemble that within: Bruno Latour, "Give Me a Laboratory and I Will Raise the World," in *Science Observed: New Perspectives on the Social Studies of Science*, edited by Knorr Cetina and M. Mulkay (Sage, 1983), 141–70. The literature on "actor-network theory" is immense. See, for example, Bruno Latour, *Reassembling the Social: An Introduction to Actor-Network Theory* (Oxford University Press, 2005).

7. The sociology of Pierre Bourdieu has been influential across the disciplines studying expertise, and also on this study. His essay "Structures, Habitus, Practices," in *The Logic of Practice* (Richard Nice, trans.; Stanford University Press, 1990), proposes a widely cited vocabulary to embrace the domain within which expertise simultaneously arises and is practiced. As I read him, the word "habitus" expresses the difficulty of articulating what people think and do together in a reciprocal relationship with the context in which they do it rather than a solution. On "tacit knowledge," see Harry Collins and Robert Evans, *Rethinking Expertise* (University of Chicago Press, 2007). However they are constituted, constellations of knowledge and modes of practice shift and stabilize in the life of a professional discipline or field. On the history of scientific conceptions of "objectivity" as an ethic of perception and representation, see Lorraine Daston and Peter Galison, *Objectivity* (Zone Books/MIT Press, 2007).

8.   See, e.g., James N. Rosenau, "Governance in the Twenty-First Century," 1 *Global Governance* 13–43 (1995); David Held, *Democracy and the Global Order: From the Modern State to Cosmopolitan Governance* (Stanford University Press, 1995); David Held, Anthony McGrew, David Goldblatt, and Jonathan Perraton, *Global Transformations: Politics, Economics and Culture* (Stanford University Press, 1999); Martin Hewson and Timothy Sinclair, *Approaches to Global Governance Theory* (SUNY Press, 1999); Craig N. Murphy, "Global Governance: Poorly Done and Poorly Understood," 76 *International Affairs* 4, 789–803 (2000); Saskia Sassen, "Neither Global nor Local: Novel Assemblages of Territory, Authority, and Rights," 1 *Ethics & Global Politics* 61–79 (2008); Mark Mazower, *Governing the World: The History of an Idea 1815 to the Present* (Penguin, 2012). For a discussion of the turn to "globalism" and "globalization" in the social sciences (focusing on anthropology), see Anna Tsing, "The Global Situation," 15 *Cultural Anthropology* 327–60 (2000).

9.   Roberto Unger, "The Critical Legal Studies Movement," 96 *Harvard Law Review* 561, 674–76 (1983).

CHAPTER 1   POLITICAL ECONOMY: WORLD-MAKING STORIES

1.   Joshua Kurlantzick, "The Great Deglobalizing: Our Interconnected World Is Shrinking Back toward Its National Borders—And That's a Problem," *Boston Sunday Globe*, Ideas, February 1, 2015, K1.

2.   Thomas L. Friedman, *The World Is Flat: A Brief History of the Twenty-First Century* (Farrar, Straus and Giroux, 2005).

3.   For a systematic recharacterization of corporate power as public, see Dan Danielsen, "How Corporations Govern: Taking Corporate Power Seriously in Transnational Regulation and Governance," 46 *Harvard International Law Journal* 411 (2005). For an analysis of the parallels between public and private administrative power, see Jerry Frug, "The Ideology of Bureaucracy in American Law," 97 *Harvard Law Review* 1276 (1984). On the role of legal arrangements in the construction of public power, see, e.g., Frug, "The City as a Legal Concept," 93 *Harvard Law Review* 1057 (1980).

4.   Paul Krugman, *Strategic Trade Policy and the New International Economics* (MIT Press, 1986).

5.   See, for example, Gerald M. Meier, *Biography of a Subject: An Evolution of Development Economics* (Oxford University Press, 2005), chap. 7, 106ff.

6.   Ibid., 106.

7.   For one example, an "ordo-liberal" economist addressing lawyers on the institutional preconditions to rebuild in the twentieth century what had come naturally in the nineteenth, see Wilhelm Roepke, "Economic Order and International Law," 86 *Recueil des Cours* 203 (1954).

8.   On the relationship between conceptual argument about sovereignty and jurisdiction—and their relationships to physical and metaphorical territory—see Péter D. Szigeti, "Text and Territory: Jurisdictional Conflict and Territorial Language in Law" (SJD diss., Harvard Law School, 2015, on file with the author).

9.   *Restatement of the Law (Third): The Foreign Relations Law of the United States*, secs. 402–3 (1987).

CHAPTER 2   STRUGGLE: TOWARD A CARTOGRAPHY OF ENGAGEMENT

1.   Thomas Hobbes, *Leviathan* (1651; Bobbs-Merrill, 1958), 106–7.

2.   Adam Smith, *An Inquiry into the Nature and Causes of the Wealth of Nations* (London, 1812), 1:21–22.

3.   Carl von Clausewitz, *On War* (Michael Howard and Peter Paret, trans. and eds.; Princeton University Press, 1976), 76.

4.   Ibid., 149.

5. Carl Schmitt, *The Concept of the Political* (George Schwab, trans.; 1932; University of Chicago Press, 1996), 26–27.

6. See Michel Callon, "Some Elements of a Sociology of Translation: Domestication of the Scallops and the Fishermen of St. Brieuc Bay," in *Power, Action and Belief: A New Sociology of Knowledge*, edited by John Law (Routledge, 1986); Bruno Latour, *Reassembling the Social: An Introduction to Actor-Network Theory* (Oxford University Press, 2005); Timothy Mitchell, *Rule of Experts: Egypt, Techno-Politics, Modernity* (University of California Press, 2002) (particularly at chap. 2, "Can the Mosquito Speak?," 19–53).

7. Hedley Bull, *The Anarchical Society: A Study of Order in World Politics* (Columbia University Press, 1977; 4th ed., 2002), ibid., xxviii.

8. Ibid., 8.

9. John Kenneth Galbraith, *The Affluent Society* (1958; Houghton Mifflin, 1971), 152.

10. See, for example, from the economic side, Anne Kreuger, "The Political Economy of Rent-Seeking Society," 64 *American Economic Review* (1974); Martin Shubik, *A Game-Theoretic Approach to Political Economy* (MIT Press, 1984); or, from political science, Peter Ordeshook, "The Emerging Discipline of Political Economy," in *Perspectives on Positive Political Economy*, edited by James E. Alt and Kenneth A. Shepsle (Cambridge University Press, 1990) and Ordeshook, *Game Theory and Political Theory* (Cambridge University Press, 1986).

11. H. Uzawa, "Walras Tâtonnement in the Theory of Exchange," 27 *Review of Economic Studies* 3, 182–94 (1960).

12. Leon Walras, "Geometrical Theory of the Determination of Prices," 3 *Annals of the American Academy of Political and Social Science* 45–64, 53 (1892).

13. See, for example, Pascal Bridel's conclusion that "[t]he internal coherence of Walras' [tâtonnement] model is eventually shown to win clearly over any pretence of 'realism.'" In Bridel, "The Normative Origins of General Equilibrium Theory: or Walras's Attempts at Reconciling Economic Efficiency with Social Justice," in *General Equilibrium Analysis: A Century after Walras*, edited by Pascal Bridel (Routledge, 2011), 21.

14. Bull, *Anarchical Society*.

15. This approach is now associated with the writings of Michel Foucault in a way that seems first to have come to the attention of the English-speaking world in Ian Mcleod's 1980 translation of Foucault's short Course Summary at the College de France under the title "War in the Filigree of Peace," 4 *Oxford Literary Review* 15–19 (1980). Foucault frames his attention to the ubiquity of contending forces as an alternative to the "privilege" accorded "law as a manifestation of power." Foucault's notion of "law" may be similar to my skepticism of system logics of various kinds. To my mind, recovering the work of legal knowledge and practice, alongside other expert discourses, in struggles is a route to revealing rather than obscuring the role of war in the routines of peace.

16. Hans J. Morgenthau, *Politics among Nations: The Struggle for Power and Peace* (1948; 7th ed., McGraw-Hill, 2006), 29.

17. Ibid., 179.

18. Ibid., 179–80.

19. Ibid., 181.

20. In the legal literature, the "systems theory" approach originally associated with Niklas Luhmann has been developed most comprehensively by Gunter Teubner. See, e.g., *Constitutional Fragments: Societal Constitutionalism in Globalization* (Oxford University Press, 2012); *Law as an Autopoietic System* (Blackwell, 1993); "Two Kinds of Legal Pluralism: Collision of Transnational Regimes in the Double Fragmentation of World Society," in *Regime Interaction in International Law: Facing Fragmentation*, edited by Margret Young (Oxford University Press, 2012), 23–54; and "Regime-Collisions: The Vain Search for Legal Unity in the Fragmentation of Global Law," 25 *Michigan Journal of International Law* 999–1046 (2004).

21. Philip Allott has stressed this theme repeatedly in his work. See, e.g., *Eunomia. New Order for a New World* (Oxford University Press, 1990).

22. This has been powerfully argued by Martti Koskenniemi in "Hegemonic Regimes," in *Regime Interaction in International Law: Facing Fragmentation*, edited by Margaret A. Young (Cambridge University Press, 2012), 305–24.

CHAPTER 3 WORLD-MAKING IDEAS: IMAGINING A WORLD TO GOVERN AND TO RESIST

1. John Dewey, "Logical Method and Law," 10 *Cornell Law Quarterly* 17–19 (1924).

2. For doctrinal analysis of Vitoria's claims, see David Kennedy, "Primitive Legal Scholarship," 27 *Harvard International Law Journal* 1 (1986).

3. A terrific longitudinal study of indigenous strategies vis-à-vis the global community is Karen Engle, *The Elusive Promise of Indigenous Development: Rights, Culture, Strategy* (Duke University Press, 2010).

CHAPTER 4 EXPERTISE: THE MACHINERY OF GLOBAL REASON

1. For an analysis of the obligation to consult advisors to determine the justice of war, particularly in the writings of Francisco Vitoria (1480–1546), see David Kennedy, "Primitive Legal Scholarship," 27 *Harvard International Law Journal* 2 (1986), 31ff.

2. Niccolo Machiavelli, *The Prince and Selected Discourses* (Daniel Donno, trans.; Bantam Books, 1966), 80.

3. For a recent example of worry at the global level in the field of economic development, see William Easterley, *The Tyranny of Experts: Economists, Dictators, and the Forgotten Rights of the Poor* (Basic Books, 2013).

4. A good overview of the contemporary discussion in political theory, see, e.g., Evan Selinger and Robert Crease, eds., *The Philosophy of Expertise* (Columbia University Press, 2006). See also Stephen Turner, *The Politics of Expertise* (Routledge, 2013); Mark Brown, *Science in Democracy: Expertise, Institutions, and Representation* (MIT Press, 2009). Lawyers have had a lot to say about when and why experts are needed in democratic policy, the institutions of government within which they can be most useful, and the best ways to keep them within the confines of their mandate, render them responsive to leaders, citizens, and stakeholders and accountable to popular political authority. Reconciling the growth of specialized agencies with democratic governance has been a consistent preoccupation of postwar thinking about public administration and the legal process. From political science, see, for example, Dwight Waldo, *The Administrative State* (Ronald Press, 1948). From law, see Henry M. Hart and Albert M. Sacks, *The Legal Process: Basic Problems in the Making and Application of Law*, edited by William Eskridge (Foundation Press, 1994). The field of "administrative law" focuses on the authority and accountability of specialized agencies in the executive branch to the legislature and the judiciary. For an early classic, see James Landis, *The Administrative Process* (Yale University Press, 1938). Even within the trial process, the respective roles of judge and jury in the face of "expert" testimony have been both theorized and developed as a rule system for credentialing, questioning, respecting, and ignoring expert opinion.

5. See Duncan Kennedy, "The Hermeneutic of Suspicion in Contemporary American Legal Thought," 25 *Law and Critique* 91–139 (2014).

6. For an otherwise fascinating study weakened by efforts to resolve such questions, see Isabel V. Hull, *A Scrap of Paper: Breaking and Making International Law during the Great War* (Cornell University Press, 2014).

7. For a comparative study of international legal disciplines, see David Kennedy, "The Disciplines of International Law and Policy," 12 *Leiden Journal of International Law* 9 (1999).

CHAPTER 5   EXPERTISE IN ACTION: RULE BY ARTICULATION

1. I develop the relationship between economic and legal expertise more fully in David Kennedy, "Law and Development Economics: Toward a New Alliance," in *Law and Economics with Chinese Characteristics: Institutions for Promoting Development in the Twenty-First Century* (Oxford University Press, 2013), 19–70. See also Kennedy, "The 'Rule of Law,' Political Choices and Development Common Sense," in *The New Law and Economic Development: A Critical Appraisal*, edited by David Trubek and Alvaro Santos (Cambridge University Press, 2006), 95–173.

2. I develop these relationships more fully in David Kennedy, *Of War and Law* (Princeton University Press, 2006).

3. I develop the difference between these two styles in David Kennedy, *The Dark Sides of Virtue: Reassessing International Humanitarianism* (Princeton University Press, 2004).

4. See Duncan Kennedy, "A Semiotics of Legal Argument," 42 *Syracuse Law Review* 75 (1991) and "Form and Substance in Private Law Adjudication," 88 *Harvard Law Review* 1685 (1976). I have undertaken parallel studies of argument in the international law field, starting with "The Sources of International Law," 2 *American University Journal of International Law and Policy* 1 (1987) and *International Legal Structures* (Nomos Verlag, 1987).

5. What I have in mind in legal argument is the "conflicting considerations" jurisprudence that Duncan Kennedy ascribes to the past half century in legal thought. The significance of "balancing" what are understood to be "competing considerations" in postwar legal argument is analyzed by Duncan Kennedy in *A Critique of Adjudication [fin de siècle]* (Harvard University Press, 1997) and "Three Globalizations of Law and Legal Thought: 1850–2000," in *The New Law and Economic Development: A Critical Appraisal*, edited by David Trubek and Alvaro Santos (Cambridge University Press, 2006). See also Kennedy, "The Hermeneutic of Suspicion in Contemporary American Legal Thought," 25 *Law and Critique* 91 (2014).

6. This structure is developed by Martti Koskenniemi as an opposition between what he terms "ascending" and "descending" arguments in *From Apology to Utopia: The Structure of International Legal Argument* (1989; Cambridge University Press, 2005). I detected a similar pattern of what I called "hard" and "soft" arguments about the sources of international law in Kennedy, *International Legal Structures*.

7. I have been particularly influenced by the comparative work of my colleague Sheila Jasanoff in the field of science and technology studies, most recently by "Epistemic Subsidiarity: Coexistence, Cosmopolitanism, Constitutionalism," 2 *European Journal of Risk Regulation* 439–52 (2013) and "The Practices of Objectivity in Regulatory Science," in *Social Knowledge in the Making*, edited by C. Camic, N. Gross, and M. Lamont (University of Chicago Press, 2011), 307–37.

CHAPTER 6   LAW AND THE GLOBAL DYNAMICS OF DISTRIBUTION

1. Oliver Wendell Holmes, "The Path of the Law," 10 *Harvard Law Review* 457 (1897), reprinted in David Kennedy and William T. Fisher, eds., *The Canon of American Legal Thought* (Princeton University Press, 2006), 28–45, 35.

2. Wesley Hohfeld, "Some Fundamental Legal Conceptions as Applied in Judicial Reasoning," 23 *Yale Law Journal* 16 (1913); and Robert Hale, "Coercion and Distribution in a Supposedly Noncoercive State," 38 *Political Science Quarterly* 470 (1923).

3. Particularly important for my own thinking were Ronald Coase, "The Problem of Social Cost," 3 *Journal of Law and Economics* 1 (1960); and Marc Galanter, "Why the 'Haves' Come Out Ahead: Speculations on the Limits of Legal Change," 9 *Law and Society Review* 95 (1974).

4. Duncan Kennedy has written extensively on distributive issues, drawing on a range of sociolegal tools and economic analytics. I have been particularly influenced by Kennedy,

"The Political States in 'Merely Technical' Issues of Contract Law," 1 *European Review of Private Law* 7 (2001); *A Critique of Adjudication [fin de siècle]* (Harvard University Press, 1997); "The Stakes of Law, or Hale and Foucault!," 15 *Legal Studies Forum* 327 (1991); and "African Poverty," 87 *Washington Law Review* 205 (2012).

5. On comparative advantage and rent, see David Ricardo, *On the Principles of Political Economy and Taxation* (1817). On the theory of rent and repeal of the Corn Laws, see Ricardo, *Essay on the Influence of a Low Price of Corn on the Profits of Stock* (1815).

6. Lucien A. Bebchuk, Jesse M. Fried, and David I. Walker, "Managerial Power and Rent Extraction in the Design of Executive Compensation," 69 *University of Chicago Law Review* 751–846 (2002), 783.

7. Ibid., 784.

8. Raphael Kaplinsky, *Globalization, Poverty and Inequality: Between a Rock and a Hard Place* (Policy Press, 2005).

9. Daniel K. Tarullo made this point clearly in "Beyond Normalcy in the Regulation of International Trade," 100 *Harvard Law Review* 546 (1987).

10. Judith Hippler Bello made this point in supporting US ratification in "The WTO Dispute Settlement Understanding: Less Is More," 90 *American Journal of International Law* 3 (1996).

11. See, e.g., Eric Wolf, *Europe and the People Without History* (University of California Press, 1982); Giovanni Arrighi, *Geometry of Imperialism* (Verso Press, 1978); Arrighi, *Adam Smith in Beijing: Lineages of the Twenty-First Century* (Verso Press, 2007); Samir Amin, *Delinking: Towards a Polycentric World* (Zed Books, 1990).

12. The most influential for my own thinking have been Raul Prebisch, *The Economic Development of Latin America and Its Principal Problems* (United Nations Economic Commission for Latin America, 1950); Andre Gunder Frank, *Capitalism and Underdevelopment in Latin America: Historical Studies of Chile and Brazil* (1967; Penguin, 1971); Andre Gunder Frank, *Dependent Accumulation and Underdevelopment* (Monthly Review Press, 1979); Fernando Henrique Cardoso and Enzo Faletto, *Dependency and Development in Latin America* (Mariory Mattingly Urquidi trans.; University of California Press, 1979); Peter Evans, *Dependent Development: The Alliance of Multinational, State and Local Capital in Brazil* (Princeton University Press, 1979).

13. Among his many works, those that have most influenced this book include Terence K. Hopkins, Immanuel Wallerstein, and Associates, *World-Systems Analysis: Theory and Methodology* (Sage, 1982) and *The Modern World-System, Vol. III: The Second Era of Great Expansion of the Capitalist World-Economy, 1730s–1840s* (University of California Press, 1989). See also Immanuel Wallerstein, *World-Systems Analysis: An Introduction* (Paradigm, 2004).

14. For an analysis of power differentials in global value chains, see Gary Gereffi, John Humphrey, and Timothy Sturgeon, "The Governance of Global Value Chains," 12 *Review of International Political Economy* 1, 78–104 (2005).

15. See, for example, Gunnar Myrdal, "Appendix 2: The Mechanism of Underdevelopment and Development and a Sketch of an Elementary Theory of Planning for Development," in *An Approach to the Asian Drama: Methodological and Theoretical Selections from Asian Drama: An Inquiry into the Poverty of Nations* (Vintage Books, 1970), 207–304.

16. Gunnar Myrdal, *Economic Theory and Underdeveloped Regions* (Harper, 1957), 13.

17. Ibid., 27.

18. Ibid., 31.

19. Ibid.

20. Myrdal is not alone. Even scholars of "law and development" underestimate the constitutive role of law in center/periphery dynamics. See, e.g., Michael W. Dowdle, John Gillespie, and Imelda Maher, eds., *Asian Capitalism and the Regulation of Competition: Towards a Regulatory Geography of Global Competition Law* (Cambridge University Press, 2013) and Dowdle, "Law, Development and Geography: On the Regulatory Logic of the Periphery and

its Implications for Law and Development" (unpublished manuscript, 2014). Dowdle analyzes the impact of economic center/periphery dynamics on national regulation in the development context. He contrasts centers that concentrate on "core industries" facing "product competition" and generating sustainable revenue streams with peripheries whose industries face "price competition" and are unable to capture or retain gains. He demonstrates the differential impact of regulatory and institutional changes thought to generate development on centers and peripheries to highlight the limitations of law as a development tool. Unfortunately, he underestimates the role of law in generating the conditions for industries to be gain-capturing and "product competitive" or "price competitive" in the first place, and therefore in the emergence and consolidation of center/periphery relations.

21. Myrdal, *Economic Theory*, 39–40.

22. Ibid., 42.

23. See Mohammed Bedjaoui, *Towards a New International Order* (Holmes and Meier, 1979); Robert F. Meagher, *An International Redistribution of Wealth and Power: A Study of the Charter of Economic Rights and Duties of States* (Pergamon, 1979).

24. Joseph Stiglitz and Andrew Charlton, *Fair Trade for All: How Trade Can Promote Development* (Oxford University Press, 2005).

25. Ibid., 108.

26. See Alvaro Santos, "Carving Out Policy Autonomy for Developing Countries in the World Trade Organization: The Experience of Brazil and Mexico," 52 *Virginia Journal of International Law* 551–632 (2012).

27. For a powerful sociological demonstration of this in sector after sector, see John Braithwaite and Peter Drahos, *Global Business Regulation* (Cambridge University Press, 2000).

28. See David Kennedy, "Some Caution about Property Rights as a Recipe for Economic Development," 1 *Accounting, Economics, and Law* 1–62 (2011); Kennedy, "The International Anti-corruption Campaign," 14 *University of Connecticut Journal of International Law* 101 (1999). See also Mushtaq Khan and Kwame Sundaram Jomo, eds., *Rents, Rent-Seeking and Economic Development and Evidence in Asia* (Cambridge University Press, 2000); "Technology Policies and Learning with Imperfect Governance," in *The Industrial Policy Revolution I: The Role of Government Beyond Ideology*, edited by Joseph Stiglitz and Justin Yifu Lin (Palgrave, 2013), 79–115; "Beyond Good Governance: An Agenda for Developmental Governance," in *Is Good Governance Good for Development?*, edited by Jomo Kwame Sundaram and Anis Chowdhury (Bloomsbury, 2012), 151–82.

29. Duncan Kennedy, "African Poverty," 87 *Washington Law Review* 205 (2012).

30. Fernando Henrique Cardoso and Enzo Faletto, *Dependency and Development in Latin America* (originally published as *Dependencia y desarrollo en America Latina*, 1971; University of California Press, 1979).

31. See David Kennedy and David Webb, "The Limits of Integration: Eastern Europe and the European Communities," 30 *Common Market Law Review* 1095 (1993); and David Kennedy, "Turning to Market Democracy: A Tale of Two Architectures," 32 *Harvard International Law Journal* 373 (1991).

32. Damjan Kukovec's doctoral dissertation developed this argument. See Kukovec, "Whose Social Europe?," talk delivered at Harvard Law School (April 16, 2010), available at http://www.harvardiglp.org/new-thinking-new-writing/whose-social-europe-the-lavalviking-judements-and-the-prosperity-gap/; Kukovec, "A Critique of the Rhetoric of Common Interest in the EU Legal Discourse," talk delivered at Harvard Law School (April 13. 2012), available at http://www.harvardiglp.org/new-thinking-new-writing/a-critique-of-rhetoric/; and Kukovec, "A Critique of the Rhetoric of Common Interest in the European Union Legal Discourse" (SJD dissertation, Harvard Law School, 2015).

33. Ermal Frasheri makes this point in "Transformation and Social Change: Legal Reform in the Modernization Process," *Nellco Legal Scholarship Repository*, September 5, 2008; and in his doctoral dissertation: "Of Knights and Squires: European Union and the Modernization of Albania" (SJD dissertation, Harvard Law School, 2012).

CHAPTER 7   INTERNATIONAL LEGAL EXPERTISE: INNOVATION, AVOIDANCE, AND PROFESSIONAL FAITH

1. I have elsewhere analyzed the process by which the field developed through a series of internal debates: between Americans and Europeans, among schools of thought or methodological tendencies, between an evolving "mainstream" and "counterpoint" sensibility. I trace the shifting relationships among mainstream and heterodoxy in the US tradition of international law in "The Twentieth Century Discipline of International Law in the United States," in *Looking Back at Law's Century*, edited by Austin Sarat et al. (Cornell University Press, 2002), 386ff; "Tom Franck and the Manhattan School," 35 *New York University Journal of International Law and Politics* 2, 397–435 (Winter 2003); "When Renewal Repeats: Thinking Against the Box," 32 *New York Journal of International Law and Politics* 2, 335 (Winter 2000); "A New World Order: Yesterday, Today and Tomorrow," 4 *Transnational Law and Contemporary Problems* 330 (1994); and "The International Style in Postwar Law and Policy," 1 *Utah Law Review* 7 (1994). The theme of internal division as mark and driver for change in international law fields is developed in Kennedy, "The Methods and Politics of Comparative Law," in *Comparative Legal Studies: Traditions and Transitions*, edited by Pierre Legrand and Roderick Munday (Cambridge University Press, 2003), 345–433. I develop a parallel argument for the expertise of specialists in economic development policy in "The 'Rule of Law,' Political Choices and Development Common Sense," in *The New Law and Economic Development: A Critical Appraisal*, edited by David Trubek and Alvaro Santos (Cambridge University Press, 2006), 95–173.

2. See, e.g., Herbert W. Briggs, "The Attorney General Invokes Rebus Sic Stantibus" 36 *American Journal of International Law* 89–96 (1942), opposing the suspension of the International Load Line Convention.

3. See Hengameh Saberi, "Descendants of Realism? Policy-Oriented International Lawyers as Guardians of Democracy," in *Critical International Law: Postrealism, Postcolonialism, and Transnationalism*, edited by Prabhakar Singh and Benoit Mayer (Oxford University Press, 2014), 29–52.

4. An early moment in the eclectic blending of opposing theories to practical ends was the reinvention of a "Grotian" middle way among opposing theoretical tendencies. See, e.g., Hersch Lauterpacht, "The Grotian Tradition," 23 *British Yearbook of International Law* 1–53 (1946).

5. See Martti Koskenniemi, *The Gentle Civilizer of Nations: The Rise and Fall of International Law 1870–1960* (Cambridge University Press, 2004). My own interpretation of the relationship between nineteenth- and twentieth-century international law has been influenced by Duncan Kennedy's "The Rise and Fall of Classical Legal Thought" (unpublished, 1975; Beard Books, 2006), particularly as reinterpreted in "Three Globalizations of Law and Legal Thought: 1850–2000," in *The New Law and Economic Development: A Critical Appraisal*, edited by David Trubek and Alvaro Santos (Cambridge University Press, 2006), 19–73. See also my "International Law in the Nineteenth Century: History of an Illusion," 65 *Nordic Journal of International Law* 385–420 (1996).

6. For a fascinating account of Nazi international law, see Detlev Vagts, "International Law in the Third Reich," 84 *American Journal of International Law* 661 (1990).

7. See Arnulf Becker Lorca, *Mestizo International Law: A Global Intellectual History 1842–1933* (Cambridge University Press, 2014).

8. John Austin, *The Province of Jurisprudence Determined* (J. Murray, 1832).

9. Ibid., 223.

10. Ibid., 148.

11. Ibid., 146.

12. See Martti Koskenniemi, *From Apology to Utopia: The Structure of International Legal Argument* (1989; Cambridge University Press, 2005). See also David Kennedy, *International Legal Structures* (Nomos Verlag, 1987).

13. The most significant for the American tradition was Emmerich de Vattel, *The Law of Nations: Or, Principles of the Law of Nature Applied to the Conduct and Affairs of Nations and Sovereigns* (1777; S. Campbell, 1796).

14. P. E. Corbett, "What Is the League of Nations?," 5 *British Yearbook of International Law* 119 (1924), 127.

15. See, for example, Koskenniemi, *Gentle Civilizer*.

16. See, for example, Nathaniel Berman, "But the Alternative Is Despair: European Nationalism and the Modernist Renewal of International Law," 106 *Harvard Law Review* 1792 (1993); Berman, "Modernism, Nationalism and the Rhetoric of Reconstruction," 4 *Yale Journal of Law and the Humanities* 351 (1992). See also David Kennedy, "The Move to Institutions," 8 *Cardozo Law Review* 841 (1987).

17. See, e.g., Sam Moyn, *Human Rights and the Uses of History* (Verso, 2014) and Louis Henkin, *The Age of Rights* (Columbia University Press, 1990).

18. See Martti Koskenniemi, "Lauterpacht: The Victorian Tradition in International Law," 2 *European Journal of International Law* 215–63 (1997), revised in Koskenniemi, *Gentle Civilizer*. See also, Koskenniemi, "Hersch Lauterpacht and the Development of International Criminal Law," 2 *Journal of International Criminal Justice* 3, 810–25 (2004).

19. See David Kennedy, "The International Style in Postwar Law and Policy," 1 *Utah Law Review* 7 (1994) comparing Hans Kelsen at midcentury with international trade and economic law expert John Jackson a half century later.

20. Hans Kelsen, *Law and Peace in International Relations: The Oliver Wendell Holmes Lectures, 1940–1941* (Harvard University Press, 1942), 69–70.

21. Ibid., 82–83.

22. Ibid., 26.

23. Ibid., 30, emphasis added.

24. Ibid., 34.

25. Ibid., 35.

26. Ibid., 54–55.

27. "Note: Constructing the State Extraterritorially: Jurisdictional Discourse, the National Interest, and Transnational Norms," 103 *Harvard Law Review* 1273 (1989–90).

28. *The Paquete Habana*, 175 US 677 (1900).

29. *The Paquete Habana*, 175 US 677 (1900), 700.

30. Oscar Schachter, "Dag Hammarskjold and the Relation of Law to Politics," 56 *American Journal of International Law* 1 (1962), 2–3.

31. Ibid., 4–5.

32. Ibid., 1–2.

33. *Corfu Channel Case (UK v Albania)*, Individual Opinion of Judge Alvarez, 1949 *ICJ* 39, 43.

34. Oscar Schachter, "The Twilight Existence of Nonbinding International Agreements," 71 *American Journal of International Law* 296 (1977).

35. Philippe Sands, ed., *The Greening of International Law* (New Press, 2004), xxx.

36. Ibid.

37. Ibid., xxxvii–xxxix.

38. See, for example, Leo Gross, "States as Organs of International Law and the Problem of Autointerpretation" (1953), reprinted in *Leo Gross: Essays on International Law and Organization*, edited by Alfred P. Rubin (Transnational, 1983), 367–98.

39. Anne-Marie Slaughter, "Good Reasons for Going Around the U.N.," *New York Times*, March 18, 2003.

40. Myres McDougal, "The Hydrogen Bomb Tests," 49 *American Journal of International Law* 357–58 (1955).

41. Myres McDougal, "Law and Power," 46 *American Journal of International Law* 102 (1952), 110.

42. Ibid., 111.

43. Ibid., 113.

44. See Philip Jessup, *Transnational Law* (Yale University Press, 1956); Harold Koh, "Transnational Legal Process," 75 *Nebraska Law Review* 181 (1996). The leading theorization of "global administrative law" is Benedict Kingsbury, Nico Krisch, and Richard Stewart, "The Emergence of Global Administrative Law," 68 *Law and Contemporary Problems* 15 (Summer/Autumn 2005). See also Koh, "The Third Globalization: Transnational Human Rights Networks," in *The Human Rights Report: US Department of State, Country Reports on Human Rights Practices for 1999* (2000), 1:xv. For an affirmative view of the potential for "networks" as global governance, see Anne-Marie Slaughter, *A New World Order* (Princeton University Press, 2005). For a more critical view, see Annelise Riles, *The Network Inside Out* (University of Michigan Press, 2000).

45. See Philip Allott, "Power-sharing in the Law of the Sea," 77 *American Journal of International Law* 1–30 (1983).

46. Koh, "Transnational Legal Process," 204.

47. Ibid., 184.

48. Ibid., 205.

49. Ibid., 206, emphasis added.

50. Ibid., 207.

51. For a more hard-boiled strategic assessment of the uses to be made of multilateral arrangements, see Ruth Wedgwood, "Unilateral Action in a Multilateral World," in *Multilateralism and U.S. Foreign Policy: Ambivalent Engagement*, edited by Stewart Patrick and Shepard Forman (Lynne Rienner, 2002), 186.

52. Oscar Schachter foreshadowed this role in his essay "The Invisible College of International Lawyers," 72 *Northwestern University Law Review* 2, 217 (1977).

53. See Kingsbury, Krisch, and Stewart, "Emergence of Global Administrative Law."

54. Ibid., 27.

55. Wilhelm Roepke, "Economic Order and International Law," 86 *Recueil des Cours* 202–71 (1954).

56. Ibid., 221, emphasis in the original.

57. Lori Fisler Damrosch, Louis Henkin, Richard Crawford Pugh, Oscar Schachter, and Hans Smit, *International Law: Cases and Materials* (4th ed., West, 2001), 586.

58. Louis Henkin, *The Age of Rights* (Columbia University Press, 1990), xvii–xviii.

59. Matthew 10:16.

60. Martti Koskenniemi traces the difficulty international lawyers and international relations theorists have had coming to terms with legal pluralism in "The Fate of Public International Law," 70 *Modern Law Review* 1, 1–30 (2007), 20ff., criticizing the recurring tendency in pluralist theories to return to metaphors of coherence rather than awareness of diversity and political possibility.

61. See, e.g., Gunther Teubner, "Constitutionalising Polycontexturality," 19 *Journal of Social and Legal Studies* (2010); Teubner, "The Project of Constitutional Sociology," 4 *Transnational Legal Theory* 1, 44–58 (2013); Teubner, *Constitutional Fragments: Societal Constitutionalism and Globalization* (Oxford University Press, 2012).

62. Martti Koskenniemi, "Law, Teleology and International Relations: An Essay in Counterdisciplinarity," 26 *International Relations* 1, 3–34 (2011), 19–20. He develops the theme of struggle amongst alternative regime consolidations in "Hegemonic Regimes," in *Regime Interaction in International Law: Facing Fragmentation*, edited by Margaret A. Young (Cambridge University Press, 2012), 305–24.

63. See Carl Schmitt, *The Concept of the Political* (George Schwab, trans.; 1932; University of Chicago Press, 1996).

64. See generally Max Weber, *Politics as a Vocation* (1918), reprinted in *From Max Weber: Essays in Sociology* (H. H. Gerth and C. Wright Mills, trans. and eds.; 1946), 77.

65. See Søren Kierkegaard, *Fear and Trembling* (1843; Howard V. Hong and Edna H Hong, trans. and eds.; Princeton University Press, 1985).

66. See Jean-Paul Sartre, *The Humanism of Existentialism* (1946), reprinted in *The Philosophy of Existentialism* (Wade Baskin, ed.; Citadel Press, 1965), 31.

67. See Jacques Derrida, *Writing and Difference* (1967; Alan Bass, trans.; University of Chicago Press, 1978).

INDEX